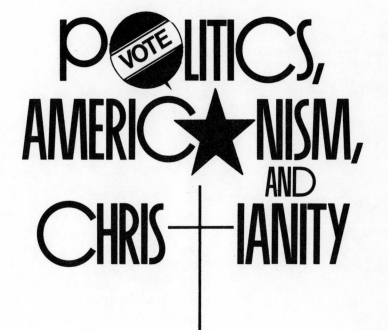

POLITICS, AMERICANISM, AND CHRISTIANITY

PERRY C. COTHAM

A CANON PRESS BOOK

BAKER BOOK HOUSE
Grand Rapids, Michigan

Copyright 1976 by
Baker Book House Company
ISBN: 0-8010-2377-7
Library of Congress Catalog Card Number: 75-39165
Printed in the United States of America

For
Teresa Lynn
Laura Michelle
Prentice Anthony

Contents

Foreword

In *Politics, Americanism, and Christianity,* Dr. Cotham adds a new dimension to our understanding of how one should relate to God and country.

When Jesus said "Render to Caesar the things that are Caesar's and to God the things that are God's," He disposed of this question in the only way possible at the time. The only alternatives were God and autocratic government; there were no other peaceful options.

Dr. Cotham now inspires us with the realization that today, in our great democracy, we have a third choice: we may shape our politics in such a way that the perplexing dichotomy of loyalty could conceivably disappear altogether.

This is an encouraging and exciting thought. It also may explain the often-posed question of why God gave man a free will. The misuse of this power often leads to difficulties, but over the centuries the gradual imposition of the free will of the people upon government has produced the democratic institutions we now have.

Dr. Cotham wisely refrains from presenting his message as a new dogmatism. He clearly states that while the right to vote in a democracy gives us a powerful instrument for furthering justice, there are many evil forces and human frailties to be reckoned with in our exercise of the third option. He does not pretend to give us a marked-up sample ballot to take into the voting booth.

The problems of decision making for a citizen in a free society are discussed broadly and deeply. In the examples he presents, he exhibits all sides with remarkable impartiality. His own convictions are moderately liberal, but he does not try to impose them upon the reader. He encourages the reader to consider carefully before he acts; but he exhorts him to act.

Dr. Cotham was raised in the Church of Christ. His father and grandfather were ministers. A minister himself, he has served in inner-city, suburban, and rural churches in the Detroit and Nashville areas. Currently at David Lipscomb College in Nashville, Tennessee, he teaches courses related to American national government, including Constitutional law. His knowledge of these subjects and his deep religious background make him singularly qualified to author a book that deals with religion and government.

The author might be called a "new evangelical." He takes the Great Commission seriously but believes the ministry of spoken discourse to be preceded and authenticated by a ministry of service. He does not compartmentalize Christian faith into a neat package, but in the last chapter of the book he suggests some of the problems to which Christian principles might be addressed in the form of Christian political action.

The book was not written for any one denomination. Dr. Cotham is affiliated with the Church of Christ, and I believe this to be the first book of its kind to be presented within that context. However, it should be read by all Americans and, in my opinion, by all citizens of democracies. As America celebrates its bicentennial, Americans should give much thought to the significance of government by the free will of the people. It is a proper time to review carefully what we have done, what we are doing, and what we should do in the future.

Dr. Cotham courageously tackles controversial questions concerning the character of America. In part 4 (chap. 12) he explores the question of whether America is a Christian nation. He then corrects what he considers to be mistaken notions of the past and defines the proper relationship between Christians, churches, and civil law in a pluralistic society. This clearly has been needed in conservative and evangelical churches.

Parts 1 and 2 are somewhat traditional in approach but very interesting. In part 2 the author discusses with eminent fairness the merits and demerits of different political life styles, and he makes clear his own choice of traditional political activism.

Part 3 contains the most extensive discussion I have seen of American civil religion from the evangelical viewpoint. There is currently much controversy over whether civil religion is Scriptural or heretical, functional or dysfunctional. The author enlightens us on this subject with rare insight.

Part 4 contains the most thorough discussion of Watergate from a theological perspective—of any kind—now in print. Enough time has passed to analyze Watergate with balanced indignation, dispassion, and compassion. Dr. Cotham views Watergate in terms of how it reflects upon American society as a whole, as there is a little of "Watergate" in all of us. Thus his concern is not with campaign reform, new laws, or mere politics, but with our entire way of life.

Most of all, I am impressed by the humility of Dr. Cotham's presentation. He has not given us a book of conclusions. He recognizes the voter's perplexity when confronted with the choice between two evils. But he clearly gives us the hope of, and prepares us for, Christian participation in politics in such a way that the choices will be broadened and that goodness may be enlarged and ultimately prevail over evil.

WILLIAM S. BANOWSKY
President, Pepperdine University

Preface

"For the very reason that Christianity addresses all life and experience, it touches man's other dilemmas. With substantial relevance Christianity penetrates every major problem of our day."[1] This was spoken by Carl F. H. Henry, one of evangelical Christianity's foremost scholars, and it is a chief premise of this book. Another premise of equal importance is that the Bible is the inspired Word of God. Though God's special revelation is contained in a canon of sacred writings that was collected many centuries ago, we cannot deny that the Universal Sovereign has a special message for individuals and nations in contemporary society. As long as history and this present dispensation continue, God will continue to speak to man through His Word. As you read these pages, keep in mind these two premises, which will be given neither apology nor defense.

The Bible is not essentially a book about politics—nor about common law, civil liberties, democratic ideals, or forms of political government. And it is certainly not a book about Americanism. Frustratingly enough for citizens in a constitutional democracy, it does not tell us how to vote. On the other hand, the Bible is full

1. *The God Who Shows Himself* (Waco, Tex.: Word, 1966), p. 2.

of politics. It speaks to citizens and nations today. The Bible includes narratives about a number of politicians and their encounters with God, their constituents, and other nations. Many of the politicians were godly men; more often they were not. We shall take Biblical doctrine and narratives as normative for Christians today.

This book deals with some of the many issues and interrelationships concerning politics, Americanism, and Christianity. But these issues cannot be examined in a vacuum, so I have drawn upon American history and recent political events as my chief sources. When I define a good civil religion (part 3), I am talking about a good civil religion for the United States, as seen from a Biblical perspective. A totalitarian regime such as Nazi Germany may have a "good" civil religion in the sense that it is technically efficient, uniting people behind national policies and goals and performing the other functions that political theorists think a civil religion should; but it is not a good civil religion when judged by the criteria we now bring to bear.

I am writing this during our bicentennial celebration, and our nation is recovering from a crisis in confidence that emerged from crucial issues in both foreign relations and domestic political affairs. The reader may expect numerous allusions to Vietnam and Watergate. We cannot afford to broach our subject matter apart from a Biblical orientation. In one sense the Biblical events read as fresh as this morning's headline story. Before we analyze some of the issues and challenges in politics and Christian ethics, we must set the backdrop for our study by surveying what the Old and New Testaments say about politics. The Old Testament is the natural beginning point. The New English Bible is used predominantly in this book; when another version is used, it is identified. Scriptural references were left in the text of all chapters.

Few, if any, general topics are more controversial than religion and politics. And for a writer to turn out a volume on a good number of specific topics where religion and politics intersect is to make oneself vulnerable to all kinds of criticism and negative reaction. No written or spoken discourse can be divorced from the unique religious and political biases and perspectives of the communicator, so I make no claims to omniscience or complete objectivity; I fully expect readers to disagree with certain arguments and lines of analysis. A certain amount of breadth was intended in this volume, and a critic may well insist that it covers too many topics for one volume. The book was not intended, as so many others are, to be read and digested in one evening's sitting. Nor is it intended for seasoned political scientists or scholars, but for interested and intelligent laymen.

In several ways the preparation of this volume was intricately linked with my work at David Lipscomb College. In a general way I am grateful to Dr. Patrick H. Deese and Dr. Robert E. Hooper for opening the opportunity for me to teach in the department of history and political science. Without this opportunity this volume would not have been possible. In a specific way I am indebted to the Lipscomb Research Committee, chaired by Dr. James Lee McDonough, for granting me a research grant for the summer of 1974, which enabled me to commence this project. Small but important contributions were made by a number of other people. Dr. Joel Anderson, a Christian political scientist at the University of Arkansas—Little Rock, sent me a number of materials and essays. Cathie King Hardeman helped collect material during the early weeks of research. Several of the chapters were read by people who were particularly qualified to react constructively to the content and style. Dr. James W. Thompson, a New Testament scholar at the University of Texas Student Ministry, read chapters 2 and 5 and offered some materials for my perusal. Other chapters were read by some colleagues at Lipscomb: Dr. Rodney Cloud (chap. 1); Dr. Robert Hooper (chaps. 3 and 4); Dr. Pat Deese (chaps. 8 and 9); and Dr. Constance Fulmer (chaps. 13 and 15). Cindy Watson, Karen Hill, Holly Halls, and my wife, Glenda, all helped type the final manuscript. And last but not least I am grateful to Dr. William S. Banowski, president of Pepperdine University and increasingly noted political activist, for taking time from his busy schedule to read the manuscript and write the foreword; and to Dan Van't Kerkhoff and Allan Fisher, editors at Baker Book House, for their assistance and perseverance in allowing the development of these themes in my own method and style. My hope is that this volume will glorify God and further His will and work in this nation.

September 1975

part one

Biblical Foundations
and Introductory Concepts

... *for you are a people holy to the Lord your God; the Lord your God chose you out of all nations on earth to be his special possession.*

Moses (Deut. 7:6)

For you alone have I cared
among all the nations of the world;
therefore will I punish you
for all your iniquities.

(Amos 3:2)

The time is coming, says the Lord, when I will make a new covenant with Israel and Judah. . . . I will set my law within them and write it on their hearts; I will become their God and they shall become my people.

(Jer. 31:31, 33)

chapter one

A Holy Nation

The study of any contemporary issue in ethics from a Christian perspective too often begins and ends with the New Testament. The Old Testament is just as inspired and often even more dramatic than the New, but, the feeling must run, God dealt with people in those days in a different manner and we have more in common with the first-century church than we do with Old Testament patriarchs and kings. Dietrich Bonhoeffer once noted that we frequently try to come to the New Testament too quickly and too easily without first studying it in relationship to the Old. This is particularly unfortunate in a study of Christianity and politics, for the Old Testament contains a rich heritage of relevant ideas and narratives. The Old Testament places much greater emphasis on the godly man's and the godly nation's sense of social justice and social responsibilities, as well as on God's sovereignty over all nations and His intervention in history.

First-generation Christians did not repudiate these concepts; indeed, they perceived themselves as standing solidly within the tradition of Old Testament doctrine about man and society, but their own commitment to the Messiah led them naturally to a greater emphasis on the life, death, resurrection, and Great Commission of Jesus Christ. Christian ethicists must view the action of God as one continuous drama that begins with the creation and ends with the spiritual blessings bestowed on the special *ekklēsia,* or called-out community of believers. As the distinguished Old Testament scholar G. Ernest Wright wrote: "When the New Testament is separated from the Old, it is a superstructure hanging in midair, a small torso of a literature filled with the presuppositions which can be misunderstood and perverted. Without the Old Testament there could be little conception of God's purposive work in and through history, which reaches its climax in Christ. . . . By itself the New Testament contains insufficient material for a doctrine of creation, of justice and the responsible society, and of man in relation to his world and people."[1] Both Testaments share a common theme—the self-disclosure of a transcendent, sovereign God to man in word and deed in history.

Any survey of politics and the Old Testament ultimately must be centered in the life and experiences of the Hebrew nation. The Hebrews always attributed their identity as the people of God to His prior action. In Old Testament theology it is God who provides the basis for becoming an identifiable and unique community. Israel had a special relationship with Jehovah, and what interests us is the rich variety of ways the ancient writers expressed this fundamental element of the national faith.

Perhaps the most significant way that this relationship was expressed was through the idea of covenant. Throughout her history, and even during the period when the concept was sparingly used, Israel understood her fundamental relationship to God in terms of the covenant which He had freely and graciously established with her. Jehovah was the dominant party in this covenant. There is a clear development of the covenant motif in Deuteronomy, and it is interesting that the covenant is presented as something contemporary for each generation: "It was not with our forefathers that the Lord made this covenant, but with us, all of us who are alive and are here this day" (Deut. 5:3). Each generation was to assume for itself the ritual, the renewal, and the social obligations of the covenant relationship.

Jehovah did not establish this relationship with Israel because of any special merit on Israel's part. Exclusively by His grace He elected her and chose her from among all nations for a special mission: ". . . for you are a people holy to the Lord your God; the

---

1. "The Faith of Israel," in George A. Buttrick, ed., *The Interpreter's Bible,* 12 vols. (Nashville: Abingdon, 1952), 1:389.

Lord your God chose you out of all nations on earth to be his special possession. It was not because you were more numerous than any other nation that the Lord cared for you and chose you, for you were the smallest of all nations; it was because the Lord loved you and stood by his oath to your forefathers. . . . Know then that the Lord your God is God, the faithful God; with those who love him and keep his commandments he keeps covenant and faith for a thousand generations" (Deut. 7:6-9).

The concept of covenant underwent considerable development and clarification throughout the course of Israel's history. New covenants were made with emerging patriarchs and spiritual leaders, and old ones were renewed. The covenant was conceived more in exclusivistic and nationalistic terms in the days of liberation from Egyptian servitude and conquest of Canaan. But in the course of her historical and spiritual development, the Hebrews realized that Jehovah's mercy and grace extend to all peoples and that the mission of ushering in and declaring salvation for all nations ultimately would be accomplished through Israel. Jeremiah prophesied a time when God would establish a new covenant with His people, a covenant written not on tables of stone but on the heart (Jer. 31:31-33). There were two major types of covenants in the Old Testament. The first type bound, or obligated, Jehovah alone. An example is God's covenant with Abraham to make him the father of many nations and through him to bless all nations of the earth (Gen. 12:1-3). God's covenant with Noah not to destroy the earthly system by water is another example (Gen. 9:8-17). The second type of covenant bound Israel to certain specified obligations. In the Sinaitic covenant God bound Israel to keep the Decalogue. But while He gave Israel the law, His sovereignty was not limited by her response to it, as we shall note.

The Hebrew drama began in Egypt. God's chosen people were struggling to survive under the heavy yoke of human bondage and earnestly seeking deliverance. Through Jehovah's providence, Moses appeared on the scene and, although having been reared in the royal family and groomed for high political office, he identified instead with the people of God. The children of God through Moses made a bid for their freedom, first by negotiation and eventually by the dramatic intervention of Jehovah in affairs of state. The story is a familiar one. It is important to note that the conflict involved two opposing conceptions of sovereignty and reality. Egyptian mythology identified the pharaoh as a divine

21

potentate who was the source of authority and order in all social, political, and religious matters; but Jehovah made a counterclaim by identifying his son as Israel rather than as the pharaoh (Exod. 3:10). God instructed Moses to confront the pharaoh with this unsettling claim: "Israel is my first-born son, I have told you to let my son go, so that he may worship me" (Exod. 4:22, 23). Unwilling to acknowledge the claim of a rival god, Pharaoh replied with a touch of both sarcasm and political realism: "Who is the Lord, that I should obey his voice to let Israel go? I know not the Lord, neither will I let Israel go" (Exod. 5:2 KJV). The struggle for power between the two deities was occasion for the fledgling Hebrew nation to determine to be loyal to Jehovah rather than to Pharaoh. This faith and loyalty frequently wavered, but it was sufficient for a great deliverance from Egypt and for receiving the law at Mt. Sinai.

The Sinai experience marked the beginning of a new epoch in Hebrew history. No longer a coalition of tribes and families, they were molded together and given identity through their participation in a common covenant. The Sinai covenant made it clear that Israel's primary loyalty was to Jehovah and not to any national state. The Decalogue was prefaced with the declaration that "I am the Lord your God who brought you out of Egypt, out of the land of slavery" (Exod. 20:2). The first four commandments gave distinctive clues to the nature of Israel's identity; they were peculiar features of Hebrew faith and practice. They set Israel apart from all other religious, social, and political communities. Should she fail to express her loyalty to Jehovah through obedience to these commands, she would be in immediate danger of losing her distinctiveness, her special identity, as the prophets continually reminded her. The remainder of the Decalogue put in minimal but concrete terms the meaning of faithfulness between members of this special community. Even now, of course, they are frequently cited as minimal requirements for the maintenance of integrity and social cohesion within *any* community. These six commandments include respect for parents and for the life, marriage, property, and honor of every other member of the nation.

For our purposes it is important to note that, while the special religion of Israel did provide a strong impetus toward the creation of an independent nation, from the beginning this goal was secondary to faithfulness to the divine will and fulfillment of her mission and destiny as a spiritual people of God. In other words, Israel was a nation-state with her own political goals. The rule of God was pervasive and absolute. We rightfully refer to Israel throughout her history as a theocracy. But from her origins and the charges given, Israel was more of a religious community than a political community. Obedience to God was paramount, and the political and economic structures of the new nation were to exemplify and foster such obedience.

We should not be surprised that various types of pharisaism or legalism developed among the Hebrews. The demand for total obedience led to schemes for locating God in a number of codes of law. They eventually substituted a mechanical, slavish, ritualistic obedience to certain law codes for the living, dynamic relationship with God intended by the covenant. They understood the covenant solely in terms of law, not of relationship. In this context the prophets appeared. By then the concept of the covenant had been so misconstrued that the old appeal and pedagogical value of a covenant relationship could not be recaptured. Consequently, prophets such as Amos, Hosea, Isaiah, and Micah introduced the symbols of sonship, marriage, kinship, judgment, sovereignty, and lordship to epitomize and restore Israel's relationship to Jehovah and to clarify what God required of His people, namely, love, trust, loyalty, justice, and integrity.

Since it was impossible to capture the inner meaning of that special relationship in any law code, Jeremiah pined for the time when God would make a new covenant with His people and write the law upon their hearts. We tend to forget that these prophets were spokesmen for hope as well as judgment: "The prophets frequently annexed to the prediction of judgment a prophecy of hope. The godly needed encouragement, and it was necessary to show the congruity between the overwhelming judgment and God's long-standing promise of the stability of David's throne and the perpetuity and triumph of God's kingdom on earth."[2]

In our survey of the Old Testament for potential relevance to politics, the teachings and writings of the prophets are crucial. The doctrine and exhortations they passed from God to this "holy nation" are of particular relevance for our study, and they may be summarized as follows:

1. *God was concerned about the corporate, or collective, life of the nation of Israel.* He was concerned about public morality and

---

2. John D. Davis, "Amos," in *Davis Dictionary of the Bible,* 4th ed. (Grand Rapids: Baker, 1954), p. 34.

social ethics. The church has emphasized individual responsibility and individual piety to such an extent that we tend to forget God is also concerned about societal standards and morality. In the Old Testament, personality is conceived corporately. To find fulfillment as a person means to be involved in a community and to participate in its life. A man's self, or soul, was perceived as extending through all his relationships, so that his family, tribe, nation, possessions, and even clothes were an integral part of himself. His neighbor was himself, so that to love his neighbor was to love himself, as the second great commandment states. John Donne's memorable line—". . . any man's death diminishes me, because I am involved in mankind. . . ."—aptly expresses the ideal view of man and his neighbor held by Israel. Disobedience to Jehovah affected more than the individual who disobeyed. This is the point in the story of Achan (cf. Josh. 7). To adequately punish Achan, not only he had to be destroyed, but also his family, animals, and property. Should any of these have been spared, Achan would have lived on, for they were all he.

This conception of the individual as inextricably bound to the community has its positive aspects. It enhances the worth and responsibility of a single man or woman, and it makes the possibilities for enrichment of community life and standards virtually limitless. One man's blessing could spread through the entire community around him and to succeeding generations. This is the meaning of the explanatory clause in the second commandment: ". . . and showing mercy unto thousands of them that love me, and keep my commandments" (Exod. 20:6 KJV).

Some of the prophets' severest warnings to Israel related to her neglect of public morality and social responsibilities. The requirements for social justice were reasonable in light of God's mighty action for Israel, and to the prophets there was no more devastating way to forget Jehovah than to forget the cries of the needy and oppressed. And forgetting the needy and oppressed is a natural outgrowth of pride, materialism, and immorality. Apparently Israelite society became so decadent that there was no sin to which the Jews did not stoop. Hosea warned them about their swearing, lying, killing, stealing, and adultery (Hos. 4:2). Amos warned against being ostentatious, dealing unjustly, indulging the rich and exploiting the poor, corrupting the courts, and committing a catalogue of social vices applicable to virtually any society, ancient or modern (cf. Amos 2, 3, 6). The judgments that the prophets saw Jehovah meting out in the calamities of history were primarily judgments against human pride. They followed inevitably when man refused to acknowledge the finite nature of his character, his dependence upon God, and when he charted out his own course according to selfish will and whim.

The iniquities of Israel were compounded by the comfortable piety that attaches the label "religious" to the oppressors and "sinners " to the victims. Amos pronounced the judgment of God upon His people at the national shrine of the North where people said their prayers and offered their sacrifices. Much like Jesus, Amos hurled his harshest censures not at the godless, but at religious people. Amos almost suggested that his people were guilty of treason, and he set out to destroy their religious traditions: "I hate, I spurn your pilgrim-feasts; I will not delight in your sacred ceremonies. When you present your sacrifices and offerings I will not accept them, nor look on the buffaloes of your shared-offerings. Spare me the sound of your songs; I cannot endure the music of your lutes. Let justice roll on like a river and righteousness like an ever-flowing stream" (Amos 5:21-24). Correct performance of worship is not enough. Despite the special bond between Jehovah and His people, Amos insisted that they were not so privileged that they could flaunt the basic rights of their neighbors or seek the protection of unjust law.

2. *God's love and concern were not limited to one people or nation, but extended to all nations on earth.* Israel's sense of Jehovah's universal activity kept her faith from becoming parochial. There was always an uneasy tension, however, between Israel's conception of Jehovah's concern for all nations of the earth and its conception of Israel as His own special people. At times, it seems, the mystery was never resolved completely. The story of God's command for Jonah to preach repentance in Nineveh was intended to instruct and remind the Hebrews of this aspect of Jehovah's nature. The perception of God as the God of all nations is much clearer in the New Testament, but it is not, of course, as slighted in the Old Testament as many believe. Israel had accepted her vocation on behalf of other nations; she was to be a living witness of Jehovah's intention for every human community.

3. *Special blessings for Israel meant special obligations.* As we have suggested already, the prophets viewed the covenant relationship in terms of demand and responsibility. It is tempting to see in the doctrine of election an election to blessing and spiritual

status that is unconditional. In the Old Testament, election is to both blessing and obligation. Israel is chosen for special deeds—to be "a light unto the Gentiles," a "polished shaft" sent forth into the darkness of unbelief to illumine life for those who have never heard of Jehovah. To Amos, who spoke for the Lord, the natural consequence of receiving God's special election and blessings was to be judged even more severely then others for one's sins: "For you alone have I cared among all the nations of the world; therefore will I punish you for all your iniquities" (Amos 3:2). This implication of election must have both startled and disturbed the Hebrews, who probably wished God had said, "You only have I known of all the nations, therefore I will see to it that all goes well with you." To be chosen is to be guaranteed not an easier time but a rougher time.

4. *The covenant reationship had to be constantly maintained by fidelity and commitment, for there was a constant temptation to neglect this vital relationship until it was destroyed.* One way in which the special relationship with Jehovah was strained was through neglecting instruction and being willfully ignorant. The fault lay with the priests, who were custodians of the law but who neither nourished their own souls by studying it nor transmitted it to their children. God told the priestly cult: "My people are ruined for lack of knowledge. . . . You have rejected knowedge, and I will reject you from serving me as priest. You have forgotten the teaching of God, and I, your God, will forget your sons" (Hos. 4:6).

Man can dissipate his relationship with God and blind himself to the peril. The prophets perceived this false security. "Woe to them that are at ease in Zion, and trust in the mountain of Samaria. . . ." warned Amos (6:1 KJV). Peace and safety, which the covenant established, were not so much a stable order between nations or individuals as a spiritual relationship with the Almighty that was informed and reformed by His Word. And what disturbed security and safety was not the enemy's attack but Israel's shifting its confidence and trust to an object other than Jehovah.

It is at this point of shifting trust and false security that politics, in the Old Testament, comes into sharpest conflict with covenantal faith. Despite her spiritual origin, the nation of Israel had a political structure. At critical junctures in her history, she was powerful and prosperous, but she was never independent from God's succor.

The catalogue of things that tempted Israel to shift her trust sounds very modern.

First were foreign alliances. Hosea's most searing condemnations were in the area of international politics, where Israel's misplaced trust clearly showed (see also I Kings 18). Hosea saw the folly of matching strength only with greater strength that was devoid of moral authority and trusting in chariots and massive retaliation (Hos. 10:13; see also Ps. 147:10; Zech. 4:6). Hosea's description of his people reads like a modern political cartoon caricaturing Uncle Sam: "Ephraim and his aliens make a sorry mixture; Ephraim has become a cake half-baked. Foreigners fed on his strength, but he was unaware; even his grey hairs turned white, but he was unaware. . . . Ephraim is a silly senseless pigeon. . . ." (Hos. 7:8, 9, 11). To Hosea those people who insisted in the superiority of their nation, right or wrong, were not the most patriotic ones. The fate of the nation was at stake, and Hosea could not be optimistic.

Besides trusting in foreign alliances, Israel trusted in fortifications (Jer. 5:17), armaments (Isa. 31:1), oppression (Isa. 30:12), wealth (Ps. 52), man and his power (Jer. 17:5) and, ever closer to home, assessments that cover unpleasant facts and realities (Jer. 7:8). Such misplaced confidence amounted not only to a breakdown in faith, but also to idolatry and, in political terms, treason. It was never Jehovah's intention to deny Israel earthly political power or national wealth. But the continual tension between Him and His chosen people hinged on Israel's not making Him the ultimate basis of her confidence, self-identity, and security. The prophets warned that a disobedient, idolatrous nation would fail in war and diplomacy. At the climax of her humiliation, Israel would receive the prophecy and hope of a Suffering Servant whose advent would bring ultimate victory and fulfill the purposes of the covenant. The description of the Suffering Servant offers the deepest insight into the meaning of suffering and the depth of God's love in the Old Testament (Isa. 42:1-4; 49:1-6; 52:13–53:12).

5. *Political leaders were also spiritual leaders, anointed to carry out the will of God.* The Old Testament gives detailed accounts of the lives of Israel's leaders. It does not cover up their flaws and misconduct, whether public or private. It considers their misdeeds violations of God's commandments, breaches of man's relationship with Jehovah. To the prophets, God's will was the essence of public interest. When a king of Israel was accused by the prophetic community of something, he was condemned not simply for acting

against the public trust but for violating God's holy law. Amos leveled his strongest censures not just at political authorities but at all those in positions of power and influence who were taking advantage of the poor. Even in the case of David, Israel's greatest king, the establishment of the monarchy depended upon a covenant between David and the people (II Sam. 5). The turning point in his career came when, just after the Bathsheba incident, Nathan accused David of having overstepped his authority and set an improper example for his subjects (II Sam. 12:9, 10).

Israelite kings, therefore, were bound by special covenantal obligations. We should not be surprised that the political leaders sought out special clerical support and blessings for all their political decisions. The king might have his own court prophet to lend the authority of Jehovah to all his grisly deeds. The true prophet of the Lord was anything but welcome in the king's court, as Amos discovered, for example. The king of Israel (Jeroboam II) and the priest of Bethel (Amaziah) accused him of conspiring against the land, forbade him to preach at Bethel, and banished him from the land (Amos 7:7-17). Amaziah both challenged and ridiculed Amos, calling him a seer and urging him to seek employment where his message might be more warmly received. But Amos saw himself not as a professional but as a man Jehovah had seized for His own designs (cf. Amos 3:8). Amaziah resorted to a propaganda device, calling him a rabble-rouser who harangued the people. But Amos's message, like Micaiah's, could not be avoided by obliterating the message-bearer (cf. I Kings 22). One may imprison the messenger, but not the truth.

6. *History was used to inspire godly people to greater planes of righteousness.* Throughout the Old Testament holy men of God, and particularly the prophets, motivated their nation to return to and remain in righteousness by appealing to the past, especially God's action on their behalf. Hosea reminded Israel of what Jehovah had done in the wilderness, at the exodus, and in the conquest of Canaan and its deities (Hos. 2:14-17). Before giving the law God instructed Moses to remind the people what He had done for them: "Speak thus to the house of Jacob, and tell this to the sons of Israel: You have seen with your own eyes what I did to Egypt, and how I carried you on eagles' wings and brought you here to me. If only you will now listen to me and keep my covenant, then out of all peoples you shall become my special possession; for the whole earth is mine. You shall be my kingdom

of priests, my holy nation. . . ." (Exod. 19:3-6). In the Old Testament the appeal to the past is at the same time a means of conveying and celebrating the presence of Jehovah in all undertakings. Numerous other passages appealing to history could be cited.

7. *God revealed His will to His people through unlikely sources.* God did not always reveal His will and Word through expected channels. The usual pattern was for Israel to make God's will known to the pagans, but the ancient readers of the message of Isaiah were in for a surprise: "The Assyrian! He is the rod that I wield in my anger; and the staff of my wrath is in his hand. I send him against a godless nation, I bid him march against a people who rouse my wrath, to spoil and plunder at will and trample them down like mud in the streets" (Isa. 10:5, 6). The Hebrew nation had forgotten God, so God would employ pagan Assyria to reveal to Israel His will and the seriousness of flouting it. Assyria was the instrument, "the rod of my anger" (KJV). To be sure, it never occurred to Assyria that it was being used by God, and the Assyrian king might well have been delighted and amused at the idea, for "howbeit he meaneth not so, neither doth his heart think so. . . ." (v. 7 KJV). Nevertheless, the pagan became God's vehicle of revelation and judgment upon His people. To all Old Testament writers God acted in both history and word. Periods of captivity were essentially periods of chastisement and moral instruction.

This survey of the Old Testament is intended to point to concepts that have particular relevance to the study of Christianity and politics. We have found the basic structure of ethics to involve God's initiative in creating a religious and political community, and Israel's response. Ethics, politics, and religion are interrelated in the Old Testament doctrines of God and man, and the central criterion for genuine community is total commitment and fidelity to God. The prophets contended that such a community involves the exclusive worship of the one true God and justice that includes the needy, the neglected, the oppressed, and strangers in the community.

Many implications are suggested by this survey, but we have deliberately avoided drawing out any of them. One might ask, for example: Is America in any sense a chosen, elected nation? Can a modern nation, a political entity with powers of enforcement, be such a covenant community? Does God expect more of us because we have enjoyed greater material prosperity? Do we have a false sense of security? Will a study of American heritage and history inspire us to greater deeds? Should our political leaders be held accountable for violating not only the public trust but certain tenets of the Scriptures? Have we attempted to silence the true prophets of God and turned instead to "court prophets"? Will God always bless America? Might we lose a war or our precious liberties if we are not faithful to God?

Most of us could provide easy answers to these questions already, but we will explore these issues in some depth in later chapters after studying the view of politics and religion held by Jesus and the early Christians.

Pay Caesar what is due to Caesar, and pay God what is due to God.

Jesus (Mark 12:17)

Every person must submit to the supreme authorities. There is no authority but by act of God, and the existing authorities are instituted by him; consequently anyone who rebels against authority is resisting a divine institution, and those who so resist have themselves to thank for the punishment they will receive.

Paul (Rom. 13:1, 2)

We are in fact of all men your best helpers and allies in securing good order, convinced as we are that no wicked man, no covetous man or conspirator, or virtuous man either, can be hidden from God.

Justin Martyr to the Emperor

We sin then against the imperial majesty in this, that we do not make him subject to his own possessions; that we do not perform a mockery by offering a service for his safety when we do not suppose that safety to rest in hands soldered with lead. . . . For we call upon God for the safety of the Emperor, upon God the eternal, God the true, God the living, whose favor beyond all others the Emperor desires.

Tertullian

chapter two

Render unto Caesar

The New Testament is from beginning to end about Jesus Christ. He alone is indispensable to its concern and content. The New Testament is about a Person and an event. In Christ, God has visited man. Every other person and every other event assume importance only in relationship to that Man and that event. All subjects of concern treated by the New Testament authors, whether doctrinal or practical, center on His life and teaching. For the early Christians the self-disclosure of God in Jesus Christ became the decisive and most complete revelation of the nature and will of God. The first Pentecost after His resurrection was the occasion for the advent of the long awaited kingdom; the *ekklēsia,* or church, was called into being. The basic premise of the New Testament church was that in and through Jesus of Nazareth and subsequently through the church, God was fulfilling His promises to Israel.

The narrative accounts of the life of Jesus and the letters of doctrine, instruction, and encouragement to various individuals and congregations of the first century constitute the core of the New Testament. Their purpose was to create faith in Jesus as Christ, the Son of God, and to inspire renewed faithfulness to His life and teachings in word and deed. All other issues were peripheral for the apostles and early disciples. Modern Christians who look to the New Testament, and especially to a key verse or passage in it, for a definitive treatment of the state and politics will be disappointed. On the surface there appears, and we emphasize *appears,* to be no single view of state and politics in the New Testament. Actually, we may conclude that Jesus and the New Testament writers did not hold contradictory viewpoints. But we must broach our subject of the New Testament view of state and politics the same way we would such subjects as the place of women, slavery, and science; we must inductively examine key passages in both their immediate social context and their broader, historical context.

The Politics of Jesus

During His earthly ministry Jesus came into contact with three levels of government: the rule of Herod Antipas in Galilee, the rule of Jewish councils culminating in the Sanhedrin, and the rule of Rome represented by the procurator, Pontius Pilate. There is no evidence that Jesus directly repudiated any of these or that He was particularly interested in political affairs. His overriding concern was with spiritual matters and, in particular, the coming of God's kingdom. In contrast with the Zealots, He rejected revolution against Rome and advised the practice of nonresistance, giving His blessing to the peacemakers. Political power held no attraction for him. One of the three great temptations Jesus overcame in the wilderness was Satan's suggestion that He assume the political lordship of the kingdoms of the world (Matt. 4:8-10 and Luke 4:5-8). In its immediate context, Jesus' statement "I have not come to bring peace, but a sword" (Matt. 10:34-39 and Luke 12:51-53) clearly refers to the dissension created in a family when one member becomes a disciple of His. No one can read the Sermon on the Mount and conclude that Jesus intended His disciples to have much in common with those who wield political power. Although the specific phrase "kingdom of God" is not in the Old Testament, it was in wide currency by the time of Jesus, due in large measure to the preaching of John the Baptist. Jesus purged the term of all its nationalistic elements and transformed it into a universal reign of God, thus beqeathing it a new and deeper meaning.

Jesus made only one directly political utterance, but it is probably the best-known and most often quoted comment on politics in the Scriptures. In reply to the question "Is it lawful to pay taxes to Caesar?" he pointed to the image of Caesar on a coin and said, "Render to Caesar the things that are Caesar's, and to God the things that are God's" (Mark 12:17 KJV). The Jews had devised a cunning trap for Jesus. Had He said it was lawful to pay tribute to Caesar, he would have offended the nationalistic sentiment of His people; had he said civil disobedience was permissible, he would have been reported to the Roman authorities and tried in their courts.

Jesus' reply, however, was more than a cunning evasion or skillful ploy. The statement had much more theological significance than political. Unmoved by local or nationalist prejudice, Jesus asserted that the authority of earthly rulers is valid in their own sphere. Those whose first allegiance is to God are not excused from paying their dues to the de facto authority responsible for law and order. Political government is legitimate, necessary, and proper. But political authority is limited to a very precise sphere, and it must not trespass upon the infinite demands of God. Absolute obedience belongs to God alone. The difference between God's realm and Caesar's is that the latter belongs to the transient order that will pass away. Jesus warned His disciples not to confuse the order of the state with the divine order, nor to give to Caesar the ultimate loyalty that belongs to God alone. When the Sanhedrin attempted to silence the apostles, Peter and John replied, "We must obey God rather than men" (Acts 5:29). When Sir Thomas More refused to compromise the authority of the church and was ordered executed by Henry VIII, he protested that he was "the king's good servant, but God's first."

Jesus' statement undoubtedly was misunderstood and misconstrued by many who heard it. It is entirely feasible that, as Luke tells us, Jesus incited the people not to pay their taxes (Luke 23:2). Our Lord's position, though simply stated, was a complex one and most difficult to translate into action. Consequently, His view was distorted by the public prejudices and political attitudes of His day. In modern times many dissenters from the absolute, or at best uncertain, claims of a state have had their position misconstrued and their allegiance questioned. But Jesus' statement is radically relevant. The political state is not the ultimate authority. It is so important, however, that it may levy taxes to finance its activity. Pay these taxes even when you have serious and legitimate reservations about certain activities and claims of your government. Do not waste time and energy resisting taxes; the mammon belongs to Caesar anyway. But do not give Caesar more than his due; give him nothing that belongs to God! We must keep this doctrine in mind when later we discuss a Christian's attitude toward American patriotism.

This conception of political power surfaced in the trial of Jesus before Pilate. Political power bears some relationship to the creating, preserving, and redeeming work of God, but Pilate would have had no authority over Jesus if it had not been given to him from on high (John 19:11). As a judge, Pilate was granted the possibility and opportunity to do what is right in a sinful world. Pilate allowed this possibility to escape him, either through a flaw in his character or by his somewhat precarious political situation. Even Pilate had a duty and responsibility to a Force greater than the will of the people. But this personal shortsightedness and failure does not nullify the principle that political authority is ordained of God to serve His purposes in the human society.

To recapitulate, Jesus accepted the state and renounced any attempt to overthrow it or deprive it of its due. On the other hand, He certainly did not regard the state in any sense a final, divine (in the sense that the church is) institution. We need not have limited ourselves to His statement on taxes in Mark 12. When Herod tried to run Him out of the country with a threat, He did not hesitate to call that public official a "fox" (Luke 13:32). On another occasion He noted the irony of civil authorities who rule by force and oppress the people, and still call themselves "their country's 'Benefactors'" (Luke 22:25). Jesus also seemed to legitimize the stereotype of tax collectors as "collaborationists," rebuking them in the same context as heathen, sinners, and prostitutes (cf. Matt. 9:10; 18:17; 21:31). And yet Jesus received tax collectors and sinners, which subjected Him to intense criticism by the religious establishment. Not only did He obediently pay taxes to the power that occupied His homeland, but he healed a Roman officer's servant and enjoined His disciples to go the extra mile with Roman mail carriers. As Oscar Cullman pointed out, "Jesus was in no sense an enemy of the State on principle, but rather a loyal citizen who offered no threat to the state's existence."[1]

A First-Century Che Guevara?

In recent times a few purportedly religious scholars have argued

---

1. *The State in the New Testament* (New York: Scribner's, 1956), p. 54. This book is brief, but it is one of the most authoritative and practical studies of this subject currently in print, and I am indebted to it for many of the lines of analysis in this chapter.

that Jesus was a political revolutionary or rebel and then read the New Testament accounts of His life accordingly. This simply cannot be done. He shunned the role of political rebel and patriot. He was a social conformist, the embodiment of Paul's admonition to render "custom to whom custom . . . honour to whom honour" is due (Rom. 13:7 KJV). The debate over the length of Jesus' hair becomes rather silly. He groomed Himself according to the custom of His time. This is evidenced by the fact that when He was arrested in the garden, the police needed someone from within the inner circle to identify Him. But those modern Christians who fervently denounce any effort to make Jesus a political revolutionary have sometimes been the least willing or able to acknowledge that He was a revolutionary of sorts—a religious revolutionary.

A reading of the Gospel narratives leaves no doubt about Jesus' priorities. Christ offered no general programs of political and social action; He did offer a planned preaching ministry for His disciples. But He showed concern for the total well-being and destiny of all men. He did not talk about man in general or the world in the abstract; He loved and dealt with men and women as He encountered them and, as in the parable of the good Samaritan, He taught His disciples to do the same. For Jesus, social ethics arise out of concrete situations, and the Gospels are a collection of such situations. He was endlessly concerned about people's daily behavior and the values by which they order their lives. He identified openly with the poor, the needy, the oppressed, and the socially ostracized. Jesus' table fellowship with despised sinners, tax collectors, and prostitutes made Him unique in contemporary Judaism. In the tradition of the Old Testament prophets, He boldly proclaimed that meticulously keeping the finer points of the ceremonial law could in no way ameliorate for neglecting the weightier matters of the law, such as justice, mercy, and love (cf. Matt. 23). His willingness to challenge society's ethnocentrism (or racism) and materialist values (note His many parables and warnings about covetousness) strike directly at two sore spots within our own society. Besides associating and dining with tax collectors and other citizens in disrepute, Jesus performed other acts that must be labeled nonconformist in nature. Included here would be His forceful disruption of crass commercialism in the temple (John 2:13-22), His way of observing the Sabbath (Matt. 12:1-8; Mark 2:23-28; Luke 6:1-5), and His method of demonstrating power over the Devil (Matt. 8:28-34; Mark 5:1-17; Luke 8:26-36). Nor is it irrelevant to recall that Jesus was executed by Rome as a political criminal.

The real question is not how a handful of writers can see the New Testament Christ as a political revolutionary, but how millions of those who wear His name can read the New Testament and miss the revolutionary demands Christ made of His followers? How did Christianity come to be the official religion of those who sanction oppression, materialism, slavery, and the divine right of kings and emperors, whether Hapsburgs, Romanoffs, Bourbons, or Stuarts? How could Mark Twain's mother never have heard slavery assailed in any pulpit but have heard it defended and sanctified in a thousand? The last situation may be atypical, at least for our times, but how did it all come about? Two factors are at work. First, people tend to read the Bible in light of their own situation. If they are power-holders, they want to defend the status quo. Psychologists have warned us about thinking autistically, confusing what we want the truth to be with what the truth is. Second, when revolutionary movements succeed, it is difficult for their beneficiaries to perceive the revolutionary nature of the original struggle. A radical cause that prevails no longer seems so radical to descendants. There was an uneasy inconsistency in the views of those Christians who condemned as too revolutionary the non-violent civil disobedience of the late Martin Luther King, Jr., but praised as national heroes men who had sneaked aboard British ships in the Boston harbor and dumped tea into the ocean. Whenever and wherever the church has challenged a sinful status quo more than defended it, it is because Christians have recaptured the revolutionary spirit of the life and teachings of Jesus Christ.

Last, but not least, Jesus acknowledged that man does not live by bread alone, that human judgment is not ultimate judgment, and that there is more to life than the here and now. Uniqueness and individuality do not reside in external forms; the true sign of discipleship emerges from a quality that is internal: "By this shall all men know that ye are my disciples, if ye have love one to another" (John 13:35 KJV). Despite a ministry of benevolence, Jesus taught that the one thing that survives the worldly order is a man's soul. He intended His teaching to add immeasurably to the quality of spiritual life.

The Church of the New Testament

The church was both a continuation and a consummation of

the covenant community of Israel. Yet at the same time it was essentially a *new*, visible community of believers, separated from the world, called by God through the power of the Holy Spirit, and made possible by the death and resurrection of Jesus Christ. God's purpose for the church was to bring salvation to all nations, peoples, and races of the earth, and thus to fulfill His promise to Abraham to bless all the nations through Abraham's descendants (cf. Gen. 22:18; Acts 3:25). The New Testament church realized that the new people of God cannot be bound to God and protected by the power of the Holy Spirit by some form of political clout or coercion, for by its very nature it is an ecumenical, not a political, community. The church is bound to God through her relationship to His Son, Jesus Christ; in Him the last vestige of religious nationalism in the covenant community is swept away. Like Israel of old, God's new Israel is called to be a merciful, faithful, and righteous people. It is to be physically defenseless in the world; it is to share the service, suffering, and sacrifice of her Lord, bearing witness to the reconciling work of God in Christ by proclaiming the gospel unto all men and becoming itself an agent of reconciliation in the world through concrete acts of love. The Christian's first loyalty is to Christ—both His teachings and His ministry. The world can never completely embody the will of God, so the church is called out from the world to be a sign and a witness to the world as well as a place of fellowship with fellow saints.

The first-century church interpreted its mission among the nations largely in evangelistic terms. The principal theme of Christian evangelism was that there is an infinite separation between evil mankind and a just God, a gap which is bridged finally by Jesus Christ. The early Christians did not involve themselves in the social and political structures of society. They were largely noninvolved or nonattached. True, they were deeply concerned for the "neighbor" who is a victim of oppressive social institutions or unjust public policies. And the early church practiced a radical reversal of our typical human attitudes toward wealth and privilege. Jesus' teaching that the last will be first and the first last (Matt. 20:16) found its place in the life and teaching of early congregations (cf. James 2:1-4). And yet the first generation of Christians did not believe it their responsibility to transform or reconstruct political and social institutions in order to harmonize them with the teachings of Christ. The first-century world was one of Roman authoritarianism in the political realm and of slavery, caste, and sexism in the social. And yet no New Testament author entertained any thought of political pressure or action to influence the political structure or the public policy of its rulers. Very few Christians accepted posts in the secular government, and most did everything within their power, consistent with loyalty to Christ, to avoid any unnecessary clash; this was not radical hostility but a cool indifference and nonattachment. While one must be careful in applying modern political terms to the ancient situation, we can say that the early Christians were conservatives or rightists.

Why this conservatism? The most obvious reason was a sense of *realpolitik.* The first Christians were a small and weak minority movement with no social prestige or political power. It was just not possible either for the church as a special community or for Christians acting individually as citizens to exercise any significant influence upon social, economic, or politcal affairs. This situation of relative political powerlessness continued up to the fourth century when Christianity became the offical religion of the empire, and it is much akin to the situation of Christians and small congregations in totalitarian nations today. In the cultural and political milieu of early Christianity, the development of a genuine social ethic was largely irrelevant.

A second reason for its conservatism was the early Christians' eschatological perspective. They entertained a strong hope for the imminent return of Christ, which would dramatically terminate the present evil age and establish a new order. There seemed to be little remaining time for reforming an unjust political or social system, nor was their any justification for it since God Himself was about to establish a new era. The existing, imperfect institutions were part of a perishing world order. Gradually, however, Christians abandoned the expectation of Christ's imminent return and the climax of history and resigned themselves to a longer future. The apostle Paul rebuked those who severed all human relations as though the end were coming the very next day (cf. II Thess. 3). The Gospel writers recorded that Jesus Himself had refused to set an exact date for His return, for only the Father knew the exact day and hour of that great event. And while an imminent return gave evangelism a sense of urgency, a delayed return did not undercut Christian doctrine or practice. Human character without God was in the same lost and alienated condition, and the answer to human spiritual needs was still to decide for Christ as the Son of God and for the kingdom.

At this point a crucial matter deserves consideration. To say that the early Christians did nothing about political, social, and economic injustices is grossly inadequate and unfair. They believed in beginning with the core, the human heart, and moving to the externals. External changes without a change of heart are inadequate and ultimately doomed to failure. In light of the fast-approaching climax of history, as we have just noted, any efforts to reconstitute governments, campaign for world peace, abolish chattel slavery, give women equal rights, or retool the economic order would be wasted. But there was time and opportunity to do something about those specific and individual relationships in which Christians found themselves. When, for example, the apostle Paul encountered a problem in human relationships (such as slavery or the second-class status of women), he in no way attempted to restructure the institutions of which the oppressed and oppressors were a part. It may have been difficult for the early Christians to imagine a world in which slavery did not exist. As a Roman citizen Paul did not call the established order into question, but he sought to transform individual relationships. He was preaching and writing to men and women who had believed in Christ and been led by the Holy Spirit into a radically new life (cf. II Cor. 5:17), one in which the demands of brotherhood must be acknowledged and acted upon. Thus Paul sent the fugitive slave Onesimus back to his rightful master and, without demanding that Philemon grant Onesimus his freedom, entreated Philemon to welcome Onesimus and treat him as a brother in Christ. And Paul suggested that Philemon would do even more than he had requested (cf. Philem. 21). The premise underlying Paul's instructions to Philemon was that being in the body of Christ transforms human relations. Nor would we expect Paul to petition the powers in Rome to pass some ancient equivalent to the modern Equal Rights Amendment, although women served in early congregations and were given a miraculous measure of the Holy Spirit (cf. I Cor. 11:5; Rom. 16:1).

In summary, the Christian community itself was the very center of early Christian activism. The church had something unique to offer, something the great philosophers and humanists could not supply—a Person and a message to satisfy man's deepest hunger and needs. This Person had transformed their lives and their relationships with those in this new community of faith. The church became the center of God's reconciling and redeeming activity in the world. In this special fellowship and fraternity there was neither slave nor free, Jew nor Greek, male nor female (Gal. 3:28). Human dignity was granted or restored to all the societal outcasts and oppressed, the widows and orphans were looked after, the aged honored, the indigent fed and clothed, the weak and fearful strengthened and given hope. This re-creation of all human relationships by the early Christians was in the long run more important and in the short run more constructive and realistic. The new human relationships they established within their community of faith could not have been produced by political coercion; they were, however, by-products of faith in Jesus Christ, who had bade His disciples to seek first the kingdom of God and His righteousness, and of joining in corporate service and worship to the same Master in heaven.

A Look at the Texts

The New Testament, as should be clear by now, is a nonpolitical book. Passive obedience based on the life and teaching of Jesus came naturally to Christians in the first century; they accepted the political order as the work of divine providence. But was their obedience absolute? And for what purposes did God ordain civil govenment? To answer this we shall survey briefly what Paul taught about civil government, chiefly in Romans 13, and then look at I Peter 2 and Revelation 13.

Paul in Romans 13 presented the longest direct discussion of civil government from a Christian perspective. This passage is remarkably optimistic:

> Every person must submit to the supreme authorities. There is no authority but by act of God, and the existing authorities are instituted by him; consequently anyone who rebels against authority is resisting a divine institution, and those who so resist have themselves to thank for the punishment they will receive. For government, a terror to crime, has no terrors for good behaviour. You wish to have no fear of the authorities? Then continue to do right and you will have their approval, for they are God's agents working for your good. But if you are doing wrong, then you will have cause to fear them; it is not for nothing that they hold the power of the sword, for they are God's agents of punishment, for retribution on the offender. That is why you are obliged to submit. It is an obligation imposed not merely by fear of retribution but by conscience. That is also why you pay taxes. The authorities are in God's service and to these duties they devote their energies. (Rom. 13:1-7)

It is instructive that Paul included this passage, his only specific discussion of the Christian's relationship to his government, in his letter to the church in Rome, the capital city. Furthermore, Paul wrote this before there was any organized persecution of Christians by the Roman authorities. The disciples could not ignore the authorities, said Paul. While the state cannot conform to the absolute perfection of God, it is ordained by God for the present sinful order. All political powers exist by divine permission, and they have their place, however great or small, in the redemptive plan of God. The function God has reserved for them is to preserve a peaceful social order, encouraging freedom and honesty and repressing violent evil. They are a sign, however ambiguous, of the mercy of God for all men; they witness to the fact that the Creator has not abandoned His world, which includes both good and bad people, to the prince of the world. To revolt against such a divinely established system of law and order is to revolt against God Himself.

Was Paul requiring absolute obedience to any and every de facto government a Christian may find himself under, and to any and every one of its demands? We must remember that Paul himself was a Roman citizen who enjoyed certain protections from the Roman authorities. When his words in this passage are taken in isolation and used as the foundation for Christian political philosophy, they are construed as a sanction for every existing order and command from a political authority rather than as an affirmation that the state is always subordinate to the authority of God. An essential corrective to this political absolutism is present in the apostle's discussion of how brethren in the church should resolve legal differences (I Cor. 6:1-11). Christians are not to make use of the state's legitimate institutions of adjudication. Paul seems to say that there is a limit to the recognition and value of any state, as well as that a public dispute of any kind reflects poorly upon the entire church. The reputation of the entire congregation is at stake. If the exclusive purpose of the state is to maintain order, then whenever the disciples of Christ can dispense with its services without threatening its existence, they should. The state's survival and validity are not endangered if Christians do not rely on it to resolve their legal disputes. Congregations must exercise their own discipline, and individuals must exercise self-discipline. And finally, the wisdom and farsightedness of political authorities is limited: "And yet I do speak words of wisdom to those who are ripe for it, not a wisdom belonging to this passing age, nor to any of its governing powers, which are declining to their end: I speak God's hidden wisdom, his secret purpose framed from the very beginning to bring us to our full glory. The powers that rule the world have never known it; if they had, they would not have crucified the Lord of glory" (I Cor. 2:6-8).

Cullman summarized his exegesis of the Pauline passages we have discussed:

> What consequences can we draw from them for the problem "Paul and the State"? The State in itself is nothing divine. But it maintains a certain dignity in that it stands in an order which is *still* willed by God. Hence it is true for Paul also: The Christian is commanded on the basis of the Gospel to maintain a critical attitude toward the State; but he has to give the State all that is necessary to its existence. He has to affirm the State as an institution. Of the totalitarian claim of the State which demands for itself what is God's, Paul does not speak directly. But there can be no doubt that he too would not have allowed the Christians to obey the State just at the point where it demands what is God's. What we know about his *life*, proves this. He would not have permitted them to say "Caesar is Lord" and "anathema Jesus" (let Jesus be accursed), as this was demanded by the same Roman State to which the Christian is to pay taxes and whose institution he is to acknowledge as willed by God.[2]

Numerous portions of the New Testament reflect situations of political persecution, and I Peter is one of them. Peter shared Paul's conviction that Christian duty demands strict obedience to the emperor: "Submit yourselves to every human institution for the sake of the Lord, whether to the sovereign as supreme, or to the governor as his deputy for the punishment of criminals and the commendation of those who do right. For it is the will of God that by your good conduct you should put ignorance and stupidity to silence" (2:13-15).

This passage is all the more striking since persecution was taking place. Some have suggested the persecution was only social ostracism, but this does not square with references elsewhere in the epistle which parallel suffering for the name of Christ with suffering as a murderer or thief (4:12-19). People are persecuted for these crimes not simply by unkind neighbors but by the police. I Peter 2:13-15 seems to be simply a prudent policy: "For it is the will of God that by your good conduct you should put ignorance and stupidity to silence." Peter is urging Christians to make sure that they give no occasion for persecution apart from their stead-

2. Ibid., pp. 64, 65.

fastness and dedication to Christ; once the magistrates generally recognize that the sole crime of the Christians is that of being Christians, political persecutions will cease. John Knox cited a letter from Pliny as evidence that the governor would not want to persecute Christians whose only crime was membership in an illegal religious group. Peter seems to be urging Christians to cooperate with authorities to clarify the nature of their religious commitment; hence, he uges them to be ready to give a defense for their Christianity to anyone, especially civil authorities, who may question them about their faith (3:15).[3]

A final passage meriting careful attention is Revelation 13. Here we face what on its surface is a radically different attitude toward the state than that in Romans 13 and I Peter 2. In the Apocalypse the power of Rome incorporates the demonic powers of evil as they are let loose on earth. Rome is " 'Babylon the great, mother of harlots and of earth's abominations. . . .' drunk with the blood of the saints and the blood of the martyrs of Jesus" (17:5, 6 RSV). We must remember, however, that Revelation, unlike Romans, came from a time of severe persecution. Revelation 13 was recorded in the context of the Roman state's demand for emperor worship. The first-century Christians had affirmed *kurios Christos*, "Christ is Lord." This seemingly inoffensive spiritual jargon, however, was loaded with political implications by the time of Domitian. Subjects of the Roman empire were required to confess a different creed: *kurios Caesar*, "Caesar is Lord." The early Christian's affirmation that "Christ is Lord" inferred that "Caesar is *not* Lord." The Roman authorities realized this, and Christians captured by the state were persecuted unless they would swear the unambiguous oath, *"Kurios Caesar, anathēma Christos,"* "Caesar is Lord, Christ is accursed."[4] If they uttered this, they were set free. Christians in Smyrna could expect to be imprisoned but were admonished to be faithful even unto death (Rev. 2:10). Antipas was martyred at Pergamum. Underneath the heavenly altar were the souls of the martyrs awaiting the day of divine vengeance upon their executioners.

---

3. "Pliny and I Peter: A Note on I Peter 4:14-16 and 3:15," *Journal of Biblical Literature* 72 (1953): 187-89.

4. This seems to be the background of the situation Paul discusses in I Cor. 12:3: "For this reason I must impress upon you that no one who says 'A curse on Jesus!' can be speaking under the influence of the Spirit of God. And no one can say 'Jesus is Lord!' except under the influence of the Holy Spirit."

The example of Rome at the turn of the century clearly illustrates how a legitimate and powerful regime can degenerate, making illegitimate demands. When the Roman state demanded emperor worship, it exceeded its proper bounds. It made absolute demands that only an infinite and omnipotent God may make. If a subject did not bow to the emperor, he, like the children of Israel who did not bow to the great image of Nebuchadnezzar on the plain, was denounced and persecuted as an enemy of the state. It is instructive that even though Revelation enjoined the disciples of Christ to reject the empire and the absolutist claims of its rulers, it did not incite them to active underground political resistance. It encouraged them only in passive spiritual resistance and faithful endurance, virtues nourished by fellowship in the community of faith and by the hope for the day of the Lord. And if early Christians could not pray *to* the emperor, at least they had early formed the habit of praying *for* the emperor. They had not forgotten the instruction of the apostle Paul to his beloved son in the gospel: "First of all, then, I urge that petitions, prayers, intercessions, and thanksgivings be offered for all men; for sovereigns and all in high office, that we may lead a tranquil and quiet life in full observance of religion and high standards of morality" (I Tim. 2:1, 2).

In I Clement we find this petition to God: "Grant that we may be obedient to . . . our rulers and governors upon the earth. . . . Thou, Master, hast given the power of sovereignty to them. . . . And to them, Lord, grant health, peace, concord, firmness that they may administer the government which thou hast given them without offense."

In summary, the New Testament documents and the great traditions of the first-century church furnish two strong warnings. The first is against anarchism, a policy of political irresponsibility and of indifference to the issue of law and order within a society. Paul in Romans 13 envisaged a state that is concerned with what we would call criminal justice and punishment; individual transgressions and crimes against the state and the people must be suppressed. There is no allusion in the New Testament to a government concerned with social justice; equal rights under law; the distribution of power, wealth, or natural resources; or welfare services. The political government of the first century was uninterested in these concerns, and it hardly penetrated the realm of social life. But since the government of the United States, as well as those of other Western democracies, are concerned with these matters, modern Christians must take especial care in making normative for the contemporary situation the New Testament passages we have surveyed. We shall return to this consideration in the next part of this book.

The other warning is against political absolutism. The state must not put itself in the place of God, for "there is no authority except from God." The interpretation of the state in the Apocalypse does not contradict Romans 13. Had Paul written the seven churches of Asia at the time Revelation was recorded on Patmos, would he not have given the same admonition? For Christians to acquiesce in the realm that belongs to God is tantamount to idolatry. Christians resist such claims even to the point of martyrdom, but to the New Testament authors there is no mandate from *their* King to destroy the state. Because the Christian considers his government a divinely ordained institution, he continually prays for renewal and restoration into its rightful role. The twin warnings against anarchism and the absolute state are relevant to every age, no less for America than for other nations of the world order.

It has been often remarked that the people of the United States come nearer to a parallel with Ancient Israel, than any other nation upon the globe. Hence OUR AMERICAN ISRAEL *is a term frequently used; and common consent allows it apt and proper.*

Abiel Abbot (1799)

They brought with them into the New World a form of Christianity which I cannot better describe than by styling it a democratic and republican faith.

Alexis de Tocqueville

To be an American is of itself almost a moral condition, an education, and a career.

George Santayana

It might be truer to say, however, that instead of finding their democratic faith in supernatural religion, Americans have tended to find their religious faith in various forms of belief about their own existence as a people.

Max Lerner

chapter three

America: God's New Israel?

Few Old-World nations have been obsessed with the search for a national identity. After all, they are products of the slow, tortuous process of history, possessing their own language, culture, mores, and traditions. Americans have not been able to take themselves for granted. *E pluribus unum,* or "out of many one," the slogan goes, and that aptly describes our beginnings. Throughout their comparatively brief history, Americans have been conscious that they constituted a new nation—a nation formed of miscellaneous peoples, languages, religions, experiences, and traditions. But a process began in the colonies and continues to this day—some indirect, subtle, but penetrating alchemy—by which Europeans (and later to a much lesser extent Africans, Asians, and Latin Americans), once exposed to the New World, have ceased to be Europeans, have revised their values and manners, and have acquired a new sense of identity. In his *Letters from an American Farmer,* de Crèvecoeur analyzed the process by which "Europeans become Americans." "In this great American asylum, the poor of Europe have by some means met together. . . . From this promiscuous breed that race now called Americans have risen. Here they become men."

Throughout their history Americans have been certain that their nation has a special character, a special mission, and a special destiny. This sense of destiny is not, of course, peculiar to Americans. Some such sense seems to be a necessary ingredient in the self-consciousness and identity of every nation, especially during its formative years. American experiences are not unique, but the interpretation of these experiences and its impact upon our collective attitudes and behavior are. Traditionally Americans have considered themselves God's New Israel, charged with a special mission among the nations of the world. America was to be a model republic or, in the words of John Winthrop, the first governor of Massachusetts Bay Colony, "a City upon a hill." Under God's infinite wisdom and providence, America was to be an asylum for the hopeless, the oppressed, and the needy, for all who seek the opportunity to begin their lives over again. Precious liberties and freedoms not found anywhere else on earth would flourish in this land of plenty. An experiment in democracy was initiated. If it did not succeed in this land, it would succeed nowhere. Consequently, Americans would not fail only themselves but all men desiring and deserving freedom. Such has been the faith of Americanism.

A Historical Sketch

The belief in the divine election to a special mission and destiny has been an integral part of the American tradition since the earliest settlements. Perry Miller captured the essence of their spirit and self-identity in the title of his history of the Puritans (itself borrowed from an election sermon preached in 1670), *Errand into the Wilderness*. Religion was a dominant motive in the lives of John Winthrop and John Cotton and a host of lesser men, all of whom considered themselves latter-day Israelites, called to establish on new soil what could not be established in England and thus bringing, by noble example, the mother country to her knees in repentance. Here the Protestant Reformation of church and society could be completed. For it was by default that America had inherited from England the role of guardian of liberty for all mankind. The American continent was the Promised Land. The New Israelites had crossed a forbidding sea, and if their errand in the wilderness succeeded, by God's grace and their own fidelity, the wide wilderness would become a new Canaan. Any success in this errand would mark a turning point in history, for their pilgrimage was part and parcel of the Almighty's scheme of redemption for the entire human race.

Like all religious people, the Puritans were prone to self-righteousness and smugness, and their desire for religious freedom for themselves did not necessarily mean that they intended it for others. Convinced that they possessed the true faith, some among them could be as intolerant of heretics in their midst as the state churches of their homeland had been toward them. The struggle for religious liberty in the new land produced its share of martyrs, but some persecuted sects (the Baptists, led by Isaac Backus and Roger Williams in Rhode Island, and the Quakers) held to religious liberty on principle. Beginning about the middle of the seventeenth century, much Puritan literature and sermons were filled with lamentations over the failure of the American experiment and calls for repentance and renewal to mission. But the mission was being secularized as the thoughts of more and more leaders of opinion in New England turned from piety to liberty and independence. Later generations of Puritans took a greater interest in economic development than spiritual growth. Religious zeal waned until the stage was set for the Great Awakening in the 1740s and the preaching of Jonathan Edwards and George Whitefield. But political and religious mission were entwined for, as H. Richard Niebuhr noted, the religious awakening was roughly simultaneous with the colonists' "awakening to national self-consciousness."[1] A few years later many churches, especially Congregationalist, Baptist, and Presbyterian churches, strongly supported the Revolution. After the conflict ended, American preachers and other orators praised God for the triumph and looked ahead with confidence to the renewed mission and destiny for a free and independent people.

The founding fathers, as the framers of our present Constitution are called, also possessed this deep sense of divine destiny. Despite their Deistic beliefs, political theorists such as Benjamin Franklin, John Adams, and Thomas Jefferson argued that God was intimately involved in the course of American undertakings. Franklin suggested that the Constitutional Convention be opened with prayer, and George Washington reminded the delegates that "it was more than probable we were now digesting a plan which in its operation would decide forever the fate of Republican Government." But few spoke as fervently and consistently about the destiny of the American Israel as Jefferson. He proposed that the seal of the United States picture "the children of Israel in the wilderness led

---

1. *The Kingdom of God in America* (New York: Harper, 1959), p. 126.

by a cloud by day and a pillar by night." This was not easily portrayed and was not adopted, but Jefferson forwarded the same
Biblical allusion again in the peroration of his second inaugural
address: "I shall need . . . the favor of that Being in whose hands
we are, who led our fathers, as Israel of old, from their native land
and planted them in a country flowing with all the necessities and
comforts of life." Despite Jefferson's isolationism, his vision of the
New Israel carried with it the seeds of national self-righteousness
which were soon to spawn a new practice of this faith.

The concept of divine mission and destiny was shaped in the
nineteenth century by westward expansion. Religious and national
sentiment were further merged. The magnitude and vastness of
the land and its rich natural resources enhanced the conviction
that Americans were the chosen people of God and that it was incumbent upon them to explore and exploit this wealth. This was
the age of "manifest destiny." The phrase was coined by John
O'Sullivan in his *Democratic Review* in 1845: "The far-reaching,
the boundless future, will be the era of American greatness. In its
magnificent domain of space and time, the nation of many nations
is destined to manifest to mankind the excellence of divine principles, to establish on earth the noblest temple ever dedicated to
the worship of the Most High." The general public swallowed this
rhetorical dose whole. America's responsibility to be a model republic was no less, but now it was responsible as well to expand without delay to its natural geographic limits—all of North
America.[2]

The same doctrine of American duty to expand waxed stronger in
the latter part of the nineteenth century until a muscular nationalism developed. American imperialism assumed perhaps its most
arrogant and unlovely forms. American churches and missionaries
were so blinded by nationalistic zeal that they could not perceive
the economic aggrandizement America received from its actions
overseas. Instead they appealed more frequently to the missionary
responsibilities of those who had benefited from the blessings of a
superior American civilization. Not only was America the superior
nation, but through the influence of racial Darwinism, the white

2. Frederick Merk, *Manifest Destiny and Mission in American History* (New
York: Vintage, 1963), pp. 33, 34. This is a good survey of how the ideology of
"manifest destiny" was associated with our expansionism. It quotes from editorials of the press, speeches in Congress, and oratory on the hustings. Merk
noted that one element of the gospel of manifest destiny was the duty of the
United States to regenerate morally backward peoples of the continent.

man had a special "burden" to be borne unselfishly. In an address entitled "For the Greater Republic, Not for Imperialism," Albert J. Beveridge, a senator from Indiana and an eloquent spokesman, declared: "God did not make the American people the mightiest human force of all time simply to feed and die. He did not give our race the brain of organization and heart of domination to no purpose and no end. No! He has given us a task equal to our talents. . . . He has made us the lords of civilization that we may administer civilization." To Beveridge and others America was "the star of the empire," and "the march of the flag" into the Philippines, Cuba, and other lands would fulfill the mission of a divinely anointed nation to civilize and Christianize savage, degenerate peoples. This would lead to "world improvement." Undoubtedly the most influential proponent of these imperialistic notions was the rough-riding president, Theodore Roosevelt, who never questioned that the will of God included the use of American power for international improvement.

The most dramatic and serious questioning of American mission and destiny during the nineteenth century occurred in the Civil War era. Abraham Lincoln continually expressed the belief that the cause of free government throughout the world hung in the balance of this great struggle, and though he could not be certain of God's will, he believed God was providentially leading the country on a steady course. During the war both Northern and Southern apologists were quick to identify their separate causes with the destiny and mission of the nation and to condemn the unorthodoxy of their opponents. Churches on both sides of the Mason-Dixon line invoked the succor of God for their respective armies. The greatness of Lincoln lay, in part, in his ability to rise above sectional interpretations of the war and to speak with greater depth and reality of God's purposes and will for mankind and the nation.

The advent of the twentieth century saw the young nation rapidly accumulating political and military power and new global responsibilities. America hesitated before entering either of the two world wars, but when she entered, her sense of mission inspired courage, stamina, and perseverance. On April 2, 1917, when the reluctant Woodrow Wilson, a staunch Presbyterian, asked Congress to declare war, he was convinced that American participation could not be justified merely on the ground of defending American interests. For Wilson and millions of Americans, this was a war to end all wars, a war to make the world safe for democracy. After the war, America's ultimate mission was to show the world that democracy was worth saving. By 1941 the nation was on another mission. Disillusioned with the fruits of the First World War, Americans generally viewed their involvement in this second global struggle more as a tragic necessity than as a glorious blow for the cause of righteousness. The Federal Council of Churches, which had hoped the proposed League of Nations would become the "political expression of the Kingdom of God on earth," saw the Second World War as merely a conflict between two irreconcilable forms of government and did not believe "that a victory of the United Nations would in itself guarantee the achievement of any Christian goals." But President Franklin Roosevelt did not hesitate to define America's role in the war in terms of national destiny. FDR, addressing a joint session of the new Seventy-seventh Congress on January 6, 1941, defied the Axis nations, denounced appeasement, and called for all-out aid to the democracies. His whole program was based on America helping to secure the "essential four freedoms": freedom of speech and expression, freedom to worship God in one's own way, freedom from want, and freedom from fear. He concluded, "There can be no end save victory."

Since the mid-twentieth century, a series of problems and dilemmas have served to focus at least indirect attention on America's national identity, mission, and destiny. Not the least of these crises have been the Korean conflict and the cold war in general, the civil rights revolution, Vietnam, Watergate, and presently the related matters of the economy and the environment. Because of the importance of these issues and their relevance to our own times, we will study in some detail the questions which they have raised.

Two Versions of American Mission

There are two distinct versions of the American sense of mission and destiny:

1. *The "militant missionary" version.* This makes America "the liberator of the oppressed." Divine election means much more than setting the proper example for the rest of the world; it means disseminating abroad American ideals and the fundamental principles of the Bill of Rights. This means preserving democratic institutions whenever and wherever they are threatened by tyranny. It means never acquiescing in the face of massive propaganda and undercover activities directed by nations that are not free. Such a

doctrine has provided ideological undergirding for the imperialism at the turn of the last century and for American involvement in two world wars and the Korean and Vietnamese wars.

In its most noble form this version of American mission makes the nation a sacrificial servant of other peoples. Unfortunately, American experience in foreign affairs has shown how easily the servant degenerates into a master and seeks to impose American ways, institutions, and economic designs on peoples and cultures that are less than elated to receive them. Advocates of the "militant missionary" approach to foreign affairs have frequently branded their opponents isolationist. This charge is inaccurate, and it does not carry the same old stigma. Responsible internationalists, rather than seeking isolation, have called for retrenchment from commitments that have become financially exorbitant, unnecessary, and dangerous both to our own domestic stability and to the traditional cultures and resources of those unlucky enough to be our "allies."

2. *The "light to the nations" version.* This version is based on the power and efficacy of example. Other nations will observe and admire how efficiently and justly democratic institutions perform in America and will seek to incorporate into their own political systems this same democratic idealism and machinery. To Clinton L. Rossiter this second version is not only the original American sense of mission and destiny, but the "true American Mission" and the "finest expression of American nationalism."

> If we must have a mission—and historically and spiritually we probably must, whether dictated by God or Providence or sheer utility—why should it not be this humane and humble version of a universal trait of national consciousness? Admittedly it can serve as a cloak for the revival of the most short-sighted, ethnocentric stamp of isolationism, but only if internationally-minded Americans permit it to be stolen from their keeping. The American Mission, a view of national destiny neither vulgar nor imperialistic, can certainly be squared with a healthy attitude of international cooperation. And at the same time it can continue to serve as a healthy spur to domestic improvement—in race relations, education, politics, labor-management relations, and all the other major areas in which we might, if we felt the world's gaze fixed upon us, be better democrats.[3]

Senator George McGovern forwarded this version when he accepted

---

3. "The American Mission," *American Scholar* 20 (1950-51): 27. Also see Winthrop S. Hudson's discussion of these two versions in *Religion in America* (New York: Scribner's, 1973), pp. 110-14.

the presidential nomination at the 1972 Democratic convention: "America must be restored to her proper role in the world. But we can do that only through the recovery of confidence in ourselves. The greatest contribution America can make to our fellow mortals is to heal our own great but deeply troubled land. We must respond to that ancient command: 'Physician, heal thyself.' "

This version presupposes that America cannot remake the Third World in her image even if she chooses to and that many nations have neither the intelligent masses essential to democratic institutions nor the natural resources needed for American patterns of industrial growth and economy, with its concomitant waste and pollution. There will always be change and revolution in the world that do not threaten our security. Once we have our own house in order, we can afford to be as indifferent to other nations' ideologies—be they Marxism, militarism, or reactionism—as they are to ours. Most of these nations are too weak to pose any threat to us, this doctrine goes, and they become our enemy only if we attack them.

While the first version of American mission contains the seeds of robust self-righteousness and muscular imperialism, which are all the more dangerous in the twentieth century with the proliferation of nuclear weapons and techniques of chemical and biological warfare, the "light to the nations" version contains the seeds of a smug isolationism that could preclude America's striving for international peace and social welfare. Throughout our history, and particularly in the decade of the Vietnam war, there have been eloquent spokesmen for both versions of American mission. A healthy tension between the two should continue, with the burden of proof resting on those who urge the "militant missionary" approach to international conflict. At least Americans have concluded finally that their nation cannot be the savior of the world. Messianic absolutism precludes an openness to alternatives, compromise, and negotiations. And while we Americans have been endowed by history and geography with unique advantages over all other nations, we can no longer afford to squander them in some irrational race to prove our power and prestige.

The Impact of Americanism

In addition to New Testament Christianity and politics, this book is about Americanism. But what is Americanism? A definition is elusive, but at its core it is a system of ideals and ideas about

America—her birth, emergence as a world power, mission, and destiny. Americanism is the one concept that continues to unify all pluralities and in devotion to which full personal life can be realized. The melting-pot motif is still alive and functional. Races, classes, denominations, and sections must be absorbed by Americanism. Peculiarities must not press for priority at the expense of the whole. Since in America one could hardly conceive of religious martyrdom, can one make a greater sacrifice than by giving his life for his country?

Schools and other public institutions must do their part to further Americanism. We have much of which to be proud, it is argued, and just as much to guard zealously lest it be irretrievably lost. "In a world torn by hatred, our country is God's reservoir of construction," declared one American. Few of our national problems would have developed "if we would have taught in our schools with the fervor they now often teach other 'isms' the greatest 'ism' of all, Americanism."[4]

This nation, in the eyes of many observers, functions as a church. We will analyze the extent to which this generalization is true when we discuss civil religion in America. But the impact of Americanism, for good or ill, is felt in all aspects of national life, even in our interpretation and application of the Scriptures. Does anyone seriously suppose that Jesus' injunction "Lay not up for yourselves treasures on earth" is understood by wealthy, self-confident Americans in the same way it is by peasants in central Europe or Latin America? Protestant America traditionally has been reluctant to believe that any agent of history can forward God's purposes in the world as efficiently as the United States can. Americanism influences our perception of social and political issues. If a politician can successfully tag his opponent's proposals "un-American," he is certain to defeat him.[5] Of course defining *un-American* is a problem. The term is sufficiently vague to be useful to name-calling extremists. Chief Justice Earl Warren once asked, "Who can define the meaning of 'un-American'? What is that single, solitary 'principle of the form of government as guaranteed by our Constitution'?"[6]

---

4. Roy W. Harper, "Changing World," *Vital Speeches* 38 (15 July 1972): 607, 608.

5. V. O. Key, Jr., *Public Opinion and American Democracy* (New York: Knopf, 1961), pp. 42ff. discusses Americanism and its effect on issue acceptance.

6. Watkins v. United States, 354 U.S. 178 (1957).

The fifties and sixties produced much oratory, editorializing, and investigations about "liberty," loyalty, and Americanism. "Any group, whether religious sect, United Nations, or World Council of Churches, which claims truth and serves purposes not its own is suspect of the ultimate sin, the sin of un-Americanism," wrote John Edwin Smylie. "When Mormons pretended that *they* were the heirs of ancient Israel, they were viewed as un-American. Could the Church of the Latter-Day Saints embody values not already in the nation? Roman Catholicism has automatically come under suspicion because it habitually acts as the true bearer of history's meaning. Only the nation bears ultimate universal purposes and has continuing historic meaning."[7] Smylie's is an interesting slant on the causes of religious prejudice in America.

In this volume we will be urging Americans to take politics seriously. As we shall see in the next section, Christians may consider politics a valid way of dealing with great socio-economic issues. But it is just as easy, and perhaps easier, for men and women to become fanatical about political ideologies and political crusades, as though demonically possessed by them. If politics must be taken seriously, religious devotion must be taken even more seriously. We must continually point to Someone beyond politics, a Cause beyond "the bounds of time and place," for Christianity eclipses in importance both politics in general and Americanism in particular.

As American Christians we have the good fortune to live in a land that is great and good in many ways. We may be gratified that our responsibilities as Christians and as Americans, while neither identical nor interchangeable, are not utterly irreconcilable. In our land Christianity need not oppose political institutions, and political institutions need not fear Christian citizens. We proceed to examine first the styles of Christian political activism available to Americans and then the religious expressions of our national experience. All the while we would do well to remember that we are strangers and pilgrims on this earth and that our allegiance is to the One who had nowhere to lay His head and who was politically executed outside the gates of the city.

---

7. "National Ethos and the Church," *Theology Today* 20 (1963): 315, 316.

part two

Styles of Christian
Political Life in America

Every foreign country is their fatherland, and every fatherland is a foreign country.

(Epistle to Diognetus)

My kingdom is not of this world. . . .

Jesus (John 18:36 KJV)

How small of all that human hearts endure, that part which laws or kings can cause or cure.

Samuel Johnson

To reconcile man with man and not with God is to reconcile no one at all.

Thomas Merton

chapter four

Should a Christian Fritter Away Time on Politics?

The evangelical Christian believes that sinful man is alienated from God, that the chasm separating men from God can be bridged through Jesus Christ, God's Son, and that those who obey the gospel are called into a radically new life that affects all personal and social relationships.[1] But what about the Christian's relationship to his government? In what sense is this relationship transformed? For the Christian who accepts as normative the New Testament, both its commands and the apostolic example it includes, does the fact that America is a democracy make a difference? In this section we will survey three general syles of political activism for Christians in America. There are of course as many separate and distinct political styles as there are citizens, and perhaps few Christians exemplify a "pure" type of consistency. We will make a case for traditional activism (in the next chapter), but we want to examine two other political life styles: radical noninvolvement (in this chapter) and revolutionary activism (in chapter 6). Most likely the average Christian takes his political life style for granted. He

---

1. For definitions of *evangelical*, see "Somehow, Let's Get Together," *Christianity Today*, 9 June 1967, p. 24; and "Who Are the Evangelicals?" *Christianity Today*, 9 June 1967, p. 22. One stimulating volume is Richard Quebedeaux, *The Young Evangelicals* (New York: Harper and Row, 1974).

gives it little thought. It may be patterned after that of his parents or of his peers. But by the very fact that he lives and works in and with a nation of people, he cannot avoid some style of political existence. Politics permeates, to varying degrees, every institution of which he is a part—the home, the office, the college, even the church. All social life is political to some extent. So what should be the Christian's relationship to the "powers that be"?

Can he afford to fritter away his time on politics and nationalism? A small but deeply committed minority of Christians has answered this question with a resounding no. These Christians adhere to the philosophy of nonattachment or noninvolvement. They do not all belong to the same denomination or sect, nor are their rationales for nonattachment the same. Some cite doctrinal reasons; others, practical reasons; perhaps most, a combination of the two. They are not just pacifists; many pacifists profess to be very much involved in the American political process. They believe it sinful to support political activities and organizations, to serve on juries, to vote, and most certainly to serve as a public official. They are Scripturally bound to pay taxes, since Jesus clearly taught and practiced this, but they find no Scriptural authorization for further political involvement. The case against political involvement is a strong one, and we would be unfair and unwise to dismiss or caricature it, as some Christian young people do. We shall examine two interrelated doctrinal objections to political involvement and three practical arguments in support of nonattachment.

The Doctrine of the Two Kingdoms

Kingdom is a political term found many times in the New Testament. It designates a king's people and territory, and especially his complete rule or sovereignty over them. As we established in surveying the Old Testament, Jehovah's relation to Israel was that of a king to His subjects. Even though we are living in a final or Christian dispensation, we are still subject to a King, the same King of Israel. Much like the Jews of our Lord's time, we persistently confuse the kingdom of God with the kingdom of the world, or the kingdom of man. Jesus instructed Pilate, "My kingdom does not belong to this world. . . ." (John 18:36), and the apostle Paul warned the Philippians against enemies of the cross whose "minds are set on earthly things. We, by contrast, are citizens of heaven, and from heaven we expect our deliverer to come. . . ." (Phil. 3:19, 20). Hence there are two kingdoms, the kingdom of man and the kingdom of God, and each person must decide which he will support. His loyalty cannot be divided or equivocal. If one is loyal to God, he is a citizen in an apolitical, anational kingdom which knows no territorial boundaries or political ideals, but consists of men of every language and nation (Rev. 7:9). Such a citizen does not fear any carnal enemy or even death itself (cf. Matt. 10:28), but lives in peace and union with his fellow citizens as they engage in a far more important battle, one not with flesh and blood but with the principalities and powers of the air who are at war with the Almighty (Eph. 6:12).

The nonattached citizen may also contend that the world is evil and that he must refrain from contact with it as much as possible. Christ has removed him from the world. Jesus told His disciples: ". . . because you do not belong to the world, because I have chosen you out of the world, for that reason the world hates you" (John 15:19); "they are strangers in the world, as I am" (John 17:16). Further, believers are enjoined not to "set your hearts on the godless world or anything in it. Anyone who loves the world is a stranger to the Father's love" (I John 2:15). James warned that "whoever chooses to be the world's friend makes himself God's enemy (4:4). Paul urged the Romans not to conform their life style to that of the world (12:2) and told the Galatians that Jesus gave His life to "rescue us out of this present age of wickedness" (1:4).

The American Restoration movement produced a number of colorful and highly influential leaders of religious thought. Their attitude toward civil government, like that toward other serious doctrinal issues, was divided.[2] In 1848, in the aftermath of the war with Mexico, Alexander Campbell went on record as opposing a Christian's involvement in military service. Campbell believed that war is rarely if ever fought for defensive purposes, and he proposed something much akin to our present United Nations for adjudicating international complaints and skirmishes. The Civil War catalyzed further thought and writing on the subject. An influential Tennessee minister and Christian educator, Tolbert Fanning, drafted a resolution, signed by many other ministers and church leaders in the South, calling on both the Union and Confederate governments to exempt Christians with "conscientious convictions" to be "relieved on terms equitable and just, from requirements repulsive to their religious faith." The two governments were gen-

2. For a brief summary see David Stewart, "The Restoration Movement and the Civil Government," *Christian Chronicle*, 5 January 1970, pp. 2-4.

erally receptive to this plea, and a number of Christians were relieved of direct involvement in the conflict. (Some adherents to the Restoration concept were not "doves"; three examples were James A. Garfield, a young Union general who later became president, B. F. Hall, and Barton Stone, Jr.)[3]

Another segment of the Restoration movement moved beyond pacifism to nonattachment and total noninvolvement in political affairs. As influential as any in this segment was David Lipscomb (1831-1917), editor of the *Gospel Advocate* from 1866 to 1917 and founder (in 1891) of the Nashville Bible School, now an established senior college named in his honor. The *Gospel Advocate* to this day is the most widely circulated and influential paper in the Church of Christ, the conservative branch of the Restoration movement. In the *Gospel Advocate* (especially during 1866-67) and his book *Civil Government* (published in 1889 and reprinted in 1913 and 1957), Lipscomb set forth his views on the Christian and government. To understand the doctrinal basis for nonattachment, we do well to survey his views.[4]

Lipscomb's position was based on the concept of the two kingdoms, one ruled by God and the other by men at the behest of Satan. All men everywhere could be ruled sufficiently if they would submit to the government of God, but as he did in the Garden, man rebels against the will of God and attempts to walk in his own ways and counsel. Political government was originally a result of man's rebellion against God. Nimrod forsook the God-ordained family system and formed families into a primitive society. Selfishness and pride were the driving forces behind the establishment of civil government.

> I am not intimating in this, that human government is not necessary. I believe that it is necessary, and that God has ordained it as a punishment to man for refusing to submit to the government of God and it must exist so long as the human family or any considerable portion of it refuses to submit to the government of God. Human government originated in the rebellion of man against his Maker, and was the organized effort of man to govern himself and to promote his own good and to conduct the affairs of the world inde-

3. Ibid.

4. A most useful synthesis is Robert E. Hooper, "The Political and Educational Ideas of David Lipscomb" (Ph.D. dissertation, George Peabody College, 1965). Chapters 3 and 4 report both Lipscomb's political ideology and his views on such issues as war, slavery, and temperance.

pendently of the government of God. It was the organized rebellion of man against God and his government.[5]

If civil government is so antipodal to the divine will, why did not God destroy it upon its very inception? To compel men to accept His government would have deprived man of free moral agency. But "so long as men refuse the rule of God, God ordains they shall be ruled by their own governments and eat the fruit of their own ways and be filled with their own devices."[6] The rule of God is so complete that there is no room for human legislation: "God is the sovereign and sole lawmaker for it and he has ruled in it to guide and bless his children."[7] If disciples are in proper relationship with God, political involvement is superfluous. "God always forbade that his subjects should join affinity or affiliate with the subjects of the human government, or that they should make any alliance with, enter into, support, maintain and defend, or appeal to, or depend upon, these human governments for aid or help."[8] The Devil possesses the world. "Everyone who honors and serves the human government and relies upon it, for good, more than he does upon the Divine government, worships and serves the creature more than he does the Creator."[9] Christ desires to destroy these governments just as much as He desires to destroy the sinfulness which necessitates them. Did not Christ point out that these earthly systems would be destroyed, anyway? (Matt. 15:13). If the ethics of the Sermon on the Mount were practiced in any earthly kingdom, that political system would disintegrate.

Put positively, the Christian is to submit himself to whatever government he may fall under; "he is to become the partisan, the supporter, the defender, of none."[10] The Christian must pay his taxes faithfully. But he must not go to war for any political government or system. And he certainly should live faithfully the Christian life to bring about eventually the downfall of all civil government and the ascendancy of the kingdom of God. Christ had informed Pilate: "My kingdom is not of this world; if my kingdom were of this world then would my servants fight. . . ." (John

---

5. *Civil Government* (Nashville: Gospel Advocate, 1889), pp. 10, 11.

6. Ibid., p. 24.

7. Ibid., p. 40.

8. Ibid., p. 41.

9. Ibid., p. 49.

10. Ibid., p. 78.

18:36 KJV). If Jesus were not willing to form a worldwide Jewish government, how can Christians participate in civil governments which are antithetical to the divine kingdom of God?

No doubt the then-recent spectacle, in the Civil War, of Christian brothers killing each other influenced Lipscomb's thinking. Lipscomb extended his argument concerning fighting to the matter of voting.

> Christians cannot fight, cannot slay one another or their fellowmen, at the behest of any earthly ruler, or to establish or maintain any human government. But if he cannot fight himself, can he vote to make another fight? What I lead or influence another to do, I do through that other. The man who votes to put another in a place or position, is in honor, bound to maintain him in that position, and is responsible for all his actions, courses or results that logically and necessarily flow from the occupancy and maintain maintenance of that position.[11]

Certainly it would be sinful for a disciple of Christ to serve a government of the Devil, for he would be fighting against God. No man can serve two masters. Garfield was once a faithful preacher of the gospel, Lipscomb argued, but after participating in the war he rightfully deemed himself unworthy to reenter the pulpit or preside at the communion service. Lipscomb publicly hoped for the defeat and discouragement of all faithful Christians who were running, or considering running, for public office.

Lipscomb deplored war, and his pacifism had a marked effect upon the faculty and students at Nashville Bible School for many years. In October 1917 they petitioned the president of the United States for a release from compulsory military service during World War I. The petition was not unlike those sent by Lipscomb and others to the Union and Confederate governments during the Civil War. Lipscomb's ideas on war influenced the school's next president, H. Leo Boles. Lipscomb was often quoted by Churches of Christ authors who wrote on war and civil government during World War II.[12] But pacifist thought in Churches of Christ was, regrettably, seldom articulated during the early stages of the Vietnam war, and the pulpit heavily emphasized national honor and service.

Lipscomb was not oblivious to the arguments of his critics, but he could always marshall a counterargument and Scriptural support for it. The Jewish state does not prove that God sanctions

---

11. Ibid., p. iv; see also p. 145.

12. Hooper, "David Lipscomb," pp. 241, 242.

political government, he argued, for it was a theocracy with Jehovah as the only king; the Jewish nation was unlike all other worldly governments. The Christian is commanded to pray for political rulers, but not to sustain them in office; prayer on their behalf is more for Christian tranquility, that is, that the Christian may be able to "lead a quiet and peaceable life in all godliness and honesty." (KJV)[13] And what about Biblical examples of service to political authorities? Lipscomb argued on shaky grounds that Joseph and Daniel "served in their position only when in slavery, and did what service they rendered in these governments as slaves of their masters, and not as officers or rulers in the state."[14] As for New Testament officeholders—including Matthew, the eunuch, Cornelius, and the Philippian jailor—Lipscomb dismissed any necessary inferences by circular reasoning: they must have surrendered their offices "because it was well understood that the Christian religion demanded the cessation of such courses; and no declaration that they ceased the practices was needed."[15] To remain in civil office would have been to work against God.

The Christian's Major Responsibility

A second doctrinal argument against political involvement is perhaps inseparable from the first: the Christian's chief responsibility is to save lost souls from sin, to win new converts for Christ. ". . . he that winneth souls is wise" (Prov. 11:30 KJV). The salvation of the world does not hinge on who is elected to any given political office; an election that seems important to us now will someday look trivial when compared with the truly crucial issues of human existence. The Great Commission that Jesus gave His disciples just prior to His ascension is totally irrelevant to political activity; it commissioned them only to proclaim the gospel. Political involvement, then, can only distract disciples from their major teaching responsibility and from concern for their own spiritual condition.

Granted that political activity can at times be profitable for human communities, why should Christians shun it completely? First, the faithful Christian simply does not have the time for it. As long as one lost soul in the world has not heard the gospel, the Christian is responsible to give him the message of hope. A Chris-

---

13. *Civil Government*, p. 80.
14. Ibid., p. 104.
15. Ibid., p. 107.

tian does not have time to do everything that is desirable or good, so he must choose and do what is best. This means of course a life of rigid discipline and constancy, not unlike that of an athlete or a soldier in training. Neither metaphor escaped the apostle Paul, who admonished the young minister Timothy: "Take your share of hardship, like a good soldier of Christ Jesus. A soldier on active service will not let himself be involved in civilian affairs; he must be wholly at his commanding officer's disposal. Again, no athlete can win a prize unless he has kept the rules" (II Tim. 2:3-5).

Second, and more important, political activism does not strike at the core of sinful man's problem; it only touches upon the periphery of his spiritual existence. Certainly we should be benevolent to people in need. But our primary task is preaching the gospel. People in sin do not need food, money, open housing, political power, or welfare nearly as much as they need salvation from sin. The only way to make a "Great Society" is to save individuals from sin. You can't take people out of slums until you take the slums out of the people. It is wrong to involve the church or her pulpit in issues like open housing, integrated quality education, anti-poverty and food programs, and civil rights for all Americans because this results in substituting the Social Gospel for the true gospel. The essential thrust of the gospel is spiritual, not social, and it relates to eternal salvation, not social and political reform. Theologian Jay G. Williams put the issue in proper perspective.

> It is true that our political and social problems are monumental and need solution, but it may very well be at their root is a deep spiritual crisis which makes any cleaning up operations frustrating illusions. The truth is we have lost touch with the depth of being and hence have become alienated from out environment as a whole. The man who is divorced from his own unconscious can hardly be reconciled with his brother. Our society, like Humpty Dumpty, cannot be put together by all the king's horses and men, no matter how well financed they be. In fact, they may only make matters worse.[16]

The church offers a special, unique remedy for individual and societal malaise, and it is not political expertise. Church leaders are usually no more qualified to speak on matters of public policy than are leaders from other segments of society, and when they do speak, the nation may assume that they speak for all of Christen-

16. "Other-Worldly Christianity: Some Positive Considerations," *Theology Today* 28 (1971): 336. Perhaps the case against organized Christian political activism that reached the widest reading audience was J. Howard Pew, "Should the Church 'Meddle' in Civil Affairs?" *Reader's Digest,* May 1966, pp. 49-54.

dom. Reo M. Christenson, a political scientist and Christian leader, wrote:

> When I hear churchmen discuss public policy, what they say usually strikes me as naive, superficial, simplistic, jargonistic, and unhistoric. Lacking real expertise, they tend to support policies that have a pleasantly humanitarian ring—and that are compatible with the dominant intellectual climate. In recent Western history this has meant compatibility with the views of the liberals (or the avantgarde), whose approval they covet above all else. Somehow the modern Christian social activist is supremely confident that the liberal —or the ultra-liberal—has a near-monopoly on social wisdom. To be out of step with them is the most dreadful fate he can imagine. Better the rack and gallows![17]

Christenson cited several examples of social legislation, especially some aimed at combatting poverty, that originally received the fervid support of liberal churchmen, but that in administration and practice proved far less effective than even its opponents had imagined.

An event in the preaching and benevolent ministry of the apostles Peter and John is instructive.[18] At the hour of prayer Peter and John walked into the temple. Among the beggars they passed at the gate was a man who had been crippled from birth. What was the response from these two Christians and chosen apostles? By conventional social ethics there were several appropriate responses: (1) make a cash donation; (2) recommend preferential treatment to the local employment agency and urge all employers in the various congregations to hire the handicapped; (3) explore the possibility of financing a special course in physical therapy, with a local congregation picking up the tab; (4) help the man live with his handicap and regain self-esteem by enrolling him in a "Dale Carnegie"-type course that stresses cybernetics. We have exaggerated the situation somewhat to show that, no matter how useful any one or all these options might be, the apostles rejected them. Peter responded: "I have no silver or gold; but what I have I give you: in the name of Jesus Christ of Nazareth, walk" (Acts 3:6); in the next scene we

---

17. "The Church and Public Policy," *Christianity Today*, 5 January 1973, p. 13. One effort to explode purported myths of political liberalism is M. Stanton Evans, *Clear and Present Dangers: A Conservative View of America's Government* (New York; Harcourt Brace Jovanovich, 1975).

18. The idea for using Acts 3 in such a manner came from Dean M. Kelley, *Why Conservative Churches Are Growing* (New York: Harper and Row, 1972), p. 135.

see this once-crippled man leaping and praising God. The point is that the church and its members have a contribution to render to a needy human society that is qualitatively different from the technological interventions of humanitarian groups, and that contribution, wrote Dean M. Kelley, is

> to give *meaning* to the situation: purpose, promise, and possibility. That does not mean that meaning should displace technological remedies—men still need food, shelter, clothing, jobs, education, medical care—or even view them as inferior to meaning. And if society or its secular agencies cannot provide the needed technological remedies, religious organizations may need to do so, but with the recognition that such stopgap measures are a distraction and diversion from their distinctive and indispensable service: making sense of the life of man.[19]

How lamentable that many Christian leaders see so little reward in fulfilling the spiritual challenge incumbent upon them that they feel they must resort to the social and secular realms.

Abstract Idealism and Concrete Situationism

The next objection to Christian political involvement is both doctrinal and practical: Christian ethics are meant for Christians, and it is extremely difficult to apply the dictates of the Christian life to the world of political power. Christian ethics are largely irrelevant and impertinent to secular power brokers. The chasm between Christian agape as understood in the New Testament and the world of political power is too wide to be bridged. How can such love apply to the statesman and the public official who is responsible to protect the national interest? How can the harsh realities of the public order be dealt with by those who intend to do the will of God?

Take war, for example. Is it conceivable that the foreign policy of a nation as powerful and as militarily oriented as the United States could for many years avoid war, skirmishes, or international conflict that might cost human life? The Christian is not so idealistic but what he realizes a strong nationalism in tandem with military might will jeopardize lives. War seems endemic to human nature. How can a Christian reconcile such tensions and temptations with the social ethic of the Sermon on the Mount—total nonresistance, even in matters that seem trivial to ordinary citizens? And what about the stockpiling of nuclear weapons? The

---

19. Ibid.

twentieth century has seen emerge a new breed of pacifists—nuclear pacifists—who logically reason that in nuclear war there can be no victors in the traditional sense. John F. Kennedy once noted that an hour of war between the United States and Russia would cost three hundred million lives. Nonattachment, then, is less an evasion than a serious response to political realities.

Domestic issues do not present much less of a challenge. The informed Christian no less than others is aware that millions of fellow citizens are alienated from their families, legal institutions, and even the church—criminals, the homeless, the aged, the hungry, the mentally ill, drug addicts, and the displaced. Injustice and even unhappiness must be extirpated wherever possible, but they cannot always be attributed to a certain public official or institution. The complexity of modern American society and the interdependence of its members mean that power is widely distributed among shareholders, consumers, voters, and workers. How often do Christians who are concerned about evils in the American system that cause suffering and dehumanization feel that they are up against faceless, impersonal forces which they are powerless and ineffectual to fight? Repentance and baptism into the body of Christ do not make anyone an expert economist-tax reformer, public welfare commissioner, social worker, or special educator.

Where does all of this bring us, then? Politically unattached Christians insist that we acknowledge how intractable political and social problems are and how little both Christian laymen and even social scientists can do to solve them. How much of the unhappiness that afflicts most people you know is due to the shortcomings of public policy? The nonattached insist that very little of it is. And political reform, do-good legislation, social engineering, and the humanitarian impulse can do comparatively little to improve the plight of an unhappy man or woman who does not know the Savior. The nonattached is, however, very much an activist, directing his activity, as did Jesus, toward improving man's relationships to other men and to God, rather than toward political activity.[20]

Politics Is Dirty

A second practical argument against Christian political involvement is that politics is so tainted with compromise, corruption, and

---

20. Christenson, "The Church and Public Policy," p. 13.

unprincipled behavior that it is sub-Christian. Put succinctly, politics is dirty. This view of politics is widely shared by the general public as well as by dedicated Christians.

Traditionally Americans have enjoyed their politics. But the term *politics* has seldom had a positive, favorable connotation. Now the nonactivists can point to Watergate and declare with renewed conviction that political government corrupts all who are drawn into it, that principles mean less than winning votes, and that predetermined ends justify any means. The popular view is that no elected official can retain his integrity; not that his motives are necessarily bad, but that the pressure to yield to expediency is overwhelming. A man who values his reputation should stay out of politics. By its very nature politics involves struggle, power, force, and behind-the-scenes finagling. Historian Oswald Spengler defined *politics* as "the art of the possible." And the possible is realized by compromise. Carl Albert once conceded that the advice that best prepared him for his long tenure as Speaker of the House came from his predecessor, Sam Rayburn: "Those who go along, get along."[21] At election time the candidates outdo one another in playing down an image of rank politician or smoke-filled-room tactician and playing themselves up as urbane statesmen. "Cast your vote for a man of principle and not of politics" a full-page advertisement for a Republican gubernatorial candidate in Tennessee declared in 1974. One congresswoman offered herself to her constituents as "unbought and unbossed." No candidate has ever lost votes by telling the public, "I'm running for office, but I'm not a politician." The nonattached Christian argues that even if such ideals are attainable, the average voter would need the supernatural gift of mind-reading to determine which of the candidates were sincere and well-intentioned.

By contrast, the Christian life is one of no compromise. Nor does it seek the comfortable neutrality or fence straddling that are so inherent in American political life. "He who is not with me is against me, and he who does not gather with me scatters," Jesus declared (Matt. 12:30). Nothing vital to Christian life and doctrine can be compromised or altered. Bargaining, back-room scheming, high-handed power plays, and the like are the very antithesis of the Christian life style. The Christian must avoid the very appearance of evil in all his relations with his fellow man.

---

21. Quoted in *Newsweek,* 2 December 1974, p. 40.

Politics Does Not Matter Anyway

Finally, the nonattached Christian may argue that political involvement has so little impact upon the course of events and upon history in general that his personal activism could not make any difference anyway. "There's nothing the nation can gain by having my vote." This is a natural reaction considering two phenomena.

The first is political apathy and indifference. Political scientists believe that historically there has been a great deal of political apathy in the United States. There is much evidence for this. Less than five percent of all Americans engage in political activity beyond voting.[22] Thirty-nine million adults did not vote in 1960; forty-three million did not vote in 1964; and forty-seven million—forty percent of those eligible—did not vote in 1968, even after a highly volatile campaign; and about forty-five percent of the electorate, some sixty-two million citizens, decided to sit out the election in 1972. And of course even fewer citizens vote in mid-term elections.

The second phenomenon is disillusionment with the political process. Disillusionment seemed rampant in the late sixties when radical youth groups of the New Left arose and many adults sympathized with them. William Kunstler, the noted civil rights lawyer, argued that "nothing will change anything in this country until the people go into the streets." Both the apathetic and the disillusioned insist there is no difference between the major parties, and opposing presidential candidates are no more diverse than Tweedledum and Tweedledee. The average citizen can do precious little to influence national affairs.

Do voting and other political activity really make a difference? To the nonattached, voting is an act of faith—faith that a certain party or candidate will keep its pledges—and this faith is misplaced. In 1940 President Roosevelt seemed to pledge to keep us out of

---

22. About one-third of the American public is largely unaware of and uninformed about political issues. About forty to sixty percent vote, but otherwise confine their political role to that of spectator, watching political television programs, reading political news in the papers, and discussing politics with their friends. About ten to twelve percent contribute money to their favorite political causes, but only three to five percent are active in party work. See Lester W. Milbrath, *Political Participation* (Skokie, Ill.: Rand McNally, 1965). For a five-country comparison with respect to levels of political knowledge and involvement, see Gabriel A. Almond and Sidney Verba, *The Civic Culture: Political Attitudes and Democracy in Five Nations* (Princeton: Princeton University, 1963). See the bibliographic note for other books on American political styles.

World War II; a year later we entered it. In 1964 Lyndon Johnson promised not to send American boys to fight Asian wars for Asian boys, and all the while, the Pentagon Papers show, he was planning to accelerate our involvement in a land war. In 1968 the true conservative felt he had finally placed *his* man in office, a man who was philosophically opposed to détente with Communist China, increased deficit spending, devaluation of the dollar, wage and price controls, territorial expansion of the war in Vietnam, and arms deals with the Russians. No wonder that by the end of Richard M. Nixon's first term, many conservatives felt betrayed. One political writer, Frank Trippett, argued that majority votes have not played a decisive, creative role in resolving the greatest political issues:

> None of the major changes in our society took place because of elections. Take the Volstead Act—both its passage and its repeal —take woman's suffrage, or the coming of the New Deal. Nobody "voted in" the New Deal. Fiscally, Roosevelt's 1932 platform was conservative. He accused Herbert Hoover of spending too much.
>
> Just as nobody "voted in" the New Deal, the New Deal government didn't "govern out" the Great Depression it strove so hard to overcome. That particular social ailment was cured only by the enormous production effort demanded by World War II—which also was scarcely a consequence of popular mandate.
>
> What may be the biggest social event of the last 20 years—the outlawing of racial segregation in schools—resulted from nobody's vote or election. And elections hardly started the related black liberation or civil rights movement.
>
> No election stopped it either. It was stopped by the Vietnam war, which students generally credit with also wrecking the economy.
>
> So what carried us into a big undeclared war? Did anyone vote for Lyndon Johnson to start it? Obviously not. And who would have voted for Richard Nixon to keep it going except someone with foreknowledge that his fervent promise to stop it was hollow?[23]

The nonattached Christian might justifiably contend that his decision not to participate in the political process should tell civil authorities something. George Will, Washington editor of *National Review* and noted conservative columnist, commented on this: "I think a word should be said on behalf of those who do not vote because they intelligently decide against it. We must accept no philosophy which does not let us respect the little old lady who,

---

23. From an article in *Intellectual Digest,* December 1972, and quoted in Robert Sherrill, *Why They Call It Politics,* 2nd ed. (New York: Harcourt Brace Jovanovich, 1974), p. 318.

when asked whom she intended to vote for, said: 'I never vote. It only encourages 'em.' "[24]

To get too involved in politics might eventually result in accepting the catchword "Caesar is messiah" and in making politics an end instead of a means. This is when we soothe our consciences with social legislation, executive orders, or new welfare programs, rather than secure complete reconciliation between God and man. "This is political messianism, Baalism," argued Will D. Campbell and James Y. Holloway. "It is blasphemous for Christians to exhaust their witness to the world in the process Caesar determines for us."[25]

In summary, Christians defend the philosophy of political non-involvement with both doctrinal and practical arguments. They acknowledge the ultimate hand of God in the affairs of men. Two Christians could concur on some issue of public policy and both be wrong. God is at work in history and His will is going to be realized no matter what political views His children hold. The government, no matter how crazily it seems to be running, is still under the hand of God and will be replaced if God so desires. A child of God can be comfortable under any government, knowing that God is on and by his side; his duty is still to be faithful to the King and to be guided by His Holy Spirit and His Word. In the Great Judgment we will be judged not for whether we stood on the right or the left politically, but whether we stood in the shadow of the cross of Jesus and followed His example.

---

24. *Washington Post,* 19 January 1973, and quoted in Sherrill, *Why They Call It Politics,* p. 318.

25. "Up to Our Steeple in Politics," *Christianity and Crisis,* 3 March 1969, p. 37.

To Wesley a scheme to reconstruct society which ignored the redemption of the individual was unthinkable, but a doctrine to save sinning men, with no aim to transform them into crusaders against social sin was equally unthinkable.

Henry Carter

Who knows whether it is not for such a time as this that you have come to royal estate?

Mordecai to Esther (Esther 4:14)

I pray thee, not to take them out of the world, but to keep them from the evil one. They are strangers in the world, as I am. . . . As thou hast sent me into the world, I have sent them into the world.

Jesus (John 17:15, 16, 18)

In Germany they came first for the Communists, and I didn't speak up because I wasn't a Communist. Then they came for the Jews, and I didn't speak up because I wasn't a Jew. Then they came for the trade unionists, and I didn't speak up because I wasn't a trade unionist. Then they came for the Catholics, and I didn't speak up because I was a Protestant. Then they came for me, and by that time no one was left to speak up.

Martin Niemöller

I am only one, but still I am one. I cannot do everything, but still I can do something, and because I cannot do everything, I will not refuse to do that something that I can do.

anonymous

chapter five

The Case for Christian Political Activism

The faithful Christian attempts to be guided by God's Word in his role as a citizen as in any other role thrust upon him. He knows that Christianity pervades all of life and transforms every relationship. Although what a Christian legally can do as a citizen will vary from nation to nation, his responsibility to take his citizenship seriously is everywhere the same. But what precisely is his proper relationship to his government? We have already surveyed as fairly as possible one response to this question—the philosophy of Christian nonparticipation. We now briefly state the case for Christian political activism, which we consider the more convincing and realistic of the two. For those Christians who elect to remain politically nonattached in America, much of what is discussed in the rest of this volume is largely irrelevant and immaterial. A thorough case for Christian political activism could consume an entire volume, and the interested reader would do well to consult a number of excellent sources.[1] Our purpose here is to suggest several lines of argument, as well as to refute some of the objections forwarded by nonparticipants.

---

1. See bibliographic note for recommended volumes on Christian political activism and sources on the social activism of the nineteenth-century evangelical churches.

Complete Neutrality Impossible

Perhaps the most obvious difficulty with the philosophy of Christian neutrality and nonparticipation is its impossibility, at least in the purest sense. The Christian born in America is still a citizen. Every Christian and every Christian church is involved in society and its problems. There are no exceptions. No matter how individualistic our ethic, we live in a social context, and our action or inaction, as the case may be, will have an impact, be it great or small, on the communities of which we are a part.

The religious and social freedom the nonparticipant enjoys in America is nourished by the rights once granted and now guaranteed by the state. He may not appreciate their value or he may take them for granted, but he needs them all the same. In times of personal crisis, he may have no reservations about relying upon legal guarantees and institutions to safeguard his freedom. At first glance this does not seem to present a problem theologically, for when the apostle Paul's life was in jeopardy, he appealed to higher authorities to enforce his legal rights as a citizen of Rome. But to what extent should noninvolved Christians rely upon the government to protect lesser liberties? Two of the most radically nonattached religious communities in America rely upon the state and legal institutions for far more than a simple guarantee to life. In 1972 the Amish, who believe that education beyond the eighth grade teaches worldly values at odds with their religious creed, asked the Supreme Court to exempt them from compulsory education requirements. Finding a record of three hundred years of Amish resistance, the court ruled in their favor.[2] The Jehovah's Witnesses, who believe that flag saluting violates the second commandment and who are active, persistent proselytizers both publicly and privately, perhaps have been subjected to more litigation than any other religious minority in America. Their victories have been among the most notable in American legal history.[3] To illustrate

2. Wisconsin v. Yoder, 406 U.S. 205 (1972). The first time the Supreme Court ruled that a specific religious group is immune from compulsory attendance requirements, the Chief Justice based the ruling on the Amish's free exercise of religion. But he made clear that this would not apply to "faddish new sects or communes." (The Amish had been on record for their resistance to compulsory attendance for three hundred years.)

3. Among the important court decisions involving Jehovah's Witnesses are the following: Cantwell v. Connecticut, 310 U.S. 296 (1940); Murdock v. Commonwealth of Pennsylvania, 319 U.S. 105 (1943); Martin v. Struthers, 319 U.S. 141 (1943); West Virginia Board of Education v. Barnette, 391 U.S. 624 (1943); and

again, conscientious objection is a political issue as well as a religious and moral issue.

In this connection many conservative and fundamental Christians who exercise the franchise but claim no further political involvement have deluded themselves. They denounce in no uncertain terms the political involvement of liberal churchmen, but they fail to see that organized demonstrations, petitions, and voting drives against gambling, pornography, the liquor traffic, and atheistic communism, are also political activities. Carl McIntire has made a career denouncing the political machinations of the National and World councils of churches, yet it is no less "political" for him to lead mass marches on the nation's capitol to press the president for "victory in Vietnam" or to protest his trip to China. Conservative Roman Catholic legions who might otherwise urge nonattachment successfully blocked the dissemination of birth control information in Massachusetts and Connecticut during the 1950s and 1960s.

The examples cited here should not be taken as inappropriate Christian responses. No moral issue is beyond the pale of Christian concern. If involvement is a sin, it is a difficult one to avoid and it is easier to see in the activity of others than in our own. Christians who attempt not to participate in political processes are making two statements: first, that Christianity is irrelevant to social problems except to the extent it can be solved through individual regeneration; and second, that the status quo on any given issue in which they choose *not* to involve themselves should prevail. The church member who contends "Christians can't afford to take sides on the race question" has already sided with the status quo, which usually favors the vested interests of power and wealth. Not to be involved is to be involved. In a democracy, no vote is just as much a vote as a vote. "Not to decide is to decide," declared an old Harvey Cox poster. Some church members, perhaps few, follow American political life closely through newspapers and magazines, express their views with no reservations, and find current election campaigns the number one topic for conversation, only to cast no ballot on election day and then contend that it is a sin for Christians to be politically involved.

Marsh v. Alabama, 326 U.S. 501 (1946). The Barnette decision was a victory for the Witnesses in the flag-salute dispute, and many of the other cases related to the right of public proclamation and the selling and distribution of religious literature. See Henry J. Abraham, *Freedom and the Court: Civil Rights and Liberties in the United States* (New York: Oxford University, 1972), pp. 206-87.

Democracy Makes a Difference

We have already examined the key passages in the New Testament that deal with the Christian's relationship to his government (especially Rom. 13 and I Peter 2). A sound hermeneutic, we insisted, demands that these passages be interpreted in the historical and cultural context of the first-century world, the *Sitz im Leben* of the Biblical writings. The political realities they presuppose differ in at least two ways from the political situation in America and other Western nations in the twentieth century.

First, government in the New Testament world was viewed as *over against* the people who were its subjects. Opposition to its policies by significant groups of people within the empire posed no threat to its legitimacy and right to rule. Granting the populace a voice in government was deemed unnecessary. But democracy makes a difference. Our national leaders derive their power directly from the people. Our legal and political institutions are bound by a Constitution written by our representatives and are staffed by men and women whom we elect or our representatives appoint. The ongoing life of this nation theoretically derives from its citizens. Involvement was unnecessary in the New Testament world, but if there were no citizen participation and activism in a democracy, the whole political structure would crumble.

One might argue that those who possess authority and wield power in a democracy do at times stand over against the people, or at least some of them. This is most apparent when a judge sentences a convicted criminal, against the criminal's will, to a prison term, or when the Selective Service drafts an unwilling youth. And who among us has not complained when the legislature increases taxes or levies new ones? And still, democracy makes a difference. The convict has been publicly tried by a jury of his peers under a system of restrictions, procedures, and guarantees called due process; draft laws provide alternatives for conscientious objectors; and tax laws are passed by representatives of the citizens.[4] The point is obvious: Paul must have instructed Christians living in authoritarian Rome somewhat differently than he would Christians living under laws that they have had a hand in writing and that are administered by institutions and agencies they have had a hand in

---

4. I acknowledge this analysis is rather simplistic. In the past the draft has discriminated against the poor and minorities. Tax reform has been weakened or aborted altogether by the power of large corporate interests. But at least in a democracy the legal mechanisms for reform exist.

staffing. The "powers that be" in America today are the laws of the land, beginning with the Constitution, and since our laws and institutions are based on participation by the people, Christians must participate if the system is to be preserved and the Constitution is not to be subverted. Built into the democratic system is participation by review, debate, reexamination, election, and defeat. Can a Christian living in this system "honor the king" by acquiescing in realities rather than engaging in these activities? The *raison d'être* of Christian activism is to see that the government is operated by its citizens just as the "powers that be" have decreed it should be. Put another way, one of the Christian's chief duties is to see that nothing more is rendered to Caesar than should be.

Second, the New Testament ascribes to government virtually a penal function alone. This is clear from Paul's statement that the civil authorities do not bear the sword in vain. The chief if not only benefit Christians could gain from submitting to and respecting the "powers that be" was that, with the government punishing and discouraging crime and thus establishing a peaceful and just order, they could live and obey the gospel. Political participation had no direct relationship to the social, cultural, and economic life of the citizens.

How far removed is the first-century society from our complex, urban, industrialized, democratic society! The twentieth century in America has been a period of turbulent change, of evolution in governmental services, and of rising expectations that our government will resolve virtually every societal problem. The American government pervades—and to some, invades—just about every aspect of our life as citizens together, either directly or indirectly. The average family sits down to a breakfast of orange juice, coffee, bacon, eggs, and toast; a half dozen agencies (especially the Food and Drug Administration of the Department of Health, Education, and Welfare) of the federal government may have dealt with the food before it arrived at the table. This book and the thousands of others issued each year by reliable publishers is protected by copyright laws. Your automobile, whether manufactured in the United States or abroad, must meet federal safety and emissions standards; and to drive it you must be licensed by your state and abide by local traffic regulations. The government even regulates such minute details as the amount of space the windshield wipers cover and even the speed of the wipers; at the fast setting, they must go "at least 45 cycles per minute."[5] An American pays taxes at three levels—local, state, and federal. He attends public schools and perhaps public colleges. He draws unemployment insurance, Medicare, Social Security, and welfare benefits. His recreation away from home is usually performed under government regulations and often only with a license. His savings and his home mortgage are guaranteed by the government. The fact escaped David Lipscomb, as Robert E. Hooper pointed out,[6] that the distribution of the *Gospel Advocate* at reasonable rates depended upon the good graces of the government. We could pile on examples of governmental inroads into our lives *ad infinitum*. From birth certificate to death certificate, civil authorities accompany the individual on his way. Even after he dies the government is not through with him; estate taxes must be collected, and his will is probated in the courts.

When government is so pervasive and far-reaching, the "evils of government" will not be extirpated by banishing politicians. To ask if politicians are indispensable, noted Gene E. Rainey, "is tantamount to inquiring if our society needs doctors, lawyers or teachers. If all citizens were Christians, politicians would still be necessary because a Christian nation requires the services of a Moses, or a Cromwell, or a Calvin." Someone must operate the machinery of state, and "the only alternative to the politician is the anarchy of a Hobbesian state or nation in which no government or sovereign ruler exists."[7]

The nonparticipating Christian argues that we cannot realistically expect the state to be controlled by agape, or Christian love. The Christian political activist concurs, but he insists that it is not impossible for the agape of many of its citizens to influence state policy for the better. To deny Christian participation in a political structure that is based on popular sovereignty and participation is to limit severely the leavening influence of good. Christians who have specialized interests and technical skills may use their talents even more responsibly, and thus serve their fellow man, in civil service. All things being equal, the public welfare commissioner who is a faithful Christian will be fairer and more benevolent in deal-

---

5. Motor Vehicle Standards 104-3 (1969).

6. "The Political and Educational Ideas of David Lipscomb" (Ph. D. dissertation, George Peabody College, 1965), p. 64.

7. "The Christian and Politics: A Problem of Misunderstanding," *Restoration Quarterly* 7 (1963): 58.

ing with the indigent and needy. The public social worker who is a Christian will be in a more strategic position for doing good as an employee of the government than of a private, charitable organization. A physician may choose to serve the community as a public health officer. Others may work in the areas of sanitation and pollution control. The public school superintendent can exert his influence to improve race relations in the schools, and indirectly in the community, by helping others to understand and accept court orders. It is true the church could also, and indeed it often does, provide many of these social services. On the other hand, the resources of local churches are limited, and since many congregations are autonomous, they simply cannot provide *all* essential social services. Christians, then, may be active in areas that congregations are not. If good and honest people avoid political participation at all levels, a serious vacuum of Christian insight and morality results. Certainly there will always be a distance between Christian love and both the policies of state and the behavior of power groups, but Christians' legitimate infiltration into all levels of government leadership and service can go a long way toward reducing that distance, bringing to bear on public policy the demands of Christian love and justice. Is there any other way to establish and maintain a Christian nation?

In sum, American Christians need to interpret Paul's doctrine of obedience to the governing authorities in light of the contemporary relationship between the "powers that be" and the people, the governors and the governed. The concept of obedience is still relevant, of course. The Christian obeys the law all the more because he has some voice in writing the law (we will discuss this in the next chapter). But more relevant for American Christians than uncritical obedience are the concepts of participation and responsibility. And the demands and priorities of Christian participation in and responsibility for his government necessarily will vary from individual to individual.

The Biblical Case for Activism

Most sincere opposition to preaching and social action aimed directly at eradicating social malaise and creating a better society is based on an inadequate understanding of the nature of man and the nature of evangelism and Christian ministry. We will examine each misconception and then cite some Biblical examples of political involvement.

The New Testament message is eminently personal; each man personally encounters God and chooses for himself to accept or reject the Savior (cf. Gal. 6:5; Phil. 2:12; II Cor. 5:10). Christians opposed to social involvement make a radical separation between man as an individual and man as a social being. If all individuals in the nation or world were genuinely converted to Christ, they reason, there would be no need for social involvement. Consider the often heard statement "You can't take the people out of the slums until you take the slums out of the people." The statement is memorable because of its antithesis; it is popular because of its gross oversimplification; it is dangerous because it may serve as either a smokescreen to hide indifference or a rationalization to justify escapism.

Accept this statement at face value and there is no reason for further investigation of the causes of poverty, discrimination in employment, substandard education and cultural deprivation, the nature of available health care, the oppression that exists, inequities in political power and tax laws, and the psychology of frustration and hopelessness. Such topics are academic and the answer is simple. Those who are jobless, drug addicts, alcoholics, mentally ill, and victims of oppression and overt violence are what they are because of personal sin. Send in a preacher to present the gospel, baptize those who believe and admonish them to attend regular worship, and in nothing flat they will be employed in a responsible white-collar position, living comfortably in a middle-class suburb, driving a late-model automobile, eating nutritious food, and, perhaps most important, wearing fine clothes so that they will no longer look out of place in a suburban church. The validity of this reasoning should be evident.

We are not discounting the value and power of collective individual piety, but is it enough? How is it possible effectively to divide private from public life? Most sin and human failure are related to both individual and social factors. The gospel is the answer to man's sin; there is but one gospel; and the gospel should not be characterized exclusively as either "individual" or "social" —it is both. Every man is enmeshed in a social situation. We are called to love our neighbors as ourselves (Matt. 22:39), and it is impossible to love God while hating our neighbor (I John 4:20, 21). Neighborly love is always social. The exalted ethics of the Sermon on the Mount are social. God extends His unmerited favor to man in his social condition. It is through group relationships in social institutions, beginning with the home, that one develops into the kind of person he is to be.[8]

If all people on earth were converted to Christ and if all of them conformed their lives to the dictates of God's Word, then we must agree that all evil in our social relationships and in our social and political institutions would be eradicated and that there would be no need for social and political activism. But this is an ideal view of evangelism that hardly seems attainable (Matt. 7:13, 14). We concur also that man's ultimate need is for reconciliation with God. Any idealism (call it "social gospel" or whatever) that would eradicate prejudice, discrimination, oppression, fear, and violence without reconciling men to God is doomed to failure, and clergymen or church leaders of any denomination who encourage this idealism while discounting this reality are doing a double disservice. But we must not allow our emphasis on a personal, future salvation in heaven to cause us to forget our Christian brethren and fellow men here on earth, thus blocking much-needed action—involvement in various ministries, attack on serious evils, sermons and studies that deal with moral issues.

Christians who oppose social and political involvement in worldly affairs also misunderstand the nature of Christian evangelism and ministry. The popular concept of public Christian ministry is one of preaching and teaching aimed at securing more conversions, restorations, and public confessions. We funnel only a small part of congregational funds into other types of ministry, giving perhaps ten or fifteen percent of the weekly contribution to orphan homes or homes for the aged. We tack this type of benevolence on the Great Commission like a footnote.

The difficulty here may be rooted in the untenable dichotomy between the spiritual and the secular. Many Christians rigidly segment their worlds into the political, the social, the economic, the civil, the religious, etc.; and they expect the pulpit and the church in general to address themselves only to ecclesiastical matters like doctrine, personal morality, and man's posthistorical destiny. Questions related to other spheres are not necessarily unimportant, but they are, because of their "this-worldly" nature, individual matters.

The problem with this kind of "hardening of the categories" should be evident: How can one be sure which aspects of ministry are sacred and to be supported by churches, and which are secular

8. See David O. Moberg, *The Church as a Social Institution* (Englewood Cliffs, N.J.: Prentice-Hall, 1962), pp. 180, 181.

and to be promoted only by other institutions or individual Christians? In Jesus' parable of the judgment scene in Matthew 25, which acts of service were religious and which belonged to ordinary individual and social work? Any belief that such a dichotomy is necessary is mere illusion!

The gospel of Christ knows no such disjunction in the affairs of man. Man himself is not some kind of bifurcated spiritual-secular amphibian who is "religious" when he prays, attends worship, and contributes to the general collection, and who is "worldly" when he donates blood, contributes money or sends his children to a Christian college, tutors deprived children in the inner-city, takes out an insurance policy to protect his family, works in a field or factory to provide for it, or even celebrates the sexual pleasures of marriage. Man is man—simply and wholly. Is he any less morally responsible when a member of the church collectively than when a member of the church in individual dispersion?

The ministry of Christ Himself provides strong clues in answering these questions. Most damaging are the portraits of Jesus that make Him a mild, almost sickly, meek and gentle do-gooder. The New Testament image of Christ is not that of a "stained-glass window" servant, but of a real person stained with dust, sweat, tears, and finally blood. He was a strong man of action who was most specific in His commands and in His answers to questions concerning His life style. He responded fully and unequivocally to the suffering, and undeniably He identified more with the societal outcasts, the poor, the sick, and the victims of oppression and degradation than with the prosperous and well situated. His teaching ministry was important, but He did much more than utter words; He made concrete the love of His Father by innumerable actions. No doubt Jesus intended His signs and wonders to support faith in Him as the Son of God, but to deny that He also used His power to help others, motivated by pure love and compassion, is to miss a vital dimension of the power and meaning of His example. Truly He was, in the words of Dietrich Bonhoeffer, "the man for others." He directed His disciples both explicitly and implicitly to concern themselves with the quality of family life, hunger, sickness, relieving the oppressed, comforting the distressed, justice, and even loneliness. These are still controversial issues today for they are part and parcel of the human condition. If we are truly His disciples, can we ignore these and similar problems to which He addressed himself without invalidating His gospel?

We examined in chapter 2 how the early church did not diminish but magnified the concern of Christ for all people and all human relationships. They believed that following Christ is the essence of being His disciple (cf. John 8:12, 31, 32; 10:27; 12:26; Eph. 5:1, 2; I John 2:6). Discipleship transcends a life of mechanical obedience to a code of laws (cf. Mark 10:42-45; Phil. 2:5-8; I Peter 2:21-24; John 13:13-17; 15:12-14). Faith without works is dead (James 2:14-18), and a Christian must let his light so shine that men will see his good works and thus glorify God (Matt. 5:16). God's will in the area of social concern is easily inferred from the greatest commandments—loving God totally and loving our fellow man as ourselves (Matt. 22:37-40).

There is another way to dramatize the Christian's ministry and involvement in the world. We are aware that God loves the world and intends to save it through our efforts; the ever-familiar John 3:16 makes this clear. Yet the same apostle who recorded those words of Jesus also admonished his brethren, "Do not love the world or the things in the world. . . ." (I John 2:15, 16 RSV). Of course it is easy enough to explain this seeming paradox with the stock comment that the church is "in the world but not of the world." Perhaps every preacher has employed that phrase on innumerable occasions, but have we caught the full significance of its twofold relationship? In view of the double requirement, it should not be surprising that throughout history large segments of Christendom have emphasized one to the exclusion of the other.

Many churches, seeking to remain uncorrupted by worldly influences, have withdrawn from culture and are radically opposed to the world. This path leads some to frequent and often bitter attacks on any human institution, whether secular or denominational, which attempts to make Christian faith relevant to contemporary life. The next step is even to deny the existence of any conflict or dilemma in contemporary culture. Perhaps we have all known people who doggedly insist there are no problems when surrounding them is a barrage of evidence to the contrary. But a church that is not *in* the world has misunderstood the meaning of the incarnation.

On the other hand, some Christians have remembered all too well that they are *in* the world and have become guardians of their particular culture. Paul's exhortation "Do not be conformed to this world but be transformed. . . ." (Rom. 12:2 RSV) falls on deaf ears. Theologians often refer to such groups as "folk churches."

Prior to World War II the Lutheran church had in essence become a *Volkskirche*. In Nazi Germany only a minority of Christians, now called the "Confessing Church," opposed Hitler's regime and programs. Hitler's takeover in 1933 had no negative effects on daily life; if anything, employment and profits increased with war preparations. The majority of ministers and Christians believed that the church and state are categorically separated, that faithful disciples must obey the state and remain neutral on all political issues so long as they are free to preach the gospel and administer the sacraments. The average German Christian had only to obey the laws, pay his taxes, and avoid dissent. Consequently they acquiesced in the suspension of civil liberties and the persecution of Jews and communists.[9]

Since America has never had a public leader to compare with the infamous Hitler, what is the implication for American Christians? The point is that people within a nation may be honest, loyal, Christian citizens and yet support, or at least share in the corporate guilt for, national evils which disgrace humanity and directly violate the ethical teachings of Scripture. The major cause for the collapse of society at any level may be traced not to the criminal activities of "bad people" (which exist and must be punished) but to the sins and silence of "good people." Christians must remember the limitations of their judgment, particularly on issues for which there is no clear Biblical directive. But the church has the same obligation to condemn gross public injustice that it had in the days of the Old Testament prophets. Christians dare not be silent over oppression, deceit, corruption, greed, and other destroyers of human personality and community well-being. The voice of protest may not be heard or heeded, but the religious institution that abandons its prophetic role for the sake of survival forfeits its right to exist.

We need to examine continually our attitudes and actions to see if we are maintaining a proper balance between being *in* but not *of* the world. It is a constant temptation to believe that Christians must be either pietists, devoted to study, prayer, worship, meditation, and personal evangelism; or activists, who assault social evils through institutional involvement. These two Christian life styles

---

9. See Roger Mehl, *The Sociology of Protestantism*, trans. James H. Farley (Philadelphia: Westminster, 1970), pp. 273, 278, 279; and Paul C. Empie, "Can Organized Religion Be Ethical?" *The Annals of the American Academy of Political and Social Science*, 363 (1966): 70-78.

are not self-contradictory but interdependent. Piety is the root of Christian life and activism its fruit. Christian ministry and evangelism are not ends in themselves, and evangelism is more than simply "getting the message out." Maybe it would be helpful to picture a continuum. At one pole is the ministry of public and private teaching; at the other is the ministry of service and benevolence. Our efforts to lead the world to Christ will employ both aspects of the ministry, or some felicitous mixture of both, depending on the circumstances. Both aspects communicate, in the broadest sense of the term; both have the goal of leading lost men back to their Creator; *without both we likely will fail.* If preachers, elders, and other church leaders will exercise their responsibilities with wisdom and maturity, surely the brotherhood of Christian believers can enter meaningfully into the life of the world and bear witness to the relevance of their faith to all of human experience without becoming captives of the modern world's misplaced values and polytheism.

One could object validly at this point that social action and political action need to be distinguished. A Christian can be socially involved in the plight of his fellow man without being politically involved. We grant that not all social involvement is political, although all political involvement is social. But the Christian must feel free to be politically active as a means of fulfilling his social responsibilities as a Christian, for which there is ample Biblical precedent. In Biblical history, men of God frequently negotiated with ungodly governments. Today's negotiations between warring parties in the Middle East are no tougher than the ones ironed out by Moses and Aaron with Pharaoh centuries earlier. As judge, Jephthah sent couriers to the Ammonites a number of times in an effort to avoid armed hostilities.

Others not only served directly in governments opposed to Jehovah, but there is clear evidence that they were placed in their positions through God's providence. Joseph's integrity and faithfulness led to his climbing the political ladder in ancient Egypt to the prime ministership, a prestigious civil office second only to Pharaoh's. Genesis describes in considerable detail his successful program to stockpile grain and food for the impending famine. In today's lingo, Joseph was an administrator or bureaucrat, and he used his power to assist vitally the people of God.

Mordecai was a Jew in exile who learned that King Ahasuerus had signed an edict to exterminate the Jews. His response was first to put on sackcloth and ashes and then to protest and demonstrate in front of the king's chancellery. Mordecai's niece, Esther, was the queen who fingered Haman as the scheming executioner of the Jews. After Haman was executed on gallows prepared for Mordecai, Mordecai assumed, as had Joseph, status second only to the king's, and he used his authority to remove the threat of Jewish genocide. The Biblical record offers this obituary for Mordecai: "For Mordecai the Jew . . . was a great man among the Jews and was popular with the mass of his countrymen, for he sought the good of his people and promoted the welfare of all their descendants" (Esther 10:3).

Daniel was a remarkable young man who was, by King Nebuchadnezzar, taken captive and carried to heathen and decadent Babylon, where he remained unswerving in his religious convictions and determination to serve God. Daniel's stern self-discipline kept him from yielding to the king's temptations, and, not coincidentally, he was selected for political service. Through four dynasties he was the first man (Dan. 6:3). Daniel survived what might as well be called a political test of envy and false accusation and was used by Jehovah to witness to the highest political authority in Babylon in the presence of his administrators, advisers, and friends, and, what is more important for New Testament Christians, he was used to keep alive the truth that God is Lord of history and the expectation that the promised Messiah was coming.

The New Testament does not give as much detail about those who were involved in civil affairs. Jesus commended the faith of one Roman official (cf. Matt. 8:10), and He exhorted Zacchaeus, the local tax official, not to relinquish his job, but to make amends for past injustices and to administer the law with fairness and equity. Cornelius, a Roman centurion, was the first Gentile convert. And Paul saluted the saints who resided in Caesar's household (Phil. 4:22).

The lives of these great Biblical saints encourage us to measure men and women not merely by what they believed but by how they discharged the responsibilities that providence and fate gave them. In light of all the Biblical evidence, the concept of two diametrically opposed kingdoms has no place in a discussion of the Christian's right to become involved in politics. When we call the church a "kingdom," we are employing a metaphor in order to underscore the saints' relationship to Christ, much the same as when we call the church the "temple of God" or the "family of God." A person's involvement in a civil order no more invalidates his relationship to God's kingdom than his membership in an earthly family invalidates his membership in the family of God. The examples we have surveyed show that God can use us where we are, that we should not forget who we are and to whom we owe ultimate allegiance, and that politics is a viable means for effecting the will of God on earth.

Miscellaneous Objections

We have argued the core of our case for Christian political activism, but before concluding we cite some remaining, lesser objections:

1. *Christians should not get involved because all politicians are crooks anyway!* The presupposition here is a gross overgeneralization. We will discuss the issue of political corruption and Christian response later when we look at Watergate. Suffice it to say here that our representatives and officials simply reflect the general morality of the country. Before judging them, perhaps we should examine ourselves. Elected officials conduct their work in the full glare of public scrutiny, watched by the other party and by the news media. The ethical affairs of big business are often enshrouded in deep secrecy. It would be extremely difficult to prove that the ethics of politicians are significantly lower than the ethics of officers of labor unions, corporation chains, banks, transportation industries, and perhaps even some colleges and churches. Perhaps Americans have a double standard. If all public officials are condemned by one corrupt official, then all religious teachers and leaders are condemned by what Annas, Caiaphas, and their company did to Jesus.

2. *Why should Christians even vote when they cannot possibly know which candidates are sincere and what they will do once in office?* But we cannot read anyone's heart or ever know the future, and still we select new employees, board chairmen, teachers, doctors, editorialists, and even gospel preachers.

3. *Politics is all compromise and no principle!* Again, another gross oversimplification. And why the prejudice against compromise? It is not only necessary to the smooth running of the legislative and executive machinery in a system based on loyal opposition, but also the key to reducing conflicts of opinion in business, church, and home. Without compromise there could be no lasting international peace.

4. *Christian political involvement does not make any difference anyway!* This charge borders on absurdity. The evidence to refute it is too overwhelming to cite here. The political and social problems of contemporary America that have moral and spiritual dimensions have been addressed by a host of Christians in recent months and years (in this context we do not use the term *Christian* in the narrow, sectarian sense). Some examples are Senator Mark Hatfield (a Baptist lay preacher who was one of the first prominent political leaders to speak out against expanded American involvement in the Vietnam conflict), Senator Harold Hughes (whose involvement in Congressional worship groups and whose confession of his one-time alcohol problem have encouraged many), Congressman John B. Anderson (an active layman in the Evangelical Free Church whose vote in the House Rules Committee enabled passage of an open-housing law), and Congressman Albert H. Quie (an active Lutheran who has helped secure passage of antipoverty and education legislation). And whatever one thinks of his political ideology, Senator George McGovern, a former Methodist minister and active layman, brought home to American voters the moral implications of our involvement in the Vietnam war. At state and local levels the list would be endless. Congressman Joe Evins of Tennessee has lent substantial support to Christian colleges in his home state (he serves on the board of David Lipscomb College). A young, newly elected judge, Steve North, single-handedly and legally removed a persistent sorespot in downtown Nashville—a number of sleazy massage parlors that were unabashed fronts for prostitution. Both Evins and North are active members of the Church of Christ.

5. *Christian involvement in politics leads to an obsession with means over ends, and eventually Caesar (the political process and public policy) becomes the new messiah!* Perhaps some religious folk in the past decade have become obsessed with politics, but to charge with apostasy those who have tried to rectify injustices and inhumanities through social and political processes is a myopic overgeneralization. Too little sophistication in using political techniques and too much reliance on the political order to accomplish the will of God can indeed lead to disillusionment or a false security, but it does not ipso facto prove allegiance to Caesar as messiah. Political activists risk becoming arrogant and dogmatic when they employ law and public policy to do what love should already have done. But, as we have insisted, what happens in the political order *does* matter, and the alternative to nonparticipation may be a com-

fortable acceptance of the ethic of escapism and total other-worldliness.

Political philosophy and ethical philosophy are, we must acknowledge, based on different premises. Political and corporate morality stresses consequences while Christian ethics stresses the intrinsic nature of deeds and the motives lying behind them.[10] Christians in politics can exercise oversight concerning impending legislation. Christian political ethicists can restate and elucidate first principles when ordinary politicians are ensconced in the quagmire of unprincipled compromise and would rather not hear about such things. After all, they should possess more insight into the moral aspects of legislation and public policy than do labor or education leaders and skilled technicians, all of whom think primarily in terms of immediate results and survival—institutional, party, or national.

The Great Reversal

In concluding our survey of the arguments for Christian political action, it may encourage Christians of the last quarter of the twentieth century to take note of evangelicalism a century ago. It may come as a surprise to learn that evangelical Christians of that day played a major role in both social welfare and social reconstruction. The latent compassion and benevolent spirit of churchgoers was whipped up by such eloquent evangelists as Charles G. Finney in this country and Charles H. Spurgeon in England. Evangelicals saw firsthand the slums, factories, and sweatshops, and they established a variety of welfare societies to help alleviate the effects of social and racial disparities. The more intelligent and activist evangelists, unlike some of their successors, were aware that new converts need more than an admonition like "Christ is the answer" or "Go and sin no more."

The organizations they began are too numerous to cite here. The Salvation Army and smaller but similar groups served the underprivileged. Florence Crittenton Homes, schools for immigrants, industrial training institutes, antislavery and temperance societies, and other associations, programs, and services for the underprivileged and culturally deprived were founded. Education played a central role in nineteenth-century evangelical activism. Revivalists and conservative Christians were anything but antiintellectual.

---

10. David Martin, "Ethical Commentary and Political Decision," *Theology* 76 (1973): 525-31.

They established schools and colleges, and at the heart of the curricula was a concern for "moral philosophy" and "the moral government of God." Moral philosophers taught that God's universal sovereignty renders it imperative to conform all aspects of society to God's moral law, and evangelicals did not confine themselves to individual acts of charity. Evangelicals attempted to get at the root causes of frustration, suffering, and poverty. It was obvious that much suffering was caused by conditions and circumstances beyond the victims' control, so many evangelicals entered the political arena to secure the right of labor to organize and strike for higher wages, better working conditions, and an end to child labor and the exploitation of women.

The early twentieth century saw evangelicals completely shift their attitude toward social and political activism, a shift that historian Timothy L. Smith has termed "the great reversal." Evangelical groups abandoned liberal economic and political perspectives; support for new institutions of social service waned to near apathy; interest in the plight of labor declined; and old, persistent problems like the liquor traffic and alcoholism were attacked almost exclusively in terms of personal salvation without regard for social conditions. True, some medical and rescue missions continued and individual acts of charity may have increased, but collective endeavors to eliminate the varied forms of injustice diminished.

Why the 180-degree turn? The great reversal was due more to ideological conflict than to any lessons learned from earlier evangelical activism. The early twentieth century was a period of war for the minds of men, war between the fundamentalists and the modernists. The social and political activism of the nineteenth-century evangelicals was assumed by the new breed of liberal churchmen. Liberal theology was firmly aligned with what came to be known as the Social Gospel, and for all practical purposes liberal Christianity was little more than a social philosophy. Fundamentalists and evangelicals became gravely concerned with the decreasing emphasis upon Biblical fundamentals and the spiritual needs of individuals. Evangelicals regarded the liberals' schemes to establish the complete kingdom of God on earth as utopian and unrealistic, but the evangelicals were losing influence in and control of many congregations and schools. Admittedly the conservative response was reactionary, for in rejecting liberal theology they rejected the entire social program as well. The phrase "social gospel" became anathema to evangelicals.

But the great reversal is now being reversed. The abundant literature and activism of the last ten years signal a return to the social and political activism of a century ago. The full impact of the Great Commission of Jesus Christ is being felt. Christians today may draw upon the experiences and lessons of both the nineteenth and the early twentieth centuries. We need not opt for the utopian, frenzied activism of so many liberal churchmen, nor must we choose the political passivity and dedication to the status quo of so many culture-denying fundamentalists. The Christian life is one of balance and perspective, and political involvement must be firmly rooted in the Word of God. We must obey Paul's dictate to the Colossian Christians: "Whatever you are doing, whether you speak or act, do everything in the name of the Lord Jesus, giving thanks to God the Father through him" (3:17).

*The tragedy is, if we fight Hitler, we will be-
come like him, too, we will turn into something
just as dirty as he is. If we are going to beat
him, we will have to.*

Thomas Merton

*But some cannot wait while the plague worsens.
They confront Caesar's stronghold, his induction
centers, his troop trains, his supply depots. They
declare that some property has no right to existence—files for the draft, nuclear installations,
slums and ghettos. They insist, moreover, that
these condemned properties are strangely related
to one another—that the military invests in
world poverty, that Harlem and Hanoi alike lie
under the threat of the occupying and encircling
power. These things being so, some Christians
insist that it is in rigorous obedience to their
Lord that they stand against Caesar and put his
idols to the torch.*

Daniel Berrigan

*You have learned that they were told, "Love
your neighbour, hate your enemy." But what I
tell you is this: Love your enemies and pray for
your persecutors; only so can you be children of
your heavenly Father. . . . There must be no
limit to your goodness, as your heavenly Father's
goodness knows no bounds.*

Jesus (Matt. 5:43, 44, 48)

chapter six

Should Christians Be Political Revolutionaries?

Consider the following three cases:

In July 1939, less than two months before the actual outbreak of the Second World War, a young German minister's peculiar decision amazed and distressed many of his friends and colleagues. Only a few weeks after his arrival in the United States for a lecture tour they had arranged for his safety, he returned to his homeland to face almost certain death if he continued in his steadfast opposition to the Nazi regime. "I must live through this difficult period of our national history with the Christian people of Germany," he wrote Reinhold Niebuhr. "I will have no right to participate in the reconstruction of Christian life in Germany after the war if I do not share the trials of this time with my people."[1] Dietrich Bonhoeffer, the son of a great doctor, was an outstanding pastor, university professor, and writer. During the period when he was writing *The Cost of Discipleship* and immediately thereafter, he had been very near to absolute pacifism—an unheard-of position in Germany at the time. Not that Bonhoeffer was politically non-involved. Only two days after Hitler assumed public office in 1933, Bonhoeffer delivered a radio address that officials actually cut off

1. Quoted in Reinhold Niebuhr, "The Death of a Martyr," *Christianity and Crisis*, 25 June 1945, p. 6.

the air when he called the Führer principle a form of idolatry. From that time forward, the conventional channels of Christian witness and protest were gradually closed to him. Barred from teaching at thirty, from preaching at thirty-four, and from publishing at thirty-five, he began to see pacifism as an illegitimate escape and courageously joined the resistance movement. Hitler was more than a madman, he was the Antichrist. The resistance movement failed, and the Nazis arrested Bonhoeffer in April 1943. After conducting a worship service for prisoners on Sunday, April 8, 1945, two guards arrived to take him to the gallows. He took aside Captain Best, a British intelligence officer, and said, "This is the end. For me the beginning of life!" Bonhoeffer died at age thirty-nine.

In April 1963, in the midst of a civil rights campaign in Birmingham, Alabama, Martin Luther King, Jr., was handed a court injunction, obtained by the city administration, to halt demonstrations until the right to such activities could be argued in court. This occasion marked a watershed in the thought and strategy of King and other leaders of the movement. Two days later, King decided to disobey the order. "We did not take this radical step without prolonged and prayerful consideration," he was to explain later. "We decided, therefore, knowing well what the consequences would be and prepared to accept them, that we had no choice but to violate such an injunction."[2] The civil rights movement had disobeyed state and local "Jim Crow" ordinances before, but not a court order. While King was in prison for disobeying the injunction, eight local clergymen of various faiths, who previously had issued "An Appeal for Law and Order and Common Sense," sent King a public letter of censure, noting that "hatred and violence have no sanction in our religious and political traditions" and that "such actions as incite to hatred and violence, however technically peaceful those actions may be, have not contributed to the resolution of our local problems."

Few clues indicated that the Berrigan brothers would develop into revolutionary priests. Two of six brothers, Philip was a decorated soldier of World War II who returned to ghetto parish work in three urban areas and Daniel taught New Testament at LeMoyne College, lived in Mexico and Paris, and visited Czechoslovakia. Philip was active in the civil rights movement, serving with CORE and SNCC and taking freedom rides. Daniel was an early antiwar

---

2. *Why We Can't Wait* (New York: Signet, 1964), pp. 69ff.

protester, deeply involved in the marching, the picketing, and the fasting. The two considered new and creative ways to protest when traditional forms seemed to no avail. Philip prayed in front of the homes of the defense secretary (Robert S. McNamara) and the joint chiefs of staff; he conferred with Secretary of State Dean Rusk and several senators. As cochairman of the Clergy and Laymen Concerned About Vietnam, Daniel had marched on the Pentagon with thousands of others in 1967. By May 1968 both brothers had concluded that traditional methods of protest were fruitless for they constituted no serious threat to the Establishment. A few days later, Philip and Daniel Berrigan and seven others (the "Catonsville Nine") forced their way into the Selective Service office at Catonsville, Maryland, and napalmed draft records. Clearly, their protest was no longer simple and legal, but militant and illegal. They also were charged with scheming to kidnap presidential adviser Henry A. Kissinger and blow up the government's heat tunnels in Washington, but they were acquitted. When Philip Berrigan poured blood on draft files, his defenders declared this symbolic act to be in the same tradition as Isaiah's walking naked through the streets of Jerusalem and Jeremiah's burying his loincloth in the river bank.

Genuine and complete surrender to Jesus Christ makes a difference, and how great, how far-reaching that difference is, may well depend upon the person's historical situation. Circumstances alter responses, whether political or otherwise. Each individual conscience is in some way unique. Bonhoeffer, King, and the Berrigans illustrate different responses to unique political and moral situations. But their three responses have one common denominator: all transgressed the boundaries of law. Bonhoeffer tried to remove clandestinely the German dictator from the scene and set in motion the movement toward peace; King and the Berrigan brothers, to protest, respectively, American racial injustice and involvement in the Vietnam war. Each response was clearly radical, even revolutionary. Was each man justified in the sight of God for his activities? Should Christians feel free to go beyond traditional activism and act above the law? Put succinctly, can Christians be political revolutionaries? And if so, under what circumstances?

Our survey of political life styles for American Christians has uncovered a number of vital issues. The question of violence in a world that is neither perfect nor perfectible is a tough one. Few issues, if any, are more difficult to resolve than this one, and undoubtedly few Christians have grappled with it. The hard fact is that resistance, both violent and nonviolent, is very costly, and most Americans are probably too comfortable and too privileged to participate willingly in revolutionary activity. We are more willing to judge others' individual acts, offer our opinions and votes, and thus in some way share in the decision to repress or not to repress. In this chapter we can do little more than lightly plow through ground that has been broken frequently before and offer suggestions for more study.[3] We are not concerned at this point with the hoary arguments for whether a Christian can participate in carnal warfare. Nor are we concerned with how a Christian living under other forms of government should react. This book is about Americanism, and it assumes that being both a Christian and an American citizen makes a difference.

The Case for Active Resistance

The Christian radical seeking to justify violence as a tactic for changing society begins with the role of violence in the human experience. Violence of one type or another is probably an ineradicable, though certainly modifiable, characteristic of human relationships. It is found in all cultures and figures prominently in the history of virtually all powerful national states. Many Third World nations were born in ugly violence and terrorism. In November 1974 Yasser Arafat, the controversial leader of the Palestine Liberation Organization, reminded delegates to the United Nations General Assembly that "many of you who are here in this Assembly hall were once considered terrorists."[4] Terrorists are the worst breed of revolutionaries. They use indiscriminate violence to achieve political goals. They present themselves as revolutionaries, freedom fighters, or guerrillas, and they argue that their tactics are the only way downtrodden peoples can combat oppressive or colonial governments. The fact that a terrorist was invited to address the United Nations shows that terrorism is becoming respectable in the world. What makes it respectable? Success. Respectability depends on what side you are on. The Mau Mau movement in Kenya, the FLN in Algeria, and the IRA in Ireland are celebrated by homeland patriots because they succeeded. Sad as it seems, the world

---

3. Consult the bibliographic note for several recommended volumes on the issues raised in this chapter.

4. Quoted in *Time,* 25 November 1974, p. 44.

appears willing to grant amnesty to—if not to forgive and eventually to honor—the terrorists it once called criminals.

American radicals note that the American missionary spirit has not been exclusively peaceful. Almost every type of violence has been accepted either officially or unofficially at one time or another. The United States was born not by natural evolution or historical necessity but by events culminating in a violent revolution. The doctrine for democratic revolution had been worked out in 1776 in the famous Declaration of Independence, perhaps the best-known "scripture" in the American civil religion. We forced the Dutch, British, French, and Spanish off territory we wanted, the argument goes, treated the Indians as though they had no rights, enslaved the black race, fought Mexico and seized California, fought a fratricidal civil war, fought Cuba and the Philippines, invented and used the great horror weapon—the nuclear bomb—in World War II, and, because of an outdated foreign policy, used near-terrorist tactics in Vietnam.

Christian revolutionaries insist that America is as violent today as ever. In the fall of 1974 there was bloodshed in the labor movement as recession deepened, in Boston as school busing for racial desegregation moved northward, and in West Virginia as the censorship of supplementary reading material in the public high schools became an issue. And too many Americans, they insist, see only the physical dimension of violence, and are completely indifferent to widespread covert or psychological violence—violence done through unjust distribution of power or resources, uneven access to power, laws that discriminate against persons because of class, race, or sex. This is sometimes called institutional or structural violence, public violence engaged in by the state through its legitimate use of "power" and "force." Revolutionaries insist that much personal pathological violence, such as homicide and rape, emanates directly from the state. For example, if a citizen believes the tax laws drastically discriminate against people in his class, he may have no qualms against stealing government property for personal use.

The revolutionary is convinced that institutions of this country are constructed, at least implicitly, to favor certain groups and exclude others from societal benefits. And since injustice already works violence against people, those who hold and benefit from power will not voluntarily relinquish that power. There is but one course left to pursue—the threat and use of violence—and it has been proven that violence does work, or it at least effects some of the desired results. It does change society. This is a powerful argument in its favor, especially when the alternative is continuation of the status quo. The traditionalist may condemn contemporary violence, but he glorifies the violence of, for example, the American Revolution. He recounts the Boston Tea Party with pride, but few white Americans do the same concerning the attempted black revolution in the 1960s in the streets of Detroit, Newark, Watts, and other cities. The principles of the Declaration of Independence are applied selectively. As someone has quipped, "A conservative is someone who worships a dead radical."

Traditionalists remind revolutionaries that American democracy provides machinery for reform, but as Senator Mark Hatfield pointed out, many on both the left and the right "believe that politics is an inevitable corrupting practice that deserves little regard, if not downright contempt."[5] Violent revolutionaries insist that democratic machinery is too sluggish, that only mass confrontation can bring immediate action, and that injuries are the inevitable cost of the pursuit of justice. Put simply, the end justifies the means. By the time Martin Luther King was assassinated, many young blacks had already concluded that their race could achieve nothing more through peaceable demonstrations.

A Response to the Violent Revolutionary

The traditionalist must confess that the revolutionary activist's case includes many impressive points. But, to get at the heart of the matter, there is no Biblical sanction for a life style of violent, political revolution. Jesus' often quoted statement that "I came not to send peace, but a sword" (Matt. 10:34 KJV) refers metaphorically to the dramatic impact discipleship has on personal relationships, as we discussed in chapter 2. The history of ancient Israel, admittedly violent on numerous occasions, provides no mandate for Christian revolution. Israel's judges and kings ruled by divine appointment. The nation's misconduct and violations of God's commandments eventually were punished by God, and often through the afflictions of political persecution and bondage. The Hebrews could appeal to God for protection and relief from an evil or oppressive potentate, and at the same time, as we have noted already, interpret political oppression as Jehovah's punishment for

---

5. *Conflict and Conscience* (Waco, Tex.: Word, 1971), p. 148.

their neglecting their relationship with Him. The situation today, even in "Christian America," is hardly analogous.

The Christian renunciation of violence is seldom the easiest option. Indeed it requires much courage and perseverance. But the Christian life style was never meant to be easy and comfortable. New Testament ethics, especially in the Sermon on the Mount, are so lofty, so demanding, as to appear idealistic and unattainable. Some of the ethical demands of Jesus fly in the face of common sense. But there is much evidence that, in the final analysis, individual commitment to this system of ethics is in the best interests of the kingdom of God among men. We will not consider the success or immediate effectiveness of this system. The committed Christian remains nonviolent even when his moral courage and patience do not immediately evoke sympathy, compassion, and restraint in his enemies. One important message of the cross is that apparent failure may be transformed into a great victory. We do not argue, however, that nations or all other institutions should completely renounce political violence. Political cultures or societies are structured around certain collectively held resources and interests, the protection of which is vital to their security. Failure to defend and protect these interests would be an abdication of political leadership. And the most effective and universally recognized method of national defense and protection is the use or threatened use of violence.

The church, unlike the nation, is concerned about reconciliation. The Christian does not counter evil with nonviolence because he considers evil weak, or because he thinks evil should not be opposed. The intelligent Christian knows a great deal about hatred, violence, and dehumanization in the modern world. And though they may be insoluble to some degree, he does not attempt to escape them or evade the fight against them. But to meet hatred with hatred and weapon with weapon is less than Christian. It may bring "victory," in which one party bitterly submits to the superior force of the other, but not reconciliation. Violence is self-perpetuating, almost invariably provoking reciprocal violence. The man who uses violence cannot complain about his opponent's use of violence. Then it is that "might makes right." Once we adopt violent tactics, we are not likely to abandon them. Once we discard rational discourse or other forms of ethical response, we do not easily resume them. And in many cases violence not only fails to solve the problem but creates several new ones of even greater magnitude.

The Christian's only real consideration is what Jesus did and taught. Jesus' overriding concern was the kingdom of God—its emergence and expansion among men. Discipleship demanded a radically new life and a radically different perspective. One was to not retaliate but respond to evil with good; one was to forgive enemies; persecution only produced blessing and spiritual strength. In the last hours before His crucifixion, in circumstances as difficult as Roman society could devise, Jesus became the perfect exemplar of what He had taught. Undoubtedly this example, more than anything else, inspired the unwavering faithfulness of so many primitive Christians in the face of political opposition and persecuton. The apostle Peter encouraged Christians by citing the example of Jesus: "When he was abused he did not retort with abuse, when he suffered he uttered no threats, but committed his cause to the One who judges justly" (I Peter 2:23). To the world, the cross of Christ signifies both weakness and foolishness (I Cor. 1:23-31), but it unveiled the power of self-giving and permitted God to reconcile sinners unto Himself. The redemptive mission remains incomplete, however, and the disciples of Christ are called to participate in it by "the way of the cross." God confounds the mighty through the weak things of the world and manifests His strength through the weakness of His Son. This is the paradox of the cross and the content of its message. The cross proves that nonviolence can resolve the crucial issues that divide mankind. "If anyone wishes to be a follower of mine," Jesus declared, "he must leave self behind; he must take up his cross and come with me. Whoever cares for his own safety is lost; but if a man will let himself be lost for my sake, he will find his true self" (Matt. 16:24, 25).

From the Christian perspective, violence represents an inadequate view of one's enemies and is incompatible with self-giving love. Violence treats people contemptuously as means to an end; their ideas and feelings are both irrelevant and dispensable. As disciples in the kingdom, ones who are under the rule of God as He is revealed in Christ, we must not write off any opponents or enemies as nonentities or subhumans, as though somehow they were beyond redemption, cut off from the aggressive love of God. Many political revolutionaries and social reformers need a sense of humility. Fighting for the right does not make one righteous. We may fail to see not only the good in our opponents' stance but the self-interest in our own. Perhaps the greatest need of revolutionaries is a respect for and faith in their fellow man—the faith that those on the other side are human and still belong to the sphere in which reconciliation and forgiveness should be sought in spite of all external difficulties. A thoroughgoing sense of sin and finiteness is not only theologically sound, it may be tactically useful at the bargaining table or on the picket line. Reconciliation never glosses over the conflict. It may require great patience and changes of circumstance, but reconciliation remains the goal. If it is to be attained, the minimal standard of love must be met: "Love cannot wrong a neighbour. . . ." (Rom. 13:10).

What About Civil Disobedience?

During the sixties and early seventies, public events repeatedly dramatized an old and troublesome problem. Advocates of civil rights disobey state and local laws in mass demonstrations to further their cause. A folk singer withholds the portion of her taxes that she tabulates would go to support the war in Vietnam. U.S. postal workers strike for better wages and benefits despite a federal law forbidding it. Students defy the State Department's ban on travel to Cuba. Young men who are drafted flee to Canada to avoid arrest and prosecution.

When is a citizen justified in acting as his own legislator and judge? More specifically, should a Christian ever break a man-made law? Does he have the moral right to decide which laws he will obey? The issue has a long and checkered history. The philosophy of civil disobedience was not developed in America, but in the very first democracy of the Greek city-states. Socrates believed that his conscience could require him to disobey statutory law, but he also believed he had to accept the legal sanctions of the state. In Sophocles' tragedy Antigone obeyed her conscience and violated the state edict against burying her brother, who had been decreed a traitor. In this country, Henry David Thoreau, the sage of Walden, transformed this philosophy into a strategy for solving the country's injustices. A generation later, Gandhi employed Thoreau's strategy of civil disobedience to wrest Indian independence from England. Perhaps the best-known practitioner of this philosophy is Martin Luther King, who led his followers to violate state laws he believed to be contrary to the federal Constitution and natural law. Racial discrimination and the Vietnam conflict evoked more mass disobedience in America than any other factors. We cannot provide here a comprehensive set of principles that will enable the Christian citizen to rule automatically and infallibly on the morality and legitimacy of specific acts of disobedience, but we can mention some basic principles.

The term *civil disobedience* properly refers only to an intentional transgression of law to preserve the individual's (or group's) integrity and to make a public, and at times a constitutional, protest against identified wrong.[6] At the outset it should be emphasized that there is no legal right to civil disobedience. The law cannot provide for its violation and still remain the law. The offender must be held liable to punishment. We may admire individuals who have defied man-made laws in obedience to higher laws, but their right to break the law cannot be a legal right; it can only be a moral right. Legality and morality are not, indeed cannot be, synonymous. The practical goals of those who disobey the law lie at the very core of genuine Biblical morality. The greatest difficulty is that our government's relationship to religion is seldom as clearly defined as was that of the government of Old Testament Israel.

Many but by no means all of those who have publicly and dramatically opposed the community and certain of its laws have done so on religious grounds and out of religious motivation. Though mainstream American Christianity has not been nonviolent, the nonviolent tradition in this country has long been closely associated with Christianity, and particularly with certain Protestant sects. One can make a strong case for the validity of civil disobedience, both by human logic and with Biblical evidence. The Christian rejects the extreme view that disobedience to the law, even in a democratic society, can never be justified regardless of the circumstances. To argue this position is to say either that every law that

6. William R. Miller, *Nonviolence: A Christian Interpretation* (New York: Schocken, 1966), pp. 61-70, speaks of levels of nonviolence. *Subtactical* or *spontaneous* nonviolence involves little long-range planning and only a limited number of people. It can be a spontaneous expression of their good will or utter despair, or it can involve a carefully conceived and executed act of witness that seeks either to maintain the actor's integrity or to dramatize his social concern. *Tactical* nonviolence is more flexible; it utilizes nonviolent resistance only when it can be expected to succeed, and it uses other means either in conjunction with or in sequence to it. The focus is on the end and the sufficiency of the means. Strategic nonviolence comes close to collective nonviolence. Such nonviolence is part of a grand strategy that has been carefully calculated as the only way to insure success. Large numbers of people may be involved. It is called a strategy because it is believed to be the most economic and effective way to achieve a particular goal, not just the most moral way. It requires much planning and skillful organization, as well as great wisdom and foresight.

exists is a just law, which is obviously false; or that breaking the law always is a greater evil than compliance to it, which was unacceptable to those founding fathers who signed the Declaration of Independence and to those Germans who refused to execute Hitler's orders. Majorities do err, even in a democracy. The clearest example of this is the century following the American Civil War when the white majorities in many parts of the United States denied the emancipated slaves their access under law to equal voting rights and to health, education, and welfare. Many responsible citizens, both black and white, began to ask if they must invariably give the results of an election greater weight than considerations of elementary justice. Disobedience to bad laws can frequently jolt democratic processes into motion and head them in the direction of equal justice. Through dramatic disobedience to the law, a minority may catch widespread attention and sensitize an apathetic public conscience. Furthermore, civil disobedience of local laws and ordinances may be the only way to test their constitutionality in a higher court.

The Christian will find no general fault with the above reasoning. A just law is a man-made law that squares with the law of God. The Bible has always taught, by command and example, that when a man-made law directly contravenes the law of God, the former must be disobeyed in order to remain obedient to the law of God. This civil disobedience even brings great uncertainty, risk, and persecution. Esther disobeyed an ordinance of the king in a desperate effort to spare her kindred. The risk of death seemed worth it: ". . . if I perish, I perish," she declared (Esther 4:16). Daniel, and then Shadrach, Meshach, and Abednego, refused to obey the laws of Nebuchadnezzar because they owed a higher allegiance to God (cf. Dan. 3). Moses was led directly by God to circumvent and thwart the unjust demands of Pharaoh, who hoped against all odds to keep the Hebrews in bondage. The apostles Peter and John could not in good conscience obey the ordinances of the Sanhedrin (cf. Acts 5:29), and Christians living in the Roman Empire near the turn of the first century courageously faced cruel death rather than uttering a civil oath of ultimate allegiance to the emperor, a mere human.

These are the arguments of Christian activists who are prepared at a moment's notice to jump headlong into dramatic public confrontations and civil disobedience. But Christian activists in America must avoid such precipitous action. The responsibility to obey the law is greater in a democracy than in an authoritarian or totalitarian state. American Christians must obey the law because presumably we have been consulted in its formulation, and because the methods and channels of legal and social reform are generally adequate. The Bill of Rights guarantees all citizens the right to assemble and discuss public issues, to use the mass media, and to organize public parades and demonstrations, and in this way to quicken sentiment, dramatize issues, and ultimately to effect reform. Public protest has never been healthier—in any other nation or at any other time—than it is now in America. The several marches on Washington by civil rights and antiwar protest groups in the 1960s provide examples of legal alternatives to civil disobedience. In fact, one operational definition of *democracy* is, a political system that provides the citizenry alternatives to civil disobedience.

In a democracy one does not have even a moral right to break the law until all legal channels for protest and reform have failed. Black revolutionaries frequently have cited the Boston Tea Party as evidence that the use of violence and civil disobedience to redress grievances are part of the American tradition and a legacy of our own revolutionary ideology. But Thomas Jefferson predicated the "inherent right of rebellion" on the dictatorial denial of democratic rights. This is not the place to compare the right of twentieth-century American blacks to revolt with that of colonial patriots, fascinating as such a topic would be. Another "sticky" issue is how long the oppressed minority should restrict itself to using guaranteed rights and legal modes of dissent when the majority refuses to be budged. Our response here would depend on which side of the discrimination we are on.

Not infrequently the activist confuses the ideals or aims of democracy with its accomplishments and current performance, particularly with respect to such problems as poverty, education, employment, race, and health care. We may admit that America is "not democratic enough," but there is a crucial difference between the procedure and the performance. Each political activist could list at least a half dozen bills Congress ought to pass or actions the president ought to take in stimulating the economy and promoting the general welfare. But one can conclude only that democracy is not as enlightened as the critic-activist, not that democracy is absent. Reform may not come, but the machinery for it is still guaranteed by our Constitution and is enforced by our courts. The electorate still has the power to choose and to elect those who will honor its choice.

An irrational commitment to, and frequent and hasty reliance on, civil disobedience as a tactic for reform can, like the use of violence, create more problems than it solves. Violations of the law, especially for less than laudable causes, not only assault the rule of law but subvert the democratic process. Democracy is eroded when the individual conscience is elevated over collective intelligence and rationality. If the children of light can so easily justify their disobedience of particular laws on grounds of conscience, so can the children of darkness (in part 4 we will see how this difficulty contributed in part to the Watergate crimes). Most anarchists refuse to generalize the principles behind their actions. If all fanatics were encouraged to violate the law when their consciences so dictated, even the imperfect political democracy we have in America would dissolve into chaos and civil disobedience would become quite uncivil. Furthermore, history has shown that widespread civil disobedience can produce a backlash, even waves of vigilantism, among influential and otherwise traditional political groups.

To recapitulate, ethical decision making is not easy, and civil disobedience is a grave enterprise. As Christians we may succeed in withdrawing ourselves from the sphere of political action, but we cannot avoid formulating an opinion about those who are involved in it. And the perplexing fact is that a great many Christians who consider civil disobedience invalid would in certain situations resort to or approve it—but giving it a different rationale. Some who condemn civil rights demonstrators for violating a local ordinance perpetuating segregation, vociferously support a governor who defies a Supreme Court order to open the state university to students of all races. As solid American citizens, some truckers have outspokenly defended "Americanism," urging police to take a hard line against youthful antiwar protesters and displaying "America: Love It or Leave It" decals on their vehicles. But in the winter of 1973-74 truckers were hit hard financially by inflation and spiraling gasoline costs, and then their bumper stickers carried less moral force. Many blockaded traffic on some of the nation's busiest turnpikes and coerced, sometimes violently, other truckers to join their protest. Combine an easy civil disobedience with a widespread national crisis, and democrary can dissolve into anarchy.

Is not the real issue "How much do I owe my country?" or "What is service to my country?" We shall return to this issue when we study civil religion in America. Whatever one's opinion of the Nürnburg trials, in which the victors judged the vanquished, they sanctioned the concept that obedience to illegal or immoral orders is not the highest or even a valid form of service to one's country. The political revolutionary may be disobeying the law on grounds of morality and principle, or on less noble grounds. He may be saint or insane. He may be enlightened, or a person obsessed with being accepted by the crowd he mindlessly follows. But his presence in our society must awaken us to the reality that we too are making choices and that we are ultimately responsible for them. Herein is the most important function of the Christian revolutionary. He reminds us that the individual who obeys the law and conforms to society's expectations is as much obligated to examine the morality of his acts and the basic decency of his society as is the person who breaks the law.

To conclude, we may return to our opening case studies. What should a Dietrich Bonhoeffer do, living in a homeland pushed deeper and deeper into senseless war and genocide by a madman with no respect for the restraints of law? Or what should a Christian have done about historic, deeply entrenched racial injustice? And what should a clergyman do who is convinced his country is involved in a senseless, needless conflict? The situations represent varying degrees of public and personal crisis. Bonhoeffer's situation seems to be the most extreme of the three, and atypical circumstances surely alter ordinary responses. Revolutionary activity is not essentially a topic for classroom debate; it is an action, a calculated risk, a commitment. Theory is secondary. Individuals of conscience act because they must. Conscience compelled Martin Luther to declare: "Here I stand; I can do none other, so help me God." Each person must stand accountable before God in the day of judgment (II Cor. 5:10), and surely His grace will cover adequately our deficiencies.

Americans are more "participation oriented" than citizens elsewhere. They are more likely to believe that they can influence the government if they want to than do citizens in other countries, and this sense of efficacy or competence makes them more likely to act. And, perhaps more important, they are more likely to express the belief that the citizen has a responsibility to be active in the life of his community.

Sidney Verba

chapter seven

When Christians Make
Political Decisions

Shortly after World War II the editors of a major Protestant denominational magazine began selecting an American political leader as the "Christian Statesman of the Year." The idea was to honor one to whom honor was due and to hold up to citizens and aspiring politicians one man as an example of Christian virtue and courage in the political realm. After much searching, the editors chose the governor of one of our southern states, a man best known for leading the forces of racial segregation and running on a racist platform for the presidency of the United States. They justified their choice this way: the governor neither smokes nor drinks, and he will not serve liquor in his official residence.

This illustrates a pitfall that evangelicals do not easily avoid when they make political decisions—that of making private purity the chief standard for fitness for public office. If we probe much deeper into such moral myopia, however, we will discover that all sincere Christian activists feel a keen sense of responsibility to make ethical evaluations of public affairs and to apply Christian principles and values to the complex processes of political and social change. They want to put a man or woman in office who is the best possible example of Christian virtue, an official their children can respect and admire. Despite these good intentions, Christians often get bogged down in moral irrelevancies and insignificant issues. How can these pitfalls be avoided?

Before concluding this study of styles of Christian political activism, we will offer some practical suggestions for how Christians should make political decisions, suggestions that presuppose the validity of traditional activism. The Christian discharges his civic responsibilites wth certain advantages. First, he brings to political decisions the proper motivation—faith in God and His divine order, faith that His will is being accomplished, and love for men. Second, he makes political decisions in the light of genuine Biblical morality. He does not neglect moral issues. Making decisions on political issues is one aspect of Christian stewardship. Third, he can rise above the narrow self-interest that has polluted too much of public life and base his decisions on what will benefit the greatest number of people. This last advantage is particularly important in light of a major "paradox of participation" in American politics. Those who need governmental help and intervention the most—victims of racial discrimination, inferior education, poverty, and cultural deprivation—are the least active, and those who need help the least are the most active. The wealth and education that make some more advantaged also provide the resources necessary for participation in politics. Citizens who are both Christian and advantaged can help our political representatives be fairer and more balanced in responding to minorities whose voices are weak.

The first political decision that many young Christians must make is how deeply involved they should be. Should I aspire to run for elective office? Should I seek employment in Civil Service or public administration? Should I join a political party and be active in party functions? Should I actively campaign for candidates? Should I influence the political process by becoming a lecturer, a teacher, or a journalist? Should I join special interest and lobby groups like John W. Gardner's Common Cause?

We dare not attempt to answer conclusively these questions for all Christians. One of the great characteristics of political participation in America is its voluntariness—no one is forced to participate. Thus the law can provide for equal opportunity to participate. No one should run for public office without fully realizing that to win, he must have a certain type of personality and much money, dedication, and perseverance. Party and campaign activism is a more realistic option for most Americans.

Although a clear majority of the public believes that political parties confuse more than clarify issues and that party conflict hurts more than helps government performance[1], our political parties (even third or splinter parties) fulfill a vital role. Political parties are one of the principal distingushing marks of modern government, and the party system evolved by a tortuous process as a way to implement democratic ideals. Party activity is the sphere of democratic decision-making beyond general elections. It simplifies issues for the voting public, moderates conflicts, promotes political consensus and legitimacy, and, perhaps most important, recruits, elects, and appoints leaders to office. It would be difficult for a democracy to function smoothly in modern America without party activism. How could hundreds of thousands of offices be filled in the absence of parties without each election becoming a confusing free-for-all? And despite obvious shortcomings, is there a more practical way to formulate and implement public policy at the various levels of government? Would the public be as well informed on the issues without adversary parties competing for public offices?

Party activists do not need to be convinced of the importance of their role. Such activism provides them with new opportunities for involvement with issues, with competition, with new associations, and with psychological satisfaction of attachment to and involvement with a special group. But not all Christian activists will gain such satisfaction from "pressing the flesh" in political campaigns or from the rough-and-tumble of ordinary partisan politics at the state and local levels. They may feel that such activism is too indirect, too petty, too ineffectual. Each citizen possesses only a limited amount of time, energy, and money; he cannot be involved in all worthwhile activities. But the American system does provide a broad means of participation—the franchise—which the Christian can and should exercise. Our concern here is how a Christian should vote.

One lesson American school children learn is that every vote is important. Regrettably it is a lesson that Americans easily forget; we have already cited statistics showing the low turnout in American elecions. Yet there is striking evidence that each vote does indeed count. John F. Kennedy won the presidency in 1960 by a margin of just .2 percent of the votes cast, and Richard M. Nixon won in 1968 by just .7 percent. When the Ninety-fourth

---

1. See Jack Dennis, "Support for the Party System by the Mass Public," *American Political Science Review* 60 (1966): 600-15.

Congress convened in January 1975, a senatorial seat from New Hampshire was vacant because of a disputed election. After two recounts Democrat John A. Durkin was declared the winner over Republican Louis C. Wyman by two votes.[2] The confusion continued, however, and a special election was scheduled. All of this could have been avoided if more New Hampshire citizens had realized the value of their votes. Only forty-nine percent of the eligible voters had taken time to go to the polls (which happened to be better than the thirty-eight percent who participated nationwide in the same election). The voter has power. Not that the power or influence of a single voter is large; indeed, it is very small. But if everyone declined to vote because of this fact, the foundations of our democracy would crumble. Democracy must reflect the wishes of the many with little power rather than those of a few with great power.

The Centrality of Issues

The major responsibility of the Christian voter is to look closely and carefully at the issues at stake in the election. Political scientists tell us that a majority of Americans vote as directed by leaders of reference groups such as labor unions, business and professional organizations, and social clubs; they are candidate-oriented or party-oriented rather than issue-oriented.[3] Millions have never voted for a candidate outside their favorite party. We must not conclude that all party-oriented voters are oblivious to moral issues, but for many that is the case. Democracy is a viable, sensible form of government only when enough citizens act on the issues. And the Christian's involvement is strategic because he can be expected to delve more deeply into the moral implications of his votes. (In part 3 we will discuss the morality inherent in political issues.)

The responsible Christian votes on the basis of issues, but his decision about how to vote is complicated by the fact that few elections revolve around a single issue. The typical election may involve three or four major issues, each with moral implications.

---

2. *Time,* 13 January 1975, p. 8.

3. Fred I. Greenstein stated that party identification is the chief consideration for most Americans in casting their votes and that probably little more than ten percent of the electorate tends to view the world in liberal or conservative terms. *The American Party System and the American People,* 2nd ed. (Englewood Cliffs, N.J.: Prentice-Hall, 1970), pp. 29, 30. There is much statistical evidence to substantiate Greenstein's conclusion.

And once the winning candidate has taken office, he may confront many other issues that were dormant on election day. The practical result of all this is that the Christian voter may not find the ideal candidate, one he can vote for with absolutely no reservations. No candidate will completely agree with him on all major issues. His voting becomes an act of both compromise and faith. Some might argue that this is a fault within the American system, that we should have a multiplicity of political parties (seventy-five to one hundred, if necessary) so that each citizen can vote for a candidate with whom he agrees on all the issues. But if such were the case, then members of the various parties, once elected to Congress, would be compelled to compromise their positions on major issues in order to establish a working consensus and conduct public business. The question is not whether we shall compromise in dealing with political issues, but when we shall compromise—in the parties themselves when selecting candidates or in Congress?[4] The Christian should not expect to find an ideal candidate. He will look for the man or woman whose position is closest to his on what he deems the major issues. He must accept the better candidate and, when worse comes to worst, the candidate who is "the lesser of two evils." Many party regulars in both parties defended their votes in the 1972 election with the "lesser-of-two-evils" rationale.

In making political decisions, the Christian must be careful to avoid judging a candidate *solely* on the basis of his personal life and his nonpolitical affiliations. It would be shortsighted to neglect completely these factors, but they are not primary criteria in determining a candidate's fitness for office. If they were, voting would be much easier. We would not need to study and analyze the issues. We would simply ask: Is the candidate a good husband and father? Has he been divorced or committed adultery? Does he use profanity? Does he smoke? Does he drink? Does he attend church services regularly? If the answers are right, then this candidate is a good one. And he's an even better one if he is a candidate of our party. What could be simpler? This is the kind of casuistry that names a racist or warmonger the "Christian Statesman of the Year." And the tragedy is that both our political processes and our religion suffer from this charade.

The Christian can hardly apply the most rigid standards of the

---

4. An excellent discussion of this line of reasoning appears in Robert A. Dahl, *Democracy in the United States: Promise and Performance,* 2nd ed. (Skokie, Ill.: Rand McNally, 1972), pp. 281-84.

fellowship of believers to people in society at large, and he must concede that even in the more conservative and fundamentalist denominations, rules against smoking, social drinking, dancing, and divorce and remarriage are not consistently enforced or even always accepted. Not that family life and personal piety are unimportant to spiritual growth, or that God will not hold us accountable for personal, private habits. Even these matters constitute part of a statesman's public image which at least indirectly influences the nation. But by in large these matters are irrelevant to the candidate's ability to perform the duties that the office requires. Knowing that many voters care most about candidates' personal piety, some candidates create a public image of great piety that may or may not correspond with reality.

Many Christians are prone to support without question any candidate who is a member of their church or denomination. If he comes from "our" group, he has to be good, or at least he cannot be all that bad, the reasoning goes. But the truth is, not many public officials are committed to more than a generalized form of religion; they deem one church to be about as good as another. If a candidate is a Baptist, for example, he should not automatically receive the votes of all Baptists. The reason is that one should vote on the basis of issues and that a candidate's church affiliation gives little clue to his position on the issues. Any large denomination includes a wide range of political persuasions. President Kennedy was a Roman Catholic, but he took as firm a stand for separation of church and state as has any president; a special envoy was sent to the Vatican not by Kennedy but by Nixon, a Quaker. And Nixon's military decisions on Vietnam leave little doubt that he no longer embraced the Quaker doctrine of pacifism. No candidate, however faithful a church member, should be evaluated apart from his public record and stand on the major issues of the day.

In this connection the church, whether the entire brotherhood or the local congregation, has no business endorsing candidates for public office. As we noted in previous chapters, the church possesses no special gift of political or bureaucratic expertise. Sometimes an endorsement is subtle, even subliminal. In the summer of 1974 a group of church leaders from a particular denomination in Tennessee signed a letter endorsing the gubernatorial candidacy of a Nashville businessman because he was a member of their denomination and a successful businessman. While this was not intended as an official endorsement by that denomination, the practical effect was about the same; the letter had been written on church stationery and was widely circulated both inside and outside the denomination. Church leaders must be niggardly in their praise of politicians and public officials, if for no other reason than to spare possible embarrassment for their lack of wisdom. In the late fifties, Church of Christ leaders, especially in the Southwest, exalted a young oilman and lay minister as an exemplar of Christian ethics. He was in demand as a Sunday school teacher and guest speaker and, whatever his topic, he convinced many that one can be a dedicated Christian and still "strike it rich." By the early sixties, the duplicity of Billie Sol Estes was splashed across the front pages of newspapers and newsmagazines throughout the world. A generation ago, Protestants praised the administration of Warren G. Harding throughout, Robert Miller has noted. Harding was a Baptist and had brought a businesslike demeanor to the presidency. After his death but before the Teapot Dome scandal came to light, one conservative religious paper stated that Harding would be numbered with the succession of men who had made the United States presidency the noblest seat of power in Christendom.[5]

It is patently obvious, then, that the Christian cannot know, nor should he become obsessively concerned with, the motives of his public officials. Our American system can work well enough if we concern ourselves only with a candidate's proposals and with whether he has the will and capacity to carry them out. History shows no exact and necessary correlation between the quality of a man's motives and the quality of his public policy, on either the foreign or the domestic front. This is true in both political and moral terms. We cannot conclude that a well-intentioned statesman will make public policy decisions that are either morally desirable or politically praiseworthy, only that he will not pursue bad policies deliberately. How often politicians, pursuing purely selfish ambitions, have achieved worthwhile accomplishments for special groups or for the nation at large; and how often statesmen, desiring only to improve the world or reform the nation, have only made it worse!

The Bible makes clear that God is as concerned with results as He is with intentions. God cares about what happens in history. Especially in the Old Testament His dealings with the sons of men made morality not an end in itself but a means to more completely

---

5. Robert Miller, *American Protestantism and Social Issues, 1919-1939* (Chapel Hill: University of North Carolina, 1958), p. 27.

effect the will of God on earth. To manifest His will to His chosen people, God did not hesitate to use men and women of mixed motives and questionable character. Must we imagine that despite the individual greatness and commitment of Moses, God cared more about that than about the liberation of His chosen people?

To recapitulate, the gospel of Christ and His church is not linked to a single political viewpoint. If it were, politics would become the whole of the Christian life. We must not seek out a congregation composed exclusively of people who agree with the elders or the majority of the ministers on the political issues of the times. Both issues and perspectives change every few years. The divine imperative is a deep commitment to Christ and His message of liberation, which, we may trust, will be relevant to the contemporary public issues of great gravity. The church must not be limited to those who profess the correct opinions, whether theological, social, or political. The church should be a mixed group of people whose needs are diverse but who are all committed unequivocally to a new life in Christ and who resolve all personal and social dilemmas in light of that. No human institution or organization is worthy of the Christian's undivided loyalty. Whatever pressures may have been exerted on Him, Jesus refused to commit Himself to any of the politico-religious parties of his day—Zealots, Herodians, Pharisees, and Sadducees. And yet He was willing to encounter and deal with all. His disciples today must make all personal, party, and philosophical loyalties tentative, changing them when necessary to remain utterly loyal to the ultimate Sovereign of heaven and earth. David O. Moberg suggested that the traditional lingo and labels of American politics, while seldom appropriate, are even less so when applied to Christian disciples: "The Christian ideally is both a conservative who tries to conserve all that is true, honest, just, pure, lovely, and gracious (Phil. 4:8) in society and a liberal who tries to liberate mankind by changing the conditions of society that violate those criteria of excellence."[6]

Preparation for Making Responsible Decisions

The Christian activist who intends to use his political power responsibly must be intelligent and well informed. He must allow time to study and analyze the issues. He must read, listen, and discuss. He is fortunate if he is a member of reference groups that

---

6. *Inasmuch: Christian Social Responsibility in the Twentieth Century* (Grand Rapids: Eerdman's, 1965), p. 94.

pressure him to vote in different ways, because this will motivate him to analyze the issues more carefully.[7]

The Christian must be aware that no sources of political information are free of bias. The newspaper or magazine that is most biased may appear to him to be least biased because its slant is the same as his. To say that all sources of political information have a bias is not to contend that a reasonable degree of fairness and objectivity is impossible; a good number of newspapers and periodicals achieve it. But none can completely eliminate subtle, even unintentional, bias.[8]

If the voter exposes himself to several varied papers, magazines, and journals, his own bias will receive the greatest challenge and he will analyze campaign issues more objectively. But a warning is in order against "selective perception," the unconscious selection of the news programs, commentaries, and editorials that reinforce one's beliefs and attitudes, and the omission of those that challenge them. In that sense, the mass media are far less effective agents of social reform and political change than they are of entertainment and interpersonal values. Studies have shown that the most effective means of political change is personal contact.[9]

These comments are, of course, just as applicable to non-Christians as to Christians who take democratic responsibility seriously, but they have a special application to well-read Christians. Everything from interdenominational forums to religious journals and magazines to church bulletins frequently offers political commentary on the times. And yet church membership does not make these spokesmen immune to the ordinary afflictions of bias and prejudice when they expatiate on political and moral issues. In fact they are tempted to develop an arrogance that first assumes and then implies that their analyses and interpretations are preferred in the divine order of things. And uncritical readers may

---

7. See Bernard R. Berelson, Paul F. Lazarsfeld, and William N. McPhee, *Voting* (Chicago: University of Chicago, 1954), pp. 215-33.

8. For example, aside from outright endorsements, newspapers show their bias in four ways: they give larger headlines to the favored candidate; they run more lead stories on him; they give more prominent position to articles on him; and they print more quotations from him and more remarks praising him. From Peter M. Sandman, David M. Rubin, and David B. Sachsman, *Media: An Introductory Analysis of American Mass Communications* (Englewood Cliffs, N.J.: Prentice-Hall, 1972), p. 102.

9. Angus Campbell et al., *The American Voter* (New York: Wiley, 1964), pp. 67-96.

unconsciously share their presuppositions. Whether for political information or, more important, for spiritual growth and contemporary relevance, the Christian should expose himself to as many, varied religious papers and journals as his time for study and reflection permits. New concepts and ideas pose no threat to the psychological security of the intelligent and mature Christian. To be afraid of ideas is to be unfit for discipleship. And if history repeats itself, some of today's more unpopular ideas will be tomorrow's truth. The mature conservative or evangelical is well advised to read the more liberal *Christian Century*, and liberal churchmen would do well to read the more conservative *Christianity Today*. A number of other periodicals, such as *Eternity*, stand somewhere between the two. *Christianity and Crisis* was established during World War II mainly to offset or balance the consistent pacifism of the *Christian Century*. And each major denomination publishes a number of provocative books, journals, and magazines that deal with the great social and moral issues. There can be no excuse for ignorance in such times as these.

We conclude with a final warning. Social scientists have discovered the "narcotizing dysfunction" of the mass media (dysfunctional rather than functional on the assumption that it is not in the best interest of a modern complex society to have large masses of the populace politically inert and apathetic).[10] The point has special relevance for Christian political activists.

Studies show that Americans, desiring to "keep abreast" of current events, spend an increasing proportion of their time taking in the offerings of mass communications systems. But this flood of information tends to "narcotize" rather than energize the average person. The more time one spends keeping well informed, the less time one has to do something about the problems depicted. The intelligent television viewer may opt for a special on unemployment or race discrimination over "Mannix" or "Friday Night at the Movies." He may read political comment in a variety of papers and magazines and avoid the cheap novels and sensationalist magazines that make fewer demands on his psyche. He may intelligently discuss the issues at his neighbor's cookout or his boss's open house. He may address civic groups or teach Sunday school

---

10. This line of analysis is discussed in Lazarsfeld and Robert K. Merton, "Mass Communication, Popular Taste and Organized Social Action," in Bernard Rosenberg and David Manning White, eds., *Mass Culture: The Popular Arts in America* (Glencoe, Ill.: Free, 1957), pp. 457-73.

classes concerning the issues. He may know the alternative solutions to problems and the advantages and disadvantages of each. But he never translates his concern and information into concrete action. He substitutes secondary contact with the real world for involvement. He is only vicariously involved. The mass media have become social narcotics.

This chapter may be unsettling. The responsible use of influence and power, however great or small, is seldom easy. We must take our cue from Jesus Himself and become personally and meaningfully involved. The servant entrusted with just one talent had to answer for his stewardship the same as those with more talents. In America we have a number of mechanisms for exerting a good influence. What a disgrace if ours is a half-hearted effort or a superficial concern rather than a sacrificial involvement in the great spiritual and temporal problems of modern society!

part three

Civil Religion
in America

There is therefore a purely civil profession of faith of which the Sovereign should fix the articles, not exactly as religious dogmas, but as social sentiments without which a man cannot be a good citizen or a faithful subject.

Jean Jacques Rousseau

Our government makes no sense unless it is founded in a deeply felt religious faith, and I don't care what it is.

Dwight D. Eisenhower

While some have argued that Christianity is the National Faith, and others that church and synagogue celebrate only the generalized religion of "the American Way of Life," few have realized that there actually exists alongside of and rather clearly differentiated from the churches an elaborate and well-institutionalized civil religion in America.

Robert N. Bellah

chapter eight

The Nation with
the Soul of a Church

G. K. Chesterton once described America as "a nation with the soul of a church." It is "the only nation in the world founded on a creed." That creed has been called many things—Americanism, democracy, the American way of life, the religion of the Republic, Americanity—but not Christianity. The creed is based on national scriptures, the canon of which remains open for any new and lofty texts that further explicate the intentions of our founding fathers. This religion is semisecular and unofficial, but a majority of Americans appeal to it when they must have recourse to inspiration. Despite the official separation of church and state in our nation, candidates for the highest executive office are competing for a religious office.

If this analysis startles you, or seems to border on blasphemy, listen to John F. Kennedy performing the "national liturgy" of an inaugural address: "With a good conscience our only sure reward, with history the final judge of deeds, let us go forth to lead the land we love, asking His blessing and His help, but knowing that here on earth God's work must truly be our own."

Now listen to Richard M. Nixon performing the same ritual twelve years later: "Let us go forward from here confident in hope, strong in our faith in God who created us, and striving always to serve His purpose."

Since the inauguration of George Washington in 1789, the president-as-priest has been consecrating, renewing, and celebrating those articles of faith which Americans share, the civil religion which arches over us all, from neo-Puritan reformers to Eastern European Catholics to descendants of chattel slaves from darkest Africa.

In 1967 Robert N. Bellah of Harvard Divinity School published an essay entitled "Civil Religion in America." He summarized his thesis in the opening statement: "There actually exists alongside of and rather clearly differentiated from the churches an elaborate and well-institutionalized civil religion in America."[1] Bellah argued that this phenomenon must be understood sympathetically because it possesses "its own seriousness and integrity and requires the same care in understanding that any other religion does."[2] While this phenomenon long escaped serious analysis, it has long been practiced. Bellah acknowledged that he took the phrase "civil religion" from Jean Jacques Rousseau's *The Social Contract*. A number of writers have examined Bellah's analysis. Many agree with him and buttress his views. Others insist that this phenomenon is no religion at all. Some see the function of civil religion as a positive and necessary one in our society, but many writers, preachers, and other opinion leaders castigate it as not only dysfunctional but idolatrous. Our purpose here is to examine civil religion as it is manifested in contemporary American culture and then to evaluate it in light of the Biblical doctrine of church and state. First we must define some basic terms.

The Term Religion

For purposes of this study, we may differentiate three distinct uses of the word *religion*.

1. *Spiritual private religion.* This type of religion is almost totally individualistic, although it may be shared wth a few intimates. Spiritual or private religion is someone's personal theology, which includes his relationship (or lack of it) to some congregation or denomination, his myriad beliefs, his manner of worshiping God, and his perspective on all problems and events that invade his consciousness. The individual may be strongly committed or gen-

---

1. *Daedalus* 96 (1967): 1. This essay is reprinted in several other sources.
2. Ibid.

erally indifferent (or somewhere in between) to his religious faith and practices. The purpose of a man's private religion is to rescue him from sin, reconcile him to God, and establish him in virtue. The precepts and values that he cherishes may have been imparted to him and nourished by the community (and the larger communities) of which he is a part, but he has selected and adapted them according to his background, conscience, personality, and psychological make-up.

2. *Culture religion.* This term is used in two ways. First, culture religion may refer to expressions of religion that do not claim to be Biblical or Christian. Included here are superstitious religions built around astrology, the occult, and other seemingly determinative phenomena, humanistic faiths like naturalism and Ethical Culture, and some expressions of the drug culture and hippie movement.[3] We may even include such political ideologies as communism or Nazism which have been, in important respects, theologies. All of these folk or culture religions have unique philosophies and creedal systems that were formulated by people struggling to discover fulfillment and a coherent set of meanings within a certain historical context. In some cases they desired to escape reality. These religions usually claim for a set of nontranscendent, nonauthoritative data, divine revelation, transcendence, universality, and authoritativeness. In contrast to this, the Christian claims that the message in the Bible is indeed transcendent, auhoritative revelation. One might include here the vague but tenacious "faiths" of contemporary man, particularly technology, reason, and human progress. Such faiths rarely become explicit religions, but culturally they challenge New Testament Christianity. By encouraging belief in the perfectibility of society through human effort and wisdom, they subvert the doctrine that man is lost without Christ; many secular humanists openly oppose religion because of apparent irrationality and absolutism.

---

3. Harvey Cox wrote: "Happiness represents a secular version of the historic American quest for a faith that warms the heart, a religion one can experience deeply and feel intensely. The love-ins are our 20th Century equivalent of the 19th Century Methodist camp meetings—with the same kind of fervor and the same thirst for a God who speaks through emotion and not through the anagrams of doctrine." Quoted in William B. Lockhart, Yale Kamisar, and Jessie H. Choper, *The American Constitution,* 3rd ed. (St. Paul: West, 1970), p. 831. See the court's opinion in Torcaso v. Watkins, 367 U.S. 488 (1961), and a discussion of it in Paul G. Kauper, *Religion and the Constitution* (Baton Rouge: Louisiana University, 1964), p. 31.

To speak of the religious pluralism of the United States is often misleading. Of course from the very beginning there has been a pluralism of religious bodies, denominations, and churches, and many of these groups have continually spoken loudly and clearly of the important walls that divide them. But most of these denominations have had a common understanding of the Christian faith, an understanding that during the Great Awakening was first called "evangelical," or "spiritual," religion.[4] This suggests the second and perhaps more typical meaning for the term *culture religion*—the "common religion," or "general" faith, of the churches. Culture religion is generalized religion, the lowest common denominator of all religious institutions, beliefs, and values presently accepted in our country.

Since the early years of our Republic, foreign visitors have been impressed with Americans' high degree of involvement in religious affairs. In contrast, institutional expressions of Christianity in the rest of the Western world have been declining for several decades. After World War II America experienced an upsurge in religious interest and activity, with church membership increasing to sixty-three percent of the population in the late 1950s (it was only ten to fifteen percent at the beginning of the nineteenth century). While church attendance has leveled off and even declined in recent years, institutional religion is still more than a marginal phenomenon in modern society.

In the late 1950s and early 1960s many began to criticize American culture religion. The "surge of piety" was decried as an interest in "religion in general" rather than a genuine search for God and concern for His ways. American religiosity was suspect because it lacked depth, consistency, and sophistication. Perhaps more than any other critic, Will Herberg saw the new awakening of the 1950s as the merging of all faiths, including Jewish and Roman Catholic, into the "culture religion" of the "American way of life." Being a Protestant, Catholic, and Jew are three alternative ways of being an American. The theology and method of each sanctions the status quo. Herberg saw in the modern revival of religion a deterioration of all ultimate religious values that paves the way for the triumph of secularism.[5]

---

4. Winthrop S. Hudson, *Religion in America* (New York: Scribner's, 1973), pp. 7-9, 80-82.

5. *Protestant-Catholic-Jew* (Garden City, N.Y.: Doubleday-Anchor, 1960), pp. 72-98.

This analysis of culture religion in America is essentially sound. American folk or culture religion has its own creed which, as suggested earlier, condenses the tenets of generalized religion but which still is quite detailed.[6] Here are some of its basic elements:

God exists. To many He is a God of comfort and peace, but He is also concerned with the affairs of men and, hence, is a transcendent God of judgment.

Jesus is the divine Son of God. To most He is the Savior of lost mankind, and to all He is at least the sacrificial servant and the ideal man.

The Bible is the revealed Word of God.

There are good Christians in all churches.[7]

An eternal reward awaits all peoples of the earth. We should emphasize progress, optimism, and the future.

Each person should produce or achieve something in life. He who will not work should not eat.

Faithful Christian living will bring inner peace and tranquillity.

Leadership in the church and leadership in the community usually go hand-in-hand. Christians need not be ashamed of seeking worldly success and material comfort.

All people are equal; freedom comes from God; individual personality is valuable; and all nations should be granted self-determination.

America is a Christian nation. We have enjoyed more of God's blessings than any other nation. We should love our nation. Communism is wrong mainly because it is godless.

Good Christians make good citizens. Citizens must obey the law at all times.

These value-orientations are essentially general and easily applied to many different areas of life, especially politics. Each church or

---

6. See Lowell D. Streiker and Gerald S. Strober, *Religion and the New Majority: Billy Graham, Middle America, and the Politics of the 70s* (New York: Association, 1972), pp. 120-98; and Rodney Stark and Charles Y. Glock, *American Piety: The Nature of Religious Commitment*, vol. 1, Patterns of Religious Commitment (Berkeley and Los Angeles: University of California, 1968).

7. The late Adlai Stevenson, two-time Democratic nominee for president, once confessed: "If it's true that politics is the art of compromise, I've had a good start; my mother was a Republican and a Unitarian, my father was a Democrat and a Presbyterian. I ended up in his party and her church." *Time*, 28 January 1952, and quoted in Daniel J. Boorstin, *The Genius of American Politics* (Chicago: University of Chicago, 1953), p. 137.

sect may, if it chooses to, add more specific tenets and applications. But it is obvious that large numbers of Americans are content to pay lip service to the above tenets of generalized religion without searching out their implications.

3. *Civil religion.* Radical pluralism is the cardinal mark of religion in America. The disestablishment of religion by both our federal and state constitutions has meant that the laws of the land favor no one religion and that the nation's churches and synagogues must be altogether "voluntaristic." Each church must recruit new members and keep old ones in the fold with persuasion rather than coercion, without the aid of any arm of the state.

This view of church and state is so ingrained in the American consciousness that it requires some effort to imagine what a radical concept and daring innovation it was when our Constitution was being framed. For more than fourteen hundred years it had been assumed, virtually universally, that the stability of the social and political order depends on the religious solidarity of the people. No ruler or statesman, no religious or social philosopher, no church official or other responsible thinker had dared to question this axiom until our founding fathers observed settling in this land peoples of different and often antagonistic religious orientations. Our founders were intelligent, practical men who came to see an experiment with religious pluralism as virtually unavoidable; if the states were to be united, there must be national religious freedom.

But the history of church and state in America has often obscured the fact that American citizens share a common religion and that American public life has a religious dimension. This is what we mean by *civil religion* in America. Rousseau noted two hundred years ago that the decline of traditional religions would require the emergence of some new religion to replace them; in the name of progress, the nation or state would become the church. In one sense this is precisely what has happened, though hopefully we are far from the ultimate extension of this process. But sociologists of religion have qualified their judgment that religious institutions have fewer "edges," mute their voices in the interests of a rapidly increasing conformity, and make less of the differences between themselves and between them and secular institutions. John Edwin Smylie's thesis is that at the very time American denominations failed to function as the church, the nation began so to function more and more, so that gradually America the nation emerged as the primary agent of God's meaningful activity in history.[8]

What, then, is civil religion? To better understand it, we may state several things that civil religion is *not*:

Civil religion is not some new phenomenon. While the term itself had not enjoyed wide currency until recent years, nor the phenomenon been seriously studied, civil religion has been practiced without interruption since the early days of the Republic.

Civil religion is not peculiar to the United States. Most if not all modern nations have their own civil religion, and it may exist with or without some strong, compatible, traditional religion like Buddhism, Hinduism, or Islam. The same Christian symbols that American patriots have adapted have been used also by patriots in France, Scotland, and Great Britain.[9] In these countries the mixture is not so subtle; Protestant cathedrals such as Westminster Abbey are adorned with representations not so much of Christian saints as of national heroes, military and otherwise.

Civil religion is not merely a diluted version of Christianity believed and practiced in the United States. It is not the "common core" of religious beliefs in America. That Biblical religion has often been reduced to a common core we do not deny, but that is one definition we offered for *culture religion*.

Nor is civil religion the sum total of what American churches believe and teach about their nation. While Christianity—and, largely through Christianity, Judaism—is symbiotically related to civil religion, with each lending plausibility to the other, the two are not the same. Organized religion and civil religion are separate forces, fulfilling separate but often overlapping values.

Finally, there is no single version of American civil religion. It is not merely "the American way of life." In its most general form it is the convergence of several philosophies, ideologies, and perspectives; they are often contradictory, and one dominates for awhile, to be replaced by another. It incorporates both revered historical documents and widely institutionalized symbols as well as new perspectives and symbols that are becoming more widely institutionalized.

Viewed positively, civil religion is always a dynamic, not a static,

---

8. "National Ethos and the Church," *Theology Today* 20 (1963): 315, 316.

9. Carlton J. H. Hayes, *Essays on Nationalism* (New York: Russell and Russell, 1966), pp. 118-23, discusses this point.

force. It is our national understanding of our history, our contemporary situation, and our future as a nation. Civil religion is an organic structure of ideas, beliefs, values, and even myths concerning our nation that is common to the diverse peoples of America and is operative in their lives. The object of faith is America and her ideals, and, as we soon shall see, this religion selects from various sources the articles of its creed and its symbols. Perhaps it is not too much of an oversimplification to say that civil religion involves the social psychology of nationalism. Nationalism is a prototype of religion in many important respects. Civil religion falls into the area where the spheres of religion, politics, and culture overlap. Rather than judge the value of civil religion, we can safely say that no nation can avoid having a civil religion of some kind.

Some have objected to using the term *religion* to describe nationalism or national self-understanding. "That certain symbols, ceremonies, and patterns of behavior within contemporary American society (as within any society past or present) are widely experienced by individuals and groups as religious is a proposition which is incontrovertible," concluded John F. Wilson. "But it is equally the case that in the United States these phenomena are not accorded the kind of status appropriate to a religion."[10] Wilson submitted several criteria for the definition and location of historic religion, and he concluded that civil "religion" is too generalized, ambiguous, and unofficial to meet these standards.

Our purpose will not be served by using Wilson's or some other criteria for locating a religion. Our concern is to evaluate societal behavior in light of authentic Biblical religion. A person's religion is his relatonship with that which he esteems as central in the very nature of things, that which is both inescapable and indubitable. This relationship provides him with effective ways to cope with painful and otherwise unmanageable experiences by giving him a frame of reference in which to interpret them. This frame of reference enables him to discern reality and determine how ultimate, valuable, dear, and redeeming each experience is. Religion sustains and stabilizes both the individual and society.

Neither man nor society can survive for long without a religion or a faith of some kind that explains man's nature, good and evil,

---

10. "The Status of 'Civil Religion' in America," in Elwyn A. Smith, ed., *The Religion of the Republic* (Philadelphia: Fortress, 1971), p. 11.

and the meaning of life and death. The noted historian Arnold Toynbee has often argued that the history of civilization is the history of society's religion. In this context, religion may be any system of thought, doctrine, or philosophy that "ties things together," imparting a satisfactory meaning to the stark realities that all nations or societies must face. The church can and should provide such religion. But in a secularized society where formal religious commitment is weak, the activities of the state may do more than any other to interpret matters of life and death and of the quality of life and citizenship. For those who retain formal religious commitment, the national experience at least supplements it. Therefore we are justified in using the term *civil religion*. We must keep in mind that, unlike traditional religions, civil religion lacks two important elements—initiation rites (except the first voting experience) and eternal reward or retribution.

American civil religion is drawn from two major sources: the Bible and liberal humanism or liberal political philosophy. Our common historical experiences cause us to select and apply tenets of this civil faith which facilitate national self-understanding. Both sources have supplied the general principles which undergird American democracy, although liberal political philosophy likely influenced the authors of our Constitution more directly. The Bible did supply some of the basic premises about man and political society, but it supplied more of the types, metaphors, analogies, and symbols of the American civil religion. This is not to say that the metaphors, symbols, and other materials from the Bible have been employed properly or consistently, but that civil religion cannot be examined apart from the Scriptures. We can describe civil religion in America in more detail by describing its beliefs, institutions, and rituals.

Doctrine of the Civil Religion

To examine the beliefs of American civil religion, we must begin with the national scriptures. Perhaps each thoughtful citizen has a different canon, but all certainly include the Declaration of Independence, the Constitution, presidential inaugural addresses, and other epideictic or special-occasion addresses by American statesmen. A study of these sources will reveal the major themes of civil religion.

If one central theme or tenet emerges, it is that God has providentially anointed America as His "New Israel," giving America a special destiny in the modern world. Americans are a chosen people, a light to all nations, a city set upon the hill. Americans, both collectively and individually, have the awesome responsibility of carrying out God's will on earth. (We have already surveyed this theme of American mission as it has been developed in the history of our rhetoric.)

John F. Kennedy's inaugural address is an example of the verbalization of the civil religion, and it provides the most ominous clue as to how the civil religion may be differentiated from spiritual or culture religion.[11] Both in his introduction and peroration Kennedy related American tasks and principles to God. In his introduction he said:

> I have sworn before you and Almighty God the same solemn oath our forebears prescribed nearly a century and three quarters ago.
> The world is very different now. For man holds in his mortal hands the power to abolish all forms of human poverty and to abolish all forms of human life. And yet the same revolutionary beliefs for which our forebears fought are still at issue around the globe—the belief that the rights of man come not from the generosity of the state but from the hand of God.

In the conclusion Kennedy reflected a conviction that keeps recurring in American sacred ceremonies:

> Finally, whether you are citizens of America or of the world, ask of us the same high standards of strength and sacrifice that we shall ask of you. With a good conscience our only sure reward, with history the final judge of our deeds, let us go forth to lead the land we love, asking His blessing and His help, but knowing that here in earth God's work must truly be our own.

The references to God are, of course, nothing novel in American ceremonial oratory. References to God appear in all inaugural addresses except Washington's second; they usually appear in other presidential ceremonial speeches; and they occasionally appear in both campaign rhetoric and the president's messages to the Congress and the public on concrete issues. For example, when President Lyndon B. Johnson asked Congress and the American public for a strong Voting Rights Bill (March 15, 1965), he noted: "Above the pyramid on the great seal of the United States it says in Latin, 'God has favored our undertaking.' God will not favor everything that we do. It is rather our duty to define His will. I

---

11. The clues to examine Kennedy's address and later to cite Johnson's address came from Bellah, "Civil Religion in America."

cannot help but believe that He truly understands and that He really favors the undertaking that we begin here tonight." In the same speech Johnson had quoted the words of Jesus: "For with a country as with a person, 'What is a man profited if he shall gain the whole world and lose his own soul?'" When President Gerald Ford unexpectedly pardoned his self-exiled predecessor, he invoked the name of God and the Biblical concepts of mercy and forgiveness several times. To the cynic who counters that presidents invoke God merely ritualistically to win elections and gain public support for their policies, Bellah countered, "What people say on solemn occasions need not be taken at face value, but it is often indicative of deep-seated . . . commitments that are not made explicit in the course of everyday life."[12] To students of our civil religion, even sincerity is not a prerequisite for cultural significance.

To return to Kennedy's address, he did not refer to Jesus Christ, to the Roman Catholic church, to Abraham, Mary, or any other Biblical character, or to any specifically Catholic doctrine. Was JFK on this occasion relaxing his Christian commitment? Was his Roman Catholic heritage a source of public embarrassment? Quite to the contrary! Consider two factors. First, any statement of his allegiance to Christ as Lord or his respect for the Catholic faith would be, as Bellah suggested, not directly relevant to his conduct of high public office and thus inappropriate to the public, civil ceremony. The religious viewpoint he was propounding was not to be confused with his Catholicism. Second, and of less importance, Kennedy had already publicly subsumed his Roman Catholic faith to his civil faith in the areas of potential conflict.[13] He mentioned that he took his oath of office before both the people and Almighty

---

12. Ibid., p. 2.

13. As evidence for this point, I would cite JFK's address to the Houston Ministerial Alliance in his 1960 presidential campaign: "Whatever issue may come before me as President, if I should be elected—on birth control, divorce, censorship, gambling, or any other such subject—I will make my decision in accordance with these views, in accordance with what my conscience tells me to be in the national interest, and without regard to outside religious pressure or dictate. And no power or threat of punishment could cause me to decide otherwise." Text of prepared remarks in Theodore H. White, *The Making of the President, 1960* (New York: Pocket, 1961), pp. 468-72. Alfred E. Smith had the same problem in the late 1920s, and he too attempted to persuade American voters that his membership in the Roman Catholic church was not incompatible with his loyalty to the United States government. Smith noted he had taken a public oath for elective office nineteen timees and had served many years. "I have never known any conflict between my official duties and my religious belief. No such conflict could exist." *Atlantic Monthly* 139 (1927): 722.

God and that "the rights of man come not from the generosity of the state but from the hand of God." Both statements attribute ultimate sovereignty to God. Finally, in declaring "here on earth God's work must truly be our own," Kennedy perpetuated the theme that America's destiny is to carry out God's will on earth.

Another doctrine of American civil religion is that "America is good." This theme was articulated more as the nation came under increasing attack in the late sixties by the New Left and antiwar protesters. To the latter, the nation had reached "the end of American innocence." Nixon became a chief spokesman for the doctrine of the intrinsic goodness of America. "I know America," he asserted in his first inaugural. "I know the heart of America is good." Americans celebrate "the simple things, and the basic things—such as goodness, decency, love, and kindness." In his second inaugural, Nixon elaborated further on this theme. "Above all else, the time has come for us to renew our faith in ourselves and in America." He noted that "that faith has been challenged" and "our children have been taught to be ashamed of their country, ashamed of their parents, ashamed of America's record at home and its role in the world." Nixon saw in Americans such qualities as generosity, creativity, progress, love of peace and freedom. He noted that new challenges are upon us and that "we shall answer to God, to history, and to our conscience for the way in which we use these years." Thus he mentioned national accountability before God in passing, but he did not underscore it. Nixon, then, unlike Lincoln in his second inaugural, emphasized American goodness and saw little need of judgment. And while a theologian of colonial days like Jonathan Edwards or one of modern times like Robert Novak would insist that American innocence is an illusion and that no nation is inherently "good" (just as none is inherently "evil"), there can be no doubt that President Nixon confirmed what millions of Americans wanted to believe about their country.

Other beliefs or themes of the American civil religion have not been as tenacious and will not be explicated in as much detail. Over two centuries of American historical experience have been interpreted through Biblical motifs to give our civil religion a substance of narrative, imagery, and myth. For nearly fourscore and six years the celebrants of civil religion interpreted the American Revolution (and all of the Constitutional period) as the culmination of the exodus. God has delivered the colonies from Pharaoh and the corrupt old order (Britain) by his divinely appointed Moses

(Washington). The new continent was the Promised Land. The Declaration of Independence and the Constitution were sacred scriptures that explain the covenant God establishes with people everywhere who love freedom (indeed both documents have exerted wide influence in other lands). After the Revolution, the Civil War became the second event that required interpretation in the civil religion. God was subjecting His chosen people to a "time of testing," testing the strength and permanence of the Union; but He was also, according to many, judging a wayward people. The Civil War elicited the new themes of death, sacrifice, and rebirth, symbolized in the life and death of Abraham Lincoln. His Gettysburg and second inagùral addresses have been added to the sacred scriptures and are considered some of the noblest expressions in American literature. Not a few historians and observers have seen Lincoln as a Christ figure—one who unselfishly dedicated himself to a united nation and whose tragic and untimely death summed up the sacrifices that redeemed the nation.

Other personalities, events, and documents in American history have been endowed with special meaning and incorporated into the civil religion. Periods of adversity such as the Great Depression and wars easily supply the moral lessons and symbolic material. In the third quarter of the twentieth century, two developments converged (very nearly overlapping chronologically) to challenge the integrity, reputation and validity of our democratic institutions —American involvement in Vietnam and Watergate. At issue in the former were the credibility and practical wisdom of our national leaders, the public's commitment to freedom of speech and the right of dissent, and, more important, the effectiveness of American democracy and the validity of applying the concept of American mission to our foreign policy in the Third World. Watergate was a crisis of confidence. And while the wounds of neither Vietnam nor Watergate have healed completely, our nation has endured this time of testing and matured. These experiences have produced few if any additions to the national scriptures, but some important lessons certainly will be incorporated into the doctrine of our civil religion.

Institutions of the Civil Religion

If doctrines are to be promulgated, it is axiomatic that they must be intimately connected with institutions that embody, clarify, interpret, and reinforce them to individuals and groups. The process by which both children and adults learn about our nation and others nations, our political institutions and processes, and by which they develop attitudes and effective responses to this information, is part of what political scientists call *political socialization.* This is to recognize that civil religion has institutional expression. What are the social structures that originate, preserve, transmit, and revise the system of beliefs of American civil religion?

The first institution that touches all of us is the home. Parents transmit to their children attitudes they consider valuable. While it is difficult to establish precisely the extent of family influence (since the attitudes it imparts are similar or identical to those imparted by other institutions), there is no doubt that the home's influence in forming attitudes conducive to good citizenship is great. Among the attitudes children acquire at home and perhaps take for granted are loyalty, respect for the symbols of government (especially the flag, Uncle Sam, the Statue of Liberty), and respect for the law and obedience to rightful authority. The family also gives children examples to emulate; parents teach at least indirectly whether voting, membership in a political party, and other forms of political activity are important.[14]

The American civil religion has also found immeasurable support from churches. The Americanization of the churches and the support they offer the American way of life has been well documented by sociologists of religious behavior. Not always has this support been indirect and subtle. Sidney E. Mead told of a young German who came to America several years ago to study our religion; after attending a number of varied worship services, he reported that the only symbol common to all of them was the American flag. American history has for many preachers been a chief source of homiletic materials, second only to the Bible. A common pulpit theme has been that America is great and good and that national sins threaten these qualities.[15] Public worship is where many youth

14. The process of political socialization in children is interesting. See Fred I. Greenstein, *Children and Politics* (New Haven: Yale University, 1965); and David Easton and Jack Dennis, *Children in the Political System* (Boston: McGraw-Hill, 1969).

15. A typical sermon might be George W. Bailey's "Will God Always Bless America?" delivered at the Abilene Christian College Bible Lectures in 1963. Bailey paralleled the United States with ancient Israel and noted that America may be "casting off the thing which is good." Bailey cited juvenile delinquency, crime in general, sexual explicitness in the media, welfare chiseling, and modernism in the churches as signs that America is declining. He hinted at racism but did not discuss it in any detail.

learn about the faith and wisdom of our founding fathers, the courage of George Washington at Valley Forge, the humility, early defeats, and patient leadership of Abraham Lincoln, and the infectious optimism of Franklin Roosevelt. Liberal ministers build entire sermons around the theme of some political figure, such as the sermons on Lincoln on the Sunday nearest Lincoln Day. Conservative and fundamentalist ministers have preached many times against "godless communism" and in defense of American heritage and liberties. All of these are obvious signs that the national faith has found a home with the Biblical faith, but one must be most cautious in defending or attacking this fact because the relationship between the two has been complex.

The place where Americans are more frequently and for greater lengths of time confronted with civil faith is in the public schools. Their role in inculcating and reinforcing the traditions of national faith is incalculable. While the First Amendment rendered a state church illegal, our public school system, it has been argued,[16] performs the role established churches have played in the Old World. The school, with its compulsory attendance, provided a setting where instruction could be offered in the "sacred history" of the national faith. To be sure, until the Supreme Court decisions on prayer and Bible reading in the early 1960s, the public schools were unabashedly Protestant in their morning prayers, devotions, and broad religious orientation. The high court did not intend to terminate instruction in the events and documents of American civil religion, but to disentangle it from the beliefs and practices of any single American church. One could still teach the national faith in the public schools but without the explicitly Judeo-Christian underpinnings. We might add that the parochial schools also have inculcated the values central to American civil religion and perhaps with even greater success since they are free to mix civil with religious faith.

The schools teach civil religion both directly and indirectly. They reinforce what the child has learned at home, and they do this in a number of ways—displaying the flag, reciting the Pledge of Allegiance, singing patriotic songs. Pictures of Abraham, Moses, Jesus, or the apostle Paul are considered wholly inappropriate for the corridors and classrooms of America's public schools, but portraits of Washington, Lincoln, and, more recently, of John F. Kennedy

16. Sidney E. Mead, *The Lively Experiment: The Shaping of Christianity in America* (New York: Harper and Row, 1963), pp. 66-71.

and Martin Luther King, Jr., abound, and it is after them that schools are named. Pictures of historic monuments and of sites of national interest are often displayed. In the early grades teachers tell numerous stories about national heroes to impress their pupils with the importance of a proper attitude toward one's country. A story that once enjoyed wide currency was *Man Without a Country*, written by a Unitarian pastor, Edward Everett Hale. It told about Philip Nolan ruining his life by trying to find meaning and personal identity apart from his nation. As the pupil advances, he is exposed more directly to the tenets of national religion in required civics classes.

What is the impact upon the child of the narratives, pictures, and patriotic rituals? A typical first-grader does not understand many of the phrases in "The Star-Spangled Banner" or the Pledge of Allegiance (nor for that matter do all adults!). Is it not significant that there is quantitative evidence that many elementary schoolchildren associate the president with God, and the Pledge of Allegiance with a prayer to God?[17] Whatever the young pupil sees as the purpose of these daily routines, he knows that adults value them highly and he seldom questions them; since the ritualistic behavior is done in groups rather than alone, it elicits and reinforces feelings of loyalty and patriotism. Perhaps the difficulty that many Americans have in disentangling God and country has inadvertently begun during the inculcation of civil religion in the public school system.[18]

One more institution of American civil religion deserves men-

---

17. From a study by Robert D. Hess and Judith V. Torney in William M. Crotty, ed., *Public Opinion and Politics* (New York: Holt, Rinehart, and Winston, 1970), p. 52. Hess and Torney authored *The Development of Political Attitudes in Children* (Chicago: Aldine, 1967). See also David Easton and Jack Dennis, "The Child's Image of Government," *The Annals of the American Academy of Political and Social Science* 361 (1965): 40-57.

18. Easton and Hess wrote that "not only do many children associate the sanctity and awe of religion with the political community, but to ages 9 or 10 they sometimes have trouble disentangling God and country. . . . The fact that as a child grows older he may be able to sort out the religious from the political setting much more clearly and restrict the pledge to a political meaning, need not thereby weaken this bond. The initial and early intermingling of potent religious sentiment with political community has by that time probably created a tie difficult to dissolve." Quoted in Lewis Lipsitz, "If, as Verba Says, the State Functions as a Religion, What Are We to Do Then to Save Our Souls?" *American Political Science Review* 62, no. 2 (1968): 529. See also Greenstein, "Popular Images of the President," *American Journal of Psychiatry* 122 (1965): 523-29.

tion. In the past half century the mass media, and especially the electronic media, have played a strategic role in promulgating, preserving, and indirectly formulating our national self-consciousness. Certainly this is not the chief function of our communications media (that, obviously, is entertainment), and any attempt to measure its influence must take into account that it is both subtle and indirect. One can always cite examples of radio and television directly promoting the civil faith. In 1974 and in connection with the bicentennial celebration, a series of short specials on events in colonial America began to appear. Television has aired a number of programs on important historic events since the medium was introduced, but finding sponsors always has been difficult, and a cursory look at a TV schedule will indicate that such programs are a rare exception, not the rule. The communications media promote the civil religion far more, by allowing Americans to celebrate together the events and rituals that unify us. To that subject we turn next.

Rituals and Ceremonies

When we think of rituals and ceremonies that relate to life and death, heroes and martyrs, past and future, the first images we conjure up may be the loose liturgy of superstitious, primitive peoples of the ancient past whose world did not extend much beyond their local tribe. Or we may think of the spontaneous dancing and crude, rhythmic music of wildly decorated natives of darkest Africa who must suddenly grapple again with death, disease, or drought in these primitive rites, so misunderstood and unappreciated by the Western world. Such imagery may cloud the simple reality that all people identify with some kind of community and that the life and spirit of that community must continually be nourished and revitalized by some type of ritual. The ceremonies of American civil religion are well entrenched in American tradition, and however much more civilized and orderly our society is than that of primeval and untutored peoples, our rites are not different in kind from theirs and serve some of the same functions. They are among the most interesting and fascinating elements of civil religion, and in large part they constitute the actual practice of that religion. We will examine three overlapping yet central functions of these rituals.

The first is to pay homage to and keep alive the memory of

our national heroes. This is done a number of ways. Our calendars remind us of the birthdays of Washington and Lincoln, and the media do not allow the birthdays of Kennedy and King to pass without notice. Boulevards, airports, schools, universities, and other public institutions are named in their honor. The most popular names for cities and towns are Madison, Franklin, and Columbus. Perhaps in no other nation do the founding fathers command as much reverence and respect as in the United States; someone has quipped that we have a founding-father complex. Their essays, letters, and other papers are poured over as though they are infallible commentaries on the Constitution. Politicians and reformers of every political persuasion—conservative, liberal, moderate, and even radical, at either end of the spectrum—attempt to "get right" with the founding fathers and other national heroes by showing how their proposals are consonant with the fathers' goals and dreams.

The hero with whom our politicians most like to identify is Lincoln. No American has had as many words spoken or written about him as has Lincoln. Historian David Donald wrote a delightful book entitled *Lincoln Reconsidered,* and in his opening chapter, "Getting Right with Lincoln," he discussed the Lincoln cult in America. For decades after his death, Republican aspirants for high office sought—and presumably secured—Lincoln's blessing. During the campaign of 1868 Edwin Stanton, speaking in Pennsylvania on behalf of U. S. Grant, read the Gettysburg Address and then declared tearfully, "That is the voice of God speaking through the lips of Abraham Lincoln. . . . You hear the voice of Father Abraham here tonight. Did he die in vain?" According to Republican campaign literature the party's candidates, including even William McKinley, William Howard Taft, and Calvin Coolidge, bore a marked physical and moral resemblance to Lincoln. By the time of the New Deal, even Democrats were making the pilgrimage to Springfield to identify themselves with the Great Emancipator, despite cries of sacrilege by Republicans.[19] When Nixon appeared on network television for his first major defense in the Watergate episode, he was flanked by a picture of his family on one side and a bust of Lincoln on the other. This was enough of a cue for his staunch supporters, through posters, placards, and literature, to

---

19. *Lincoln Reconsidered: Essays on the Civil War Era* (New York: Vintage, 1956), pp. 3-18.

identify the two men as the most castigated and railed-against leaders in our Republic's history.[20]

Pilgrimages to the sacred cities also are a part of the religion of nationalism. A foreign visitor who would locate the places and buildings that are most dear and sacred to the vast majority of Americans would not be led to many church buildings or cathedrals but to Independence Hall in Philadelphia, possibly Faneuil Hall in Boston, the Grant tomb in New York, and, most important, to Washington, D.C. Whether in an emotionally charged march or demonstration, or in the ranks of compulsively curious school-children who are kept in line by frustrated and exhausted teachers, or in the throngs from the undiscriminating and indifferent middle classes, Americans make the pilgrimage to "Mecca" on behalf of the American civil faith. The most dominant feature of the city's "imperial architecture" is the outsize phallus memorializing the "father of his country." The Lincoln and Jefferson memorials are like classic temples raised in honor of two great charismatic lead-ers, one of the eighteenth century and one of the nineteenth. Ken-nedy is commemorated by the eternal flame and simple burial plot in Arlington Cemetery and by the Center of Performing Arts on the Potomac that bears his name.[21] Much like Congresswoman Barbara Jordan of Texas during the House Judiciary Committee's hearings on impeachment, throngs of people climb the long stairs to the National Archives to read the original manuscripts of the national scriptures—the Constitution and the Declaration of In-dependence—to gain special inspiration.[22] And multitudes visit the

---

20. For a comment on Nixon's use of the Lincoln image, see Hugh Sidey, "Try-ing to Get Right with Lincoln," *Time*, 25 February 1974, p. 14. Sidey contended that Harry Truman, not Nixon, has been the most maligned president since Lincoln.

21. John F. Wilson was irreverent enough to suggest that the American civil religion has a trinity, Washington and Lincoln being the first and second persons of the godhead. "It may not be entirely accidental that the Kennedy memorial evokes the imagery usually associated with the Holy Spirit; cer-tainly the eternal flame and the open burial plot permit this construction." "The Status of 'Civil Religion' in America," p. 4.

22. Like the American flag, the Declaration of Independence is raised each morning and lowered every evening. Settled since 1951 in a helium-filled, glass-and-bronze case designed to protect it from destructive oxygen, the old parch-ment scroll spends its daytime hours on display in a special "shrine," protected by armed guards at the National Archives in the nation's capital. At night, along with the Bill of Rights and the Constitution, the Declaration is electrically lowered into a fifty-ton vault that is fireproof and bombproof.

White House, Capitol, and Supreme Court building to see where the work of these heroes and martyrs is continued.

Heroes of America's past are not commemorated only in the capital but throughout the land. Thousands of regional and local heroes are honored by statues in the middle of town squares. The homes of many of our more recent presidents, such as FDR's in Hyde Park, New York, and Eisenhower's in Abilene, Kansas, are visited each summer by thousands of citizens. And when President Nixon's resignation seemed imminent, the VA took off the market an abandoned house on Union Street in Grand Rapids that would not sell even for $5,000, anticipating the time when Americans would want to tour the boyhood home of Gerald R. Ford. Merchants of pictures, paintings, statuettes, and relics owe their financial success to the practice of Americanism. In his study of "Nationalism as a Religion," Carlton J. H. Hayes caught this irony:

> Moderns, especially Americans, are inclined to regard the medieval veneration of images, icons, and relics as savouring of "superstition," but let them replace a statue of St. George by a graven image of General George Washington, an icon of the Blessed Virgin Mary by a lithograph of the brave Molly Pitcher, and a relic of the Holy Cross by a tattered battle-flag, and they display a reverence which they deem beautiful and ennobling. If one calls to mind the images of national heroes with which every town is plentifully supplied and the icons of national fathers which adorn both the sumptuous clubs of the rich and the simple cottages of the poor, one can appreciate the basic religious appeal of modern nationalism.[23]

A second function of the rituals and ceremonies of civil religion is to enable citizens to cope with death and tragedy by infusing them with meaning. W. Lloyd Warner creatively analyzed how certain of our rituals and ceremonies give religious sanction to American society as an entity. Memorial Day, which grew out of the Civil War, is "both sacred and secular, it is a holy day as well as a holiday and is accordingly celebrated."[24] It is a modern cult of the dead, a sacred day when the war dead are mourned, the ancient theme of redemptive sacrifice is expounded, and Protestants, Jews, and Catholics unite in renewing American freedom and ideals. Warner argued that churches provide members with a personal, individual faith that helps each one cope with calamity, but that

---

23. *Essays on Nationalism,* p. 109.

24. *American Life: Dream and Reality* (Chicago: University of Chicago, 1953), p. 1.

they do not provide a set of social beliefs and rituals that enable him to unite with all his fellows of *other* spiritual faiths in confronting the common enemy of death. "The Memorial Day rite and other subsidiary rituals connected with it form a cult which partially satisfies this need for common action on a common problem," he stated. "It dramatically expresses the sentiments of unity of all the living among themselves, of all the living to all the dead, and of all the living and dead as a group to the gods."[25]

Memorial Day is only a holiday for early summer swimming, picnicking, and auto racing, some might argue. But in towns and small cities across the land and by relatives of those who have died in foreign wars, it is taken seriously. To such folk the lowered flag leads to lingering reflection. The special sermons and speeches for that sacred day develop the theme of America fulfilling its God-given destiny. American fighting men have offered themselves on the altar of history for the sake of America's sacred mission to liberate oppressed peoples, to be the beacon of liberty for all the globe, and to safeguard the precious rights and liberties forwarded in the Declaration of Independence and the Constitution.

Special holidays are not the only way in which Americans as citizens cope with death. The public funerals for America's great citizens, especially political leaders and reformers, impart meaning to life and death that transcends sectarian religious differences. Most Americans can recall the tragic deaths of John and Robert Kennedy and Martin Luther King, Jr.—a president, a senator, and a civil rights leader. The electronic media enabled millions of Americans—Protestant and Catholic, black and white, rich and poor, young and old—to participate vicariously in the death rituals for each of these men. The funeral services themselves constituted only a minimal part, in terms of time at least, of these rituals. Images of a riderless black horse marching through the crowded but hushed avenues of Washington, a mule-drawn wagon creaking along a crowded Atlanta avenue bearing a plain casket, and a funeral train slowly winding its way through silent onlookers crowding the tracks from New York to the nation's capital come readily to mind.

These public funerals were, to be sure, *religious* in the sense that most of us use that term. Hymns or sacred music were played and sung, the Bible was read, and a pastor or priest eulogized the dead

---

25. Ibid., p. 24.

to comfort the family. The funerals for the Kennedys were characteristically Roman Catholic, and King's funeral had the spontaneity and style of a service that was both black and southern Baptist. But at the same time the funerals were civil-religious ceremonies with meaning and significance for all Americans regardless of their denominational affiliations. All could find great consolation in the fact that these leaders had met their tragic, untimely deaths in the midst of valiant efforts to secure rights and freedom for all citizens. They had done their part to fulfill America's destiny and further its dream. Their most lofty statements (e.g., "And so my fellow citizens, ask not what your country shall do for you" or "I have a dream . . .") are being added to the canon of national scriptures. Although these men could have chosen a less arduous life style, they were driven by American idealism. The proper response to their tragic deaths, the ceremonies imply, is for all of us to capture their vision of America's destiny and complete their unfinished tasks.[26] Thus, in both Memorial Day ceremonies and last rites for great leaders is the same symbolic and thematic structure—the living are united with one another, the living are united with the honored dead, and all are united with God and His grand purposes in history. And despite their obvious sectarian overtones, these ceremonies are conducted in such a way that they unite Americans of all religious persuasions.

Social psychologists and psychiatrists have located a degree of ceremonial and ritualistic behavior in other acts by public officialdom. Here is one example. In the early days of August 1974, Americans were faced with the prospect of removing a president, whether by impeaching him or forcing him to resign. When one survives some atrocity or life-threatening experience, he can either attempt to erase it from his consciousness or undergo a genuine ritual of mourning followed by renewal of spirit. A nation has the same choice. It is more difficult but also more responsible to confront the symbolic death image or tragedy, acknowledge involvement in it, and seek some sort of illumination or perspective on it. Since,

---

26. These three are not the only canonized martyrs. Conrad Cherry wrote: "American history is, in fact, replete with leaders who have been canonized in the national consciousness as exemplars of American ideals and as particular bearers of America's destiny under God. When those leaders have met their deaths they have become, in the national memory as well as in the ceremonies and speeches that surround their deaths, martyrs for the American cause, even in some cases redeemers." *God's New Israel: Religious Interpretations of American Destiny* (Englewood Cliffs, N.J.: Prentice-Hall, 1971), p. 6.

it may be argued, there is some "Watergate" in all of us, President Nixon's resignation and departure from the national scene are part of a national cleansing ritual—a ritual of atonement—that greatly strengthens the resolve of all citizens to live and act more carefully within the boundaries of the law.[27] Newspapers and television enabled all willing citizens (the audience for prime-time summer TV more than doubled on the resignation evening) to participate in this ritual. Outlines for newsclips, old films, career highlights, and interviews were drafted weeks earlier in anticipation of a Nixon departure. Large headlines were prepared for the morning dailies. The ritual of atonement communicated the atmosphere of a national tragedy. News commentators spoke in hushed tones. No one was unmoved; even CBS correspondent Dan Rather, a long-time thorn in the president's flesh, was misty-eyed when he said that the oration was Nixon's "finest hour" and that Nixon gave the occasion a "touch of majesty." The events of that week were covered almost continuously until Air Force One touched down in southern California and Nixon emerged as an ordinary citizen.[28]

In passing we note that Americans have plenty of rituals and ceremonies to celebrate the glorious and uplifting, whether victory in the world arena or a moon landing[29] or the return of POWs. One need only tune in a political convention or attend a political rally to hear partisans strain credulity in claiming responsibility for the good times. The meaning of God's blessing and guidance has traditionally been taught on a special day—Thanksgiving—but that lesson seems to have been submerged in modern times in family fellowship and a laden dinner table.

The third function of the rituals and ceremonies of American civil religion is to quicken and sustain corporate faith in the

---

27. This idea was suggested by Robert Jay Lifton, *Time*, 19 August 1974, pp. 65, 66. Smylie once suggested that during the days Congress was investigating alleged subversive activity, the occasional television spectacle of witness after witness spelling out national sins before a committee and the nation at large (confession under oath) allowed a national catharsis.

28. Journalistic accounts of how the media covered this event are presented in *Time*, 19 August 1974, pp. 73, 74; and *Newsweek*, 19 August 1974, pp. 77, 78.

29. Roger Shinn noted that the moon landing was a ritual celebrating the movement from mystery to mastery. "Apollo was a search for transcendence. The President rightly called it a 'moment of transcendent drama.' Man, frustrated by defeats in his hunger for domestic tranquility and international peace, now could celebrate a liberating achievement." Shinn stated that Neil Armstrong's first words on the moon have a liturgical ring. "Apollo as Ritual," *Christianity and Crisis*, 14 August 1969, p. 223.

national ideals and American way of life. Admittedly, this function overlaps the other two. Paying respect to national heroes and coping with death as a community does much to keep this faith alive. But a number of rituals fulfill this final function exclusively.

One of these, already alluded to, is the pageantry of the presidential inauguration, held ordinarily only every fourth year. On this momentous occasion the new president traditionally informs the nation in general terms of his political philosophy and then invokes the blessing of God. This ceremony, among other things, reaffirms the religious legitimacy of the highest political office. All presidents from George Washington to Gerald Ford have referred to the sovereignty of the Supreme Being, although none used the word *God* until James Monroe did in 1821 in his second inaugural. In his first inaugural Washington referred to God as the "Almighty Being who rules over the universe, who presides in the councils of nations, and whose providential aids can supply every human defect," the "Great Author of every public and private good," the "Invisible Hand," and the "benign Parent of the Human Race." In his brief inaugural address Ford declared: "Our Constitution works; our great Republic is a Government of laws and not of men. Here the people rule. But there is a higher power, by whatever name we honor Him, who ordains not only righteousness but love, not only justice but mercy." The new president asked that "the golden rule" be applied and "brotherly love" be shown, and after requesting prayers for himself and for Richard Nixon and his family, Ford concluded: "God helping me, I will not let you down." After taking the oath of office the first time, Eisenhower asked, "Would you permit me the privilege of uttering a little private prayer of my own?" and requested those in the audience to bow their heads. The ceremonial music performed and prayers offered during inaugurations also serve this legitimizing function.[30]

The ritual of the American flag is one of the most unique. It is

---

30. Excerpts from inaugural addresses that refer to God are published in Benjamin Weiss, *God in American History: A Documentation of America's Religious Heritage* (Grand Rapids: Zondervan, 1966). At Nixon's first inauguration Billy Graham prayed: "Thou hast said, 'Promotion comes not from the east nor from the west, but from thee.' We acknowledge thy divine help in the selection of our leadership each four years. We acknowledge, our Lord, that in thy sovereignty thou hast permitted Richard Nixon to lead us at this momentous hour of history." The full text of this prayer is in *Christianity Today*, 14 February 1969, p. 27.

the national faith's most important, most loved, and most easily identified symbol. All modern nations use flags, displaying them in all kinds of public gathering places. But the ritual of the flag—the almost rabbinic rules for raising, lowering, saluting, dipping, and hoisting Old Glory—are peculiar to America. On all solemn occasions and ceremonies of civil religion, the flag is prominently displayed. To refuse to remove one's hat or cap when the flag is hoisted before a ball game or when it passes in parade is an act of sacrilege.

Proper respect for the flag has been one of the most litigated subjects in American judicial history. In 1940 the Supreme Court upheld the right of school districts to require all students, even Jehovah's Witnesses, to salute the flag. Justice Frankfurter explained the important role of the flag in our society: "We live by symbols. The flag is the symbol of our national unity, transcending all internal differences, however large, within the framework of the Constitution." He rejected the plea that children of Jehovah's Witnesses should be excused from "conduct required of all other children in the promotion of national cohesion," adding that "we are dealing with an interest inferior to none in the hierarchy of legal values. National unity is the basis of national security."[31] Retrospectively, this near-unanimous (eight to one) decision was one of the high court's greatest miscarriages of justice, and in a similar case three years later,[32] the court overruled the earlier verdict. But all court decisions related to the place and use of the flag have acknowledged its value as a symbol of the national faith and ideas. Desecration cannot be given legal sanction.

Often associated with the flag are the ritual of the Pledge of Allegiance and patriotic hymns, especially the national anthem. Pledges, confessions, and sacred music have always been a part of man's religious behavior, but Americans seem to have a fetish for signing loyalty oaths and condensing political philosophy into brief, recitable mottoes and statements. "Perhaps never before in history has a people talked so much and said so little about its basic

---

31. Minersville School District v. Gobitis, 310 U.S. 568 (1940). Frankfurter quoted an earlier court decision (Halter v. Nebraska) in explaining what the flag stands for: "The flag is the symbol of the Nation's power, the emblem of freedom in its truest, best sense. . . . it signifies government resting on the consent of the governed; liberty regulated by law; the protection of the weak against the strong; security against the exercise of arbitrary power; and absolute safety for free institutions against foreign aggression."

32. West Virginia State Board of Education v. Barnette, 319 U.S. 624 (1943).

beliefs," commented noted historian Daniel J. Boorstin. "Perhaps never before has a people been fuller of pledges and creeds and oaths, of high-sounding speeches and worthy maxims and mottoes. Nor have these ever before been so widely diffused—on the mast-heads of newspapers, on the walls of grocery stores and filling sta-tions and insurance offices, over the apple pie of the Rotary Club; . . . from countless, endless voices in the halls of Congress; and now from countless voices on television."[33] Our courts have also had to rule on the use of loyalty oaths,[34] but more significant than the content of the oaths is the widely held assumption that the essence of patriotic doctrine can be contained in an oath and that reciting or signing it enhances national unity and intensifies per-sonal commitment to American ideals.

The Pledge of Allegiance and the national anthem are the best-known and most frequently recited group rites. The words are learned early in life—usually in kindergarten or the first grade—and repeated in unison at appropriate times. As with liturgies, a citizen may never understand or even think about the words he is uttering; even worse, he may consciously fail to live up to the ideals and values they verbalize. But he adamantly opposed any tampering with these rites. Music critics are unanimous that the national anthem is poorly composed, but it must not be revised. Men feel secure with unchanging traditions, and sacred music of the civil religion is above textual and musical criticism. In October 1968 at Detroit's Tiger Stadium, prior to the start of a World Series game, José Feliciano sang the old anthem to an entirely new score. The general response was negative; while some people liked it, most felt the blind singer had taken too much liberty with Ameri-can tradition. Ironically, most agreed they had listened to the words of the anthem for the first time in years.

One change in the Pledge of Allegiance was gladly welcomed. The pledge was written in 1892 for a Columbus Day ceremony by an ex-Baptist minister, Francis Bellamy, and was adopted by Congress in December 1945. In June 1954 President Eisenhower signed into law a bill adding the words "under God" to the phrase "one nation." That law was one of the most popular of the Eighty-third Congress; no congressman dared oppose it, and the only floor argument was over who would earn the credit for its passage. The

33. *The Genius of American Politics,* p. 150.

34. See the court cases and readings in Lockhart, Kamisar, and Choper, *The American Constitution,* pp. 563-637.

president argued that the two words strengthened America's spiritual resources in times of trial and affirmed her heritage as well as her future.[35] On July 11, 1955, Congress passed a bill requiring that "In God We Trust" be inscribed on all currency. And then, on July 3, 1956, President Eisenhower signed a bill that made the phrase "In God we trust" the national motto of the United States. Cynics might dismiss all of this as political reflex to the "surge of piety" in the 1950s. But, as we have noted, religion is always a source of societal stability. These bills were part of the cold-war atmosphere. There was a battle for the minds of men. If freedom of religion and the right to worship distinguished Western democracies from Soviet communism, Americans needed to be reminded of that distinction. And in light of this conflict, surely the differences between Protestantism and Roman Catholicism were not so significant; hence, both House and Senate, Republican and Democrat, Protestant and Catholic could together claim credit for this legislation.[36]

Slightly changing the Pledge of Allegiance and adopting an official motto added no new doctrine or ideal to the American national faith, nor did reciting the motto or seeing it on currency, we are skeptical enough to suggest, have much psychological impact. All congressmen conceded that nothing new was being added. What had been an implication of the national faith was made explicit: this nation has a special destiny and responsibility under the providence of the Almighty God. And this is the concept preserved and reinforced by all the rituals and ceremonies of American civil religion.

Our survey of civil religion in America has attempted to divide it into its various components and to examine them separately. Whenever possible we have avoided making value judgments, but our study is incomplete until we evaluate our national self-consciousness in the context of Biblical teachings about man and his world. To that consideration we turn next.

---

35. *New York Times,* 15 June 1954.

36. See Gerald Kaye and Ferenc M. Szasz, "Adding 'Under God' to the Pledge of Allegiance," *Encounter* 34 (1973): 52-56.

Before any man can be considered a member of civil society, he must be considered as a subject of the governor of the universe; and if a member of civil society, who enters into any subordinate association must always do it with a reservation of his duty to the general authority, much more must every man who becomes a member of any particular civil society do it with the saving his allegiance to the universal sovereign. We maintain, therefore, that in matters of religion no man's right is abridged by the institution of civil society.

James Madison (1784)

There is no better measure of a country's belief in its own professed values than the ease or difficulty with which it betrays them. America is having an exceedingly difficult time in repudiating the ideals of Jefferson, Lincoln, and Wilson in favor of the new militarism which our leaders have said is our destiny and responsibility. This shows the authenticity of our attachment to democracy, but it does not guarantee democracy's survival.

J. William Fulbright

Where there is no vision, the people perish. . . .
Solomon (Prov. 29:18 KJV)

chapter nine

One Nation Under God:
A Value and a Danger

Most Americans are not comfortable with the idea of a civil religion. There is a certain reluctance and insecurity about crossing what are supposed to be the boundaries of religion and politics. These feelings are largely unfounded because the Supreme Court has been a tenacious watchdog, keeping the separate provinces from unduly encroaching upon each other. Still, to many people the term *civil religion* has a negative connotation. Some have argued that civil religion in any form is idolatrous. In an article entitled "Patriotism—or Civil Religion," Anne Tansey contended that misplaced "patriotism" grows into civil religion and can cause great losses in church membership. "Parents are unaware of the danger of civil religion, and the young people are blaming the churches for the mistakes of government. Religion has become the victim."[1] But are civil religion and Biblical religion totally irreconcilable? And can a nation avoid, if it chooses, having a civil religion of some kind?

Before we evaluate the place of civil religion in our national life, we offer two propositions. First, a civil religion of some kind inevitably will be formulated and practiced by all societies. Civil

---

1. *Marriage and Family Living* 56 (1974): 3-6. Tansey's statement relates to the silence of the churches in the early years of the Vietnam conflict.

religion, as we have defined it, is not something that can be avoided. A society is above all else a faith, a spiritual entity, a set of shared convictions. All decent societies must have a common religion. If they do not, unchecked individualism may lead to anarchy. In fact the absence of a civil religion may be taken as a "faith" of some kind. So the question for America is not whether we as a people shall possess a national faith, but what kind of faith we will share? And obviously the First Amendment to our Constitution guarantees that our civil faith cannot be the express doctrine and practices of any one denomination.

Second, there is no single version or interpretation of the American civil religion. The various challenges that have confronted the American people—colonizing a new land, forging a new nation, expanding westward, fighting civil and foreign wars, and grappling with domestic unrest—have evoked different versions, or at least different emphases, of the national faith, each attempting to put these challenges in perspective and to make them manageable. Persuasive voices can keep two conflicting versions alive during the same time period. Each president and other high public officials have had their own versions of the civil religion and the place that God occupies in it. We may say that in the 1972 presidential campaign Richard Nixon and George McGovern articulated conflicting versions of the national faith. Not always will a public official or candidate make his interpretation of the national faith explicit, but it is always there in the background, undergirding and coloring his words and policies. Michael Novak has delineated five different Protestant civil religions operative in the United States: the classic, mainline Protestantism of New England (the "high-church" tradition); the populist tradition of the lower classes, especially in the Bible Belt; the denominational, commerce-instructed moralism of middle-class churches in the heartland; the Awakening type of reform churches (e.g., Quaker); and black Protestantism. But rather than offering separate civil religions, each group has a unique interpretation of the singular, commonly shared faith. As Novak pointed out, each has its own favorite metaphors, stereotypes, methods of proceeding, thought pattern and even fears; each has its own aspirations and dream-like images of fulfillment.[2]

If civil religion is inevitable for a people aspiring to be unified into a great nation, it is important that that faith be as rich, mean-

---

2. *Choosing Our King: Powerful Symbols in Presidential Politics* (New York: Macmillan, 1974), pp. 131-36.

ingful, vital, and Biblical as possible. We must zealously guard against a national forgetfulness of the nobler tenets of this faith and the exploitation of it for narrow or mean purposes. We shall see that the American civil religion possesses one great value but also poses an omnipresent danger to our system.

The Value

Americans are the most numbered, the most labeled people in the world. Our young men have Selective Service numbers. Most people over the age of fifteen have operators' license numbers. We have student or worker identification numbers, bank card numbers, numerous credit card numbers, various insurance policy numbers, a telephone number, and a zip code. Our automobiles have an engine number, a license-tag number, and, as often as not, a county or city sticker number and a parking permit number. We are also the most ethnically and culturally diverse nation; barely one-third of the nation today is of Anglo-Saxon stock. We are a nation of hyphenated Americans: Polish-Americans, Chinese-Americans, Irish-Americans, Afro-Americans, Mexican-Americans, and Italian-Americans, to name a few. Perhaps no nation has as many reference groups with which one associates on a voluntary basis; we are Roman Catholics, Jews, Rotarians, Republicans, Elks, Baptists, Protestants, Democrats, independents, Shriners, unionists, Methodists, vegetarians, Civitans, Masons, and so on, *ad infinitum*.

The many labels that Americans wear and groups with which they associate are all subsumed not under the label of some denomination but under the label "American." This is the great value of the American civil religion: it promotes a keen sense of corporate identity. No nation on earth owes its sense of community more explicitly to fidelity to an idea. Our country was born "dedicated to a proposition." Historically, the viability of American society has depended upon the dedication of public officials and the general citizenry to the realization of certain "self-evident" moral propositions. "What holds the United States together is not, as it is with other nations, geographic proximity, ethnic loyalty, dynastic loyalty, religious conformity," declared Hans J. Morgenthau, noted professor of political science, "but the common purpose, however inadequately conceived and ineffectively put into practice, of living up to certain moral propositions, which can be defined as equality in freedom. Put into question the viability of this purpose and you have put in jeopardy the very existence of

America as a distinct social and political entity."[3] Our society must continue to discuss seriously its common core of ideas and values. The problem during great political and social dissension is not that our national values fail us but that we fail them. We do not need new values and moral propositions as much as we need renewed commitment to old ones.

The great Americans who are venerated in the national self-consciousness—the Jeffersons, the Lincolns, the Woodrow Wilsons, the Franklin Roosevelts—were great not simply because they achieved some political victory during times of national crisis and testing, but because their words and actions in some way strengthened these moral propositions both at home and abroad. The occupant of the White House, his appointees to the high court, our elected representatives in the chambers of Congress are more than faceless administrators or bureaucrats, more than the writers of our laws and adjudicators. They are the custodians of our national faith, our national ideals, and of our shared hopes and dreams. From diverse backgrounds themselves, they symbolize our unity. While they advocate conflicting policies, all attempt to further the common purpose, enlarge the American spirit, and realize the American dream. When our political leaders are unfaithful to this trust in either word or example, they contribute in some way, large or small, to the dis-spiriting and disintegration of the American common will.

There is, of course, the constant danger that this element of common purpose and shared vision will vanish almost entirely, and two forces operate together and individually to diminish it. One is complacency. The late, two-time Democratic presidential aspirant Adlai Stevenson once pointed out that, when multitudes gathered over one hundred years ago and listened for hours to Lincoln and Stephen Douglas debate the issue of slavery in the territories, citizens had fewer responsibilities and duties than they do today. Yet many citizens today are content with what candidates say about great issues of the day in fifteen-second television spots. "Is it not possible that the pressures of personal responsibilities are not greater but that the dedication and selflessness needed to discern and influence public issues have shrunk?"[4] The answer is

---

3. Quoted in Dean William Rudoy, "The Imperative of Redefining National Security," *Church and Society* 63 (1973): 19. This article is taken from Rudoy's book, *Armed and Alone* (New York: Braziller, 1972).

4. "Politics and Morality," *Saturday Review,* 7 February 1959, p. 39.

probably no. Political apathy may not be markedly more or less now than in bygone days. But when so many mentors of the public mind—from psychiatrists to advertising men—address us in terms of "what we owe ourselves," there is the danger, as Stevenson pointed out, that our devotion and concern may slacken for what man owes to God and his neighbor. If this danger materializes, our society cannot hope to be truly secure. Internal concord provides a people the strength and confidence to progress.

The other force that can destroy common purpose and spirit is cynicism—cynicism about our national goals, our leaders, and our institutions. This leads first to the withdrawal of trust in other Americans and finally to unbridled individualism and anarchy. Before regressing to that point the political community may experience radical forms of protest, repression and violation of certain civil liberties, and increased violence. Each century of our history has brought a great test to our common faith and corporate purpose. In the eighteenth century it was the Revolution; in the nineteenth, the Civil War. In the twentieth century, despite unprecedented extension of American liberties and rights, there has been a precipitate loss of morale, common purpose, and social solidarity. The signs of polarization and cynicism were all about us. The drastic impairment of our sense of purpose in the sixties and seventies resulted from three fundamental causes: the Indochina conflict, the accumulated neglect and mismanagement of urgent domestic problems (especially racial discrimination and inflation) and the lack of integrity and common decency in some elected officials (as illustrated by the Watergate scandals).

Since the almost accidental ascendancy of Gerald Ford to the presidency, rampant cynicism has slowed and some measure of equilibrium has returned. The spirit of common purpose did not expire, in large part because the doctrines of the civil religion supported the necessary reform and changes needed. Part of the dynamics of the common religion is the tremendous faith in and respect for the Constitution and political institutions, especially the judicial system, that it engenders. This faith affirms that we must not silence the voice of protest and that no man, be he president or city sanitation employee, is above the demands of the law.

The point is obvious. There is a direct link between civil religion and the extraordinary stability of the American political system. If this common purpose or, to borrow the language of Hannah Arendt, this *consensus universalis* is ever irreparably broken down, we Americans would lose not only our sense of identity and mission, but our influence among nations throughout the world that have looked to us for the inspiration of a free people. It is remarkable that throughout our history other nations, like us, have looked upon the American enterprise as a political and social experiment not only for ourselves but also for other nations, particularly those groping toward an identity and a governmental structure of their own. What we were building on this continent was worthy of emulation elsewhere.

The central and most often repeated theme of the American civil religion is that America, as our Pledge of Allegiance affirms, is "one nation under God." As church historian Sidney E. Mead put it, the "one most constant strand in its theology has been the assertion of the primacy of God over all human institutions."[5]

The words on back of our Great Seal read, "God hath ordained our undertakings." Our money is emblazoned with "In God we trust." But what do we mean when we affirm that America is "one nation under God?" Undoubtedly this concept is often misunderstood. It does not mean that God has sanctioned any single, denominational, public expression of religion in America. Nor does it mean that in some vague and indefinable way "God is on our side," for it is deceptively easy to claim the blessing of some nebulous Supreme Being for our political cause, whatever it is. Was it not the infidel Voltaire who bitingly declared that "God is always on the side of the big battalions"? It is a careless and dangerous hermeneutic that selects isolated verses or episodes from the Bible and makes them normative. A community, either religious or political, could bring together a number of such proof texts to support total war, the annihilation of the enemy, and a vindictive and self-righteous spirit. But it is precisely this spirit that has no place in the Christian approach to politics. Our national decisions have not always been right, and it would be folly for us to claim the approval of God for everything we have done in the past and will do in the future.

Stating what the phrase "one nation under God" does not mean may be easier than stating what it does mean. But, put succinctly, it means that the nation is not God. Nor is the nation to compete with God for the worship and allegiance that belong to Him alone. The Christian sees that *all* political communities, systems, and

---

5. "The 'Nation with the Soul of a Church,'" *Church History* 36 (1967): 276.

policies are under the judgment and mercy of God. Nor do we enlist some vague Supreme Being in "our cause." The God whom we are under is revealed in the Holy Scriptures. The God of the Bible is eternal, transcendent, omniscient, and omnipresent. In Him is our trust reposed, but America cannot "trust in God" unless its citizens do. Internal strife and moral decay cannot end until God is in the hearts of men, at both the individual and societal levels. This concept also means that while a nation may be blessed by God, it is never immune from God's judgment and chastisement. In a much greater sense than the United States, the Hebrew nation was "under God." And yet Amos, the prophet of the Lord, after warning of judgment upon Damascus, Edom, Moab, Gaza, and the Ammonites, spoke this word of the Lord to Amos's own people: "For crime after crime . . . I will grant them no reprieve, because they sell the innocent for silver and the destitute for a pair of shoes" (Amos 2:6). Being a recipient of God's grace entailed an even more severe judgment: "For you alone have I cared among all the nations of the world; therefore will I punish you for all your iniquities" (3:2).

The best of our political leaders have believed in a transcendent God who is sovereign over all nations. Thomas Jefferson once declared, "I tremble for my country when I reflect that God is just." Perhaps no one furthered the concept of "one nation under God" more than the great saint of American civil religion, Abraham Lincoln. Reinhold Niebuhr liked to say that Lincoln was one of the greatest American theologians, though he was not a member of any one church (the claims of many churches notwithstanding) and only a few of his statements can be called strictly theological. To Mead, Lincoln is the spiritual center of American history. Lincoln had no blind allegiance to the status quo, nor did he absolutize the American system; rather he believed profoundly in a sovereign, transcendent God, and in the nation's liability to His immediate, searing judgment. In fact, all the deeds of man stand under the judgment of an infinite God.

The Civil War, of course, evoked Lincoln's maturest application of his civil faith. Few citizens were able to rise above sectional interpretations of national destiny and speak of the fierce conflict as a judgment of God upon the young nation as a whole. But as the war dragged on and casualties mounted, the president agonized over the meaning of the protracted strife. He was convinced that the will of God, while not perfectly perceived by finite men, will be accomplished. In a meditation written probably after the Union's defeat at the second battle of Manassas, or Bull Run, Lincoln reflected:

> The will of God prevails. In great contests each party claims to act in accordance with the will of God. Both *may* be, and one *must* be wrong. God cannot be *for,* and *against* the same thing at the same time. In the present civil war it is quite possible that God's purpose is something different from the purpose of either party—and yet the human instrumentalities, working just as they do, are of the best adaptation to effect His purpose. I am almost ready to say this is probably true—that God wills this contest, and wills that it shall not end yet.[6]

Lincoln's brooding over providence, however, did not make him reluctant to pursue a Union victory. Instead it increased his resolve to conclude the war rapidly, restore a union of separate states, and renew the country's dedication to freedom, the "last, best hope of the earth." The most that finite men could do was to stand "with firmness in the right, as God gives us to see the right," Lincoln reasoned. His paramount purpose was to save the Union. "If I could save the Union without freeing *any* slave I would do it, and if I could save it by freeing *all* the slaves I would do it; and if I could save it by freeing some and leaving others alone I would also do that," he wrote Horace Greeley, responding to the *New York Tribune* publisher's attack on the president's refusal to adopt an antislavery policy. "What I do about slavery, and the colored race, I do because I believe it helps to save the Union; and what I forbear, I forbear because I do *not* believe it will help to save the Union."[7]

Unlike his predecessors and successors who have served as Commander-in-Chief during years of war, Lincoln never gave a doctrinaire defense of the Union cause. In his few public appearances he usually presented the conflict as a part of the great experiment which "embraces more than the fate of these United States." In the most famous oration in American history, the brief eulogy delivered at Gettysburg in November 1863, the beleaguered president did not celebrate an imminent victory or claim that his policies had guaranteed the world a full generation of peace; he reminded the nation that the war was "testing whether that nation or any nation so con-

---

6. In T. Harry Williams, ed., *Abraham Lincoln: Selected Speeches, Messages, and Letters* (New York: Holt, Rinehart, and Winston, 1957), p. 191.

7. Ibid.

ceived and so dedicated can long endure." Then he urged Americans to renew their commitment to the country's destiny under God: "It is for us the living . . . to be here dedicated to the great task remaining before us—that from these honored dead we take increased devotion to that cause for which they gave the last full measure of devotion . . . that this nation, under God, shall have a new birth of freedom."

Lincoln's second inaugural address is the greatest single scripture in the American civil religion. It brings together the various strands of the president's mature religious interpretation, and it, like the Gettysburg Address, is replete with Biblical allusions and terminology.

> Neither party expected for the war, the magnitude, or the duration, which it has already attained. Neither anticipated that the *cause* of the conflict might cease with, or even before, the conflict itself should cease. Each looked for an easier triumph, and a result less fundamental and astounding. Both read the same Bible, and pray to the same God; and each invokes His aid against the other. It may seem strange that any men should dare to ask a just God's assistance in wringing their bread from the sweat of other men's faces; but let us judge not that we be not judged. The prayers of both could not be answered; that of neither has been answered fully. The Almighty has His own purposes. "Woe unto the world because of offenses! for it must needs be that offenses come; but woe to that man by whom the offense cometh!" If we shall suppose that American slavery is one of those offenses which, in the providence of God, must needs come, but which, having continued through His appointed time, He now wills to remove, and that He gives to both North and South, this terrible war, as the woe due to those by whom the offense came, shall we discern therein any departure from those divine attributes which the believers in a Living God always ascribe to Him? Fondly do we hope—fervently do we pray—that this mighty scourge of war may speedily pass away. Yet, if God wills that it continue, until all the wealth piled by the bondman's two hundred and fifty years of unrequited toil shall be sunk, and until every drop of blood drawn with the lash, shall be paid by another drawn with the sword, as was said three thousand years ago, so still it must be said "the judgments of the Lord, are true and righteous altogether."
>
> With malice toward none; with charity for all; with firmness in the right, as God gives us to see the right, let us strive on to finish the work we are in; to bind up the nation's wounds; to care for him who shall have borne the battle, and for his widow, and his orphan —to do all which may achieve and cherish a just, and a lasting peace, among ourselves, and with all nations.[8]

8. Ibid., pp. 282, 283.

Lincoln here rejected the apocalyptic language of the abolitionists and the radical rhetoric of the southern "fire-eaters." He disdained the sense of moral superiority that sustains zealous warfare and advised moderation and deference to the Almighty. Such a speech is not "immediately popular," Lincoln wrote Thurlow Weed, because "men are not flattered by being shown that there has been a difference of purpose between the Almighty and them."[9] In Lincoln's civil religion, the president is accountable to God for his decisions. Alexander Solzhenitsyn offered the interesting thought that "authoritarian regimes as such are not frightening—only those which are answerable to no one and nothing. The autocrats of earlier, religious ages, though their power was ostensibly unlimited, felt themselves responsible before God and their own consciences." The Russian novelist concluded that "the autocrats of our own time are dangerous precisely because it is difficult to find higher values which would bind them."[10]

We conclude by noting that if this high form of the American civil religion provides the proper view of God in His relationship to all nations of the earth, it concomitantly provides a lofty view of man that has been a sometimes slow but certain corrective to social injustice. In the past the doctrine of Americanism has been applied restrictively. The white, more affluent middle-class mainstream has systematically excluded fellow citizens who were poor, black, Indian, Spanish-speaking, or members of other minority ethnic or religious groups. But to the degree that this has been corrected—and it has been to a significant degree—it has been inspired by the great scriptures of the national faith, to which our great reformers in all generations have returned again and again for inspiration. The civil religion served as a repository of moral resources for securing the rights of all men; its beliefs and rituals have made Americans sensitive to and appreciative of moral and spiritual values common to Christianity and Judaism, including gratitude for the bounty of the country and for civil liberties. As our history unfolded, more and more Americans concluded that the ideas of Thomas Jefferson and other great founding fathers are inconsistent with the deprivation of some citizens' God-given

---

9. In Don E. Fehrenbacher, ed., *Abraham Lincoln: A Documentary Portrait Through His Speeches and Writings* (New York: Signet, 1964), p. 279.

10. Alexander Solzhenitsyn et al., *From Under the Rubble* (Boston: Little and Brown, 1974), pp. 23, 24.

"natural rights." Sometimes, however, it took fervid rhetoric and civil disobedience to get an intransigent majority to discover new interpretations and applications of our Declaration of Independence and the Bill of Rights.

How inclusive can the American civil religion become without imperiling its doctrine? We have noted that for Americans to make their civil faith valid and relevant, they must set aside their prejudices and subcultural trappings and embrace, or at least tolerate, a plurality of viewpoints and values. A watershed in the history of the national self-understanding occurred in 1960 when Americans for the first time elected to the highest political office in the land a Roman Catholic. It is not inconceivable that either a Jew or a black will be elected to the same office before the turn of the century. Far less likely, however, is that we will elect as president an avowed agnostic or atheist. This consideration relates directly to the issue of how inclusive our national faith can be. While it guarantees minorities and dissenters of all persuasions the freedom to believe what they want, it has found no way to qualify self-confessed agnostics or atheists for positions of political leadership. During the early national period several states required all office-holders to vow that they believed in God. Perhaps it is asking too much of a civil *religion* to embrace such nonconforming elements in our society, but a *civil* religion definitely has a responsibility to those who hold unpopular opinions, as the high court has been quick to realize. Popular as it may be with the masses to do so, the civil religion must not be used to obstruct the full participation of *all* Americans in the public life of the nation; it must be used to stimulate this. A long-cherished, if not always honored, tenet in the democratic creed is that no person or group shall be politically disadvantaged by either their religious beliefs and practices or their total lack of formal religious commitment.[11] Should an atheist or agnostic be elected president, the traditional civil faith will be shaken at its very foundations. But perhaps the effect woud be no worse than the elevation of a person whose version of the civil religion is heretical. To that consideration we turn next.

---

11. I am indebted to Conrad Cherry, *God's New Israel* (Englewood Cliffs, N.J.: Prentice-Hall, 1971), p. 19, for the idea expressed in this paragraph and for some of the phrases. In the early sixties the Supreme Court struck down state requirements for a declaration of belief in the existence of God, but not all states have complied by amending their constitutions. See Torcaso v. Watkins, 367 U.S. 488 (1961).

The Danger

Any religion is capable of distortion and misuse. Any system of beliefs can degenerate into heresies of various import, and its adherents can apostatize. This is the central danger confronting the American civil religion—the ever-present tendency to forget the primary principle that a just and transcendent God is above all nations and to make the nation itself the object of ultimate loyalty. In other words, the nation becomes god. It is the sole center and bearer of our aspirations, dreams, and ultimate values. There is no hope beyond it. What is good for the nation is good for all other institutions—the church, the home, and business; conversely, what is bad for the nation is bad for all other institutions. Having lost sight of a transcendent God, the God of the Bible is packaged as a middle-class American god. The designs of the Almighty are identical with the goals of the nation. The churches that pay homage to this national god offer to the unbelieving world a religion that is an amalgamation of New Testament Christianity and Americanism. The members of these churches are unable to distinguish between the Christian way and the national way. The churches that are affected by this distorted form of national faith work in concert with other American institutions to give sanctity to middle-class values and political principles; they purport to be Christian, but they would choose Americanism and the interests of the middle class if they could be convinced that genuine Christianity and their watered-down version of it are different.

While orthodox civil religion binds a diverse people together in pursuit of noble goals, ideals, and national policy, apostate civil religion goes beyond this and demands unconditional reverence for the nation, its political system, and its pretended or real goals. The distinction here is between *national religion* and *religious nationalism*.[12] We expect the civil religion, like all other religions, to serve a legitimizing function; religion, as we noted, offers stability and permanent, even eternal, values to its adherents, who must cope with a world of change. But the apostate civil religion legitimizes little more than the status quo. It has no prophetic vision, no saving criticism. It is uncomfortable with the sensitive conscience of the church. Current national goals are law and gospel; they must receive uncritical endorsement from all opinion-making communities of citizens.

---

12. Cherry made this distinction in *God's New Israel*.

Such a form of the national faith denies the Biblical theology of God and state. Modern-day Christians have experienced a measure of difficulty in finding contemporary relevance in the first of the Ten Commandments—"Thou shalt have no other gods before me." We conjure up the golden calf, the tall image of Nebuchadnezzar, or, in more recent times, some fat-bellied Buddha of the Orient. Is it not possible that a false god that has been unknowingly and consistently worshiped by millions of Americans is America itself? Unlimited reverence for our nation is idolatry, pure and simple. The church ceases to function as a worldwide, supranational, called-out community that extends from the ancient world and commands a higher loyalty than the nation. Instead it becomes an unofficial organ of the nation and a propagandist for Americanism. Effective Christian witness on urgent national problems is rejected and denounced as some form of heresy. In the 1960s we saw how this happened; when some responsible Christians spoke out for racial justice and for an end to American involvement in Vietnam, many churches denounced them. Instead of being about their task of "Christianizing" the nation, the Christian churches had become nationalized.

The nation does bear genuinely worthwhile values, and, as Reinhold Niebuhr pointed out, it "is thus ethically ambiguous. Its very claim to unqualified moral worth is the basis of its demonic character. In other words, it belongs to the devil precisely because it claims to be God."[13] An American Christian may believe the United States to be the greatest nation in the world. He may hold this belief with a great deal of emotional intensity. He may believe, as did Daniel Webster, that dedicated Christian living and good citizenship go hand-in-hand. But no nation deserves his unconditional devotion, for it is neither the universal community nor the bearer of man's highest hopes and aspirations. Imagine the followers of Christ in apostolic days pinning their hopes on Rome! Are we American Christians without hope if the United States does not survive? Is our religion solely a civil religion that depends on the survival and success of our nation? Have we made such an idol out of "national security" that we have forgotten that ultimately only God can guard our true livelihood and safety? Then, whatever one calls it, this is not the faith of our Lord Jesus Christ. Seek first the kingdom of heaven and its righteousness (Matt. 6:33). Would it

---

13. "Do the State and Nation Belong to God or the Devil?" in Ronald H. Stone, ed., *Faith and Politics* (New York: Braziller, 1968), p. 85.

not be fair to adapt the words of the apostle Paul here for our purpose? "If in this life we have hope only in America, we are of all men most miserable" (cf. I Cor. 15:19).

How is it possible for us to slip from the valid and noble version of our civil religion into a counterfeit version? The transition is usually unconscious and gradual, and it is to be expected during a national crisis when deep disagreement develops over the meaning of our experience and the direction of national policy. This happened during the sixties and early seventies when crises were precipitated by race relations, urban unrest, and our foreign policy in the Far East. During such times we expect the civil religion to provide more reassurance and stability than it can deliver.

Other factors also contribute to this transition from orthodoxy to heresy. The rise of our national faith to a position of supremacy over our Biblical faith may be due less to the strength of the former than to the weakness of the latter. People need to cling to higher values and sacrificially commit themselves to a worthy cause that will survive them. If people do not find this commitment and these values in Biblical faith and the church, they turn to the nation-state. In his study of the extraordinary depth of public reaction to the assassination of John F. Kennedy, political scientist Sidney Verba offered the following interpretation:

> What this suggests is that complete separation of church and state may be possible only in a formal sense. In a secular society where formal religious commitment is weak, the activities of the state may be the nearest one comes to activities of ultimate importance, activities that fundamentally determine matters of death and life and the quality of life. In short, governmental institutions may have significance of a religious kind. The awe inspired by the ultimate power of the church in more pious times may be akin to the awe inspired in modern secular societies by the ultimate power of the state.[14]

Other political scientists also have argued that skepticism and a waning spiritual religion, be it Christianity or some pagan religion, give rise to the worship of the political state. Man transfers his inherent awe and reverence from a "supernatural" religion to a political religion, the latter having the two-fold advantage of being both "real" and physically powerful enough to coerce a diverse population into forms of social harmony. During the second and third centuries when pagan skepticism was prevalent among Roman

---

14. Quoted in Lewis Lipsitz, "If, as Verba Says, the State Functions as a Religion, What Are We to Do Then to Save Our Souls?" *American Political Science Review* 62, no. 2 (1968): 529.

and Greek intellectuals and when philosophers and mystics were experimenting with new cults, the deification of the Roman emperor was completed and his worship became widely and popularly accepted. And in the sixteenth century when doubt about Roman Catholicism reached a peak, not only did Protestantism develop but the populace, following intellectuals like Machiavelli and Erastus, exalted the lay state.[15]

Another factor contributing to a misplaced allegiance is our tendency to believe that democracy as a political system is the very basis of Christian faith, rather than that Christianity is one source of our democratic tradition. We benignly accept all spiritual religions under the aegis of the civil community, inasmuch as they are congregational and private concerns, and view them as expressions of the individual liberties and freedoms afforded and protected only by a democracy. But this makes democracy a patron of Christianity. Hence, God needs democracy and the American way of life in order to accomplish His will on earth. The practical effect is to render the God of Biblical faith subservient to the American style of democracy. Should the American experiment fail, God will have to retire.

A distorted civil faith is readily exploited by political leaders, demagogues, certain charismatic figures on the American scene, and political and religious fanatics of all stripes. All citizens must guard against attempts to insure the permanence of partisan political policies and experiments by connecting them with some tenets or expression of the national faith. For example, not infrequently American presidents have used religious rhetoric and Biblical motifs to gain public support for their principles and policies, and there is always the danger that a chief executive will dramatically dominate the civil religion and appropriate it for his own narrow purposes. The possibility of this is much greater than ever before because the civil religion's chief symbol, the word *God,* unfortunately has become ambiguous while retaining its evocative powers; the same thing has happened to a lesser degree with all other religious symbols. The evolution of this rhetoric of equivocation was largely unavoidable in a pluralistic society where a public official must address Southern Baptists, Methodists, Unitarians, Pentecostals, Black Muslims, Jews, and agnostics—all of whose concep-

---

15. Carlton J. H. Hayes, *Essays on Nationalism* (New York: Russell and Russell, 1966), p. 100.

tions of the Almighty vary at least slightly.[16] But politicians know that, according to polls, at least ninety-five percent of the American people believe in a Supreme Being. So in their political orations they seldom neglect to invoke His name and blessing; but their references to him are vague because they know that the more specific they are the more they will alienate their audiences. *God,* says the unwritten glossary of American politics, is a word in the last paragraph of political speeches. All Washington eulogies of religion are suspect on the ground that they may be self-serving.[17] And the astute politician knows that to call an American institution —such as the public schools—or another political philosophy "godless" is to charge it with the unpardonable sin.

From the Christian perspective the problem is far greater than a semantic one. A political society loses its vision of a just and righteous God whose ways are past finding out, who in the words of Niebuhr "laughs at human pretensions without being hostile to human aspirations," who reveals Himself in the Holy Scriptures and in Jesus Christ, when it finds ease and comfort in the darkness of idolatry. Not that God is dead, but He is transformed into a sentimental deity who smiles innocuously at everything labeled "American" and frowns upon everything labeled "un-American." He is a loyal, superspiritual Adviser to the power and prestige that is ours alone. His wrath is for other nations and other peoples, but not for us.

The use of religious sentiment for partisan purposes took an interesting turn when President Nixon introduced church services in the East Room of the White House. When Gerald Ford succeeded Nixon, he immediately discontinued the services and began going *out* to worship. The White House worship services were

16. As for the word *God*, American philosopher George Santayana once observed that "all mutual understanding is impossible. It is a floating literary symbol, with a value which if we define it scientifically becomes quite algebraic. As no experienced object corresponds to it, it is without fixed indicative force and admits any sense which its context may happen to give it." Quoted in H. M. Kallen, "Democracy's True Religion," *Saturday Review,* 28 July 1951, p. 6.

17. John F. Wilson wrote: "There simply isn't much theological reflection undergirding the ready and relatively numerous presidential references to morality and the deity. *Ad hoc* God allusions simply do not constitute a theology; there must be some consistent exploration of relevant issues in such a way that a frame of reference oriented to the deity or to the fundamental premises of a culture—whatever the particular coloration—has a logical status or plays an effective and shaping role." "A Historian's Approach to Civil Religion," in Russell E. Richey and Donald G. Jones, eds., *American Civil Religion* (New York: Harper and Row, 1974), p. 121.

symbolic acts for the general public, and we should evaluate what they symbolized. We need not conclude that the president established the services solely out of partisan considerations. He possessed a genuine religious faith and wanted to set a good example, but he had an "intense dislike of 'going to church for show.'"[18] And there is certainly no problem with a man worshiping with his family and friends (even if they number over three hundred and include congressional leaders, ambassadors, cabinet members, and Supreme Court justices) in his home, or anywhere else for that matter. There is certainly more Scriptural authority for worshiping at home than in elaborate edifices constructed solely for that purpose. In his first inaugural address Nixon declared, "To the crisis of the spirit, we need an answer of the spirit." To the extent that these services said to the public that the president acknowledged his dependence on God and believed in the value of public assembly for worship, the services made a worthwhile contribution to national morality, a contribution that harsh liberal critics have neglected. But far outweighing this contribution were two grave dangers to both the nation as a whole and the religious communities of our land.

The first is the temptation to *use* God and religion for political purposes. Any president could orchestrate piety into some political strategy. To use God for human purposes, however noble, is idolatry. The location of the services is more a national shrine than simply another American home. Having the services there not only may constitute a subtle circumvention of the First Amendment's disestablishment clause, but it encourages the public subconsciously to identify organized religion with national values and, to a lesser extent, with the policies of the current president. This greatly facilitates, as we will discuss in the next chapter, political moralism.

In the spring of 1974, Congress proclaimed a National Day of Humiliation, Fasting, and Prayer. The proclamation noted that America had become "intoxicated with unbroken success" and "failed to respond, personally and collectively, with sacrifice and uncompromised commitment to the unmet needs of our fellow man, both at home and abroad." It closed with a call "to repent of national sins." Whether the state should promote theological ideas, however sound, was one issue critics raised, but the most crucial

18. Richard M. Nixon, in Ben Hibbs, ed., *White House Sermons* (New York: Harper and Row, 1972).

issue is whether our elected officials truly desire to make these noble sentiments concrete in public policy. If they do not, such proclamations are in stark contrast with the action of the king of Nineveh in the Book of Jonah: he repented, putting on sackcloth and sitting in ashes, and amended his sinful ways. Unless Christian congressmen allow their Christianity to affect significantly their votes and proposals, such proclamations constitute paper repentance—another effort to manipulate God for partisan purposes. When such proclamations seem sincerely motivated but are ignored by the citizenry, the church should conclude that it has been too silent on these pressing issues.

The second possibility, just as real and dangerous, is that organized Christianity may be drawn so closely to the throne of power that the healthy tension that should exist between the political and religious communities is threatened. The critical faculties of the church become blunted, and its witness to the world weakened. Not only is the distance between church and state reduced, but the antiseptic ritual of a self-selected elite in a well-secured salon is likely to be confused by the public with authentic Christian worship. The services brought together everyone from the head of a Jewish seminary, to Protestant fundamentalists, to Roman Catholic cardinals; this generalized format indicated that religion can thrive when divorced from a deep, worshipful experience rooted in a single religious tradition. Both preachers and hearers were carefully selected. Amaziah, the priest of Bethel who was appointed court prophet by the king of Israel, wanted Amos to depart from Bethel because he was prophetic and critical rather than conforming and sanctioning. Might the White House preachers have felt comfortable with Amaziah? "We do not know the architectural proportions of Bethel," Reinhold Niebuhr commented caustically, "but we do know that it is, metaphorically, the description of the East Room of the White House, which President Nixon has turned into a kind of sanctuary. By a curious combination of innocence and guile, he has circumvented the Bill of Rights' first article. Thus, he has established a conforming religion by semi-officially inviting representatives of all disestablished religions, of whose moral criticism we were naturally so proud."[19]

This criticism, offered early in Nixon's first administration, was not premature, nor is the analogy it draws unfair. A cursory reading

---

19. "The King's Chapel and the King's Court," *Christianity and Crisis,* 4 August 1969, p. 211.

of *White House Sermons* reveals more praise and adulation than Christian witness and judgment. Motifs are drawn as much from the space program and the world of sports as from the Bible (Bobby Richardson, preaching on the rich young ruler, said that the ruler was probably an athlete because he came *running* to Jesus!). The preacher for July 20, 1969, the Sunday of the anticipated moon landing, rhapsodized: "And my hope for mankind is strengthened in the knowledge our President himself will soon go into orbit, reaching boldly for the moon of peace. God grant that he, too, may return in glory and that countless millions of prayers that follow him shall not have been in vain."[20]

Jesus once had a message for Herod, Paul for Felix and Agrippa, and Nathan for David; and proclaimers of the ancient gospel should proclaim it to public leaders today. But they should take great care in establishing the relationships and contexts in which they deliver that message. The Watergate experience, for one, has vividly illustrated that clergymen who get too cozy with ruling politicians find themselves compromised—unwilling and unable to pronounce the harsh moral judgments that help to keep government within the pale of decency. Like journalists, preachers can be politically biased. To ask or expect our preachers to be totally apolitical, to have or reveal no political ideology, is unrealistic. But it would serve the causes of both religion and politics for ministers to observe scrupulously the principle of church and state separation. In the future our presidents should go to a specific church before they bring church into the White House. That way our most prominent ministers can remain sufficiently aloof and uncompromised to leave no doubt about for whom they speak when great moral issues confront the nation.[21]

---

20. For an interesting journalistic account and analysis of White House worship during the Nixon years, see Edward B. Fiske, "Praying with the President in the White House," *New York Times Magazine*, 8 August 1971, pp. 14, 15. See also John Fry's review of *White House Sermons* entitled "The Moon of Peace," *Christianity and Crisis*, 24 July 1972, pp. 179, 180.

21. In recent years a new phenomenon has developed in Washington political circles—a resurgence of religious worship and activities among elected officials. There are regular prayer groups, worship services, and sharing sessions. I have chosen not to deal with this rather recent development. John Warwick Montgomery treated "Washington Christianity" in critical terms: "In baldest terms, Washington Christianity is *superficial, non-doctrinal,* and *experientialistic.* It lacks theological substance. . . . There is almost never deep and penetrating study of scriptural teaching." Washington evangelicals dislike doctrine, Montgomery contended, and emphasize "personal experience." *Christianity Today,* 8 August 1975, pp. 37, 38.

The real danger of a perverted civil faith is national pharisaism, whereby the civil faith lends philosophical and moral support to national self-righteousness and sanctifies a double standard. Perhaps no one in our time has contributed more to our understanding of how national self-righteousness operates in the public mind and public policy, or has placed this phenomenon in better theological perspective, than Reinhold Niebuhr, the late professor of Union Theological Seminary to whom we have already referred in this analysis. In his numerous writings on politics and Christianity, Niebuhr explained how men can collectively tolerate and perpetuate acts of social injustice that are at odds with the Christian individualism they fervently espouse (see especially his *Moral Man and Immoral Society*). He noted that every nation has some form of spiritual pride, but Americans' belief that they have totally turned their backs upon the vices of Europe and made a new beginning has nourished a degree of self-righteousness of which people in the Old World are incapable. The messianic consciousness and inherent righteousness of our cause is rooted in both the Calvinist and the Jeffersonian concepts of our national destiny. And while America inadvertently has achieved great power, ironically it is now less the master of its own destiny than it was before it became so powerful. Niebuhr's conclusion is at complete odds with the rhetoric of all presidents since World War II. And while all nations are troubled by spiritual pride, the powerful ones pose the greatest danger to world community. They are so obsessed with their own honor that it is nearly impossible for them to confess the error of a policy. If ever a nation required the spirit of genuine contrition and humility, it is America. One of the most important missions of the Christian church, then, is to disturb the nation when it is in a mood of self-congratulation and to sensitize its conscience to social injustice.[22]

While Niebuhr did most of his writing during the Second World War, postwar experiences have demonstrated the basic soundness of his analysis. The realm of foreign relations is where we, like other nations, have instinctively assumed the justice of our policies and been blind to our particular vices. The Christian West, not the currently communist countries, introduced imperialism and colonialism. Of the nineteenth-century nations, the United States was the most expansionist and aggressive; in a half century we

22. See Harry R. Davis and Robert C. Good, eds., *Reinhold Niebuhr on Politics* (New York: Scribner's, 1960), pp. 269-83.

trebled our territory at the expense of France, Spain, Mexico, and Great Britain. We installed military bases all over the world, close to other great world powers to keep them under close surveillance; but we would have been disturbed if Communist China or Russia had installed as many bases as close to the U.S. for the same reasons. For over a decade we claimed, in all sincerity, a vital interest in Vietnam, but we found recklessly irresponsible the Soviet Union's claim to a vital interest in an island ninety miles from our mainland. Through the sixties and seventies we have become increasingly alarmed at the development of nuclear weapons by nations like India and the warring states in the Middle East (Lyndon Johnson said when China detonated an atomic bomb that it was a "dark day"). Have we forgotten that the U.S. is the only nation to employ the atomic bomb as a weapon of war and that we dropped it on a nonwhite people? We must not imagine that the Japanese have forgotten this![23] The concern of certain of our people, spearheaded by Washington's Senator Henry Jackson, for the plight of Jews in the Soviet Union is genuinely motivated, but we must not forget our own sordid past: our ancestors drove the Indians from their rightful lands and territories and decimated them, and subjected another entire race to chattel slavery in one section of our great land.

We have long featured ourselves as God's anointed defenders of liberty, always coming to the defense of the "democratic governments" and "free institutions" of other peoples. Can we not be realistic enough to admit that, as well-intentioned as we have been, and presidential rhetoric to the contrary, we also have aided military dictatorships (as in Santo Domingo and Vietnam) and opposed duly constituted regimes (such as Allende's in Chile) when we believed it served our national interests? And can we not also admit that even America, with her illustrious and glorious past, can be only as great as her people and the leaders they elect; and that we, being as human as other people, are also as susceptible to national

23. This is not to say that Truman's decision was rooted in racism. But it is essential to see how outsiders view our nation and its policies, something into which we do not ordinarily inquire. For an interesting discussion on the wisdom of HST's "irreversible decision," see Paul R. Baker, ed., *The Atomic Bomb: The Great Decision* (New York: Holt, Rinehart, and Winston, 1968). Some of the examples in this paragraph were suggested by a statement from Henry Steele Commager before the Senate Committee on Foreign Relations, *Hearings on Changing American Attitudes Toward Foreign Policy*, 90th Congress, 1st Session, 20 February 1967, pp. 5-13.

pride, mistakes, and poor judgments, all of which are better acknowledged and studied than glossed over? Would not the national psyche be healthier if we admitted that America has "lost" and still can "lose." Cannot the familiar words of Jesus, ". . . everyone who exalts himself shall be humbled. . . ." (Luke 14:11), apply as much to nations as to individuals?

The dynamics of the apostate civil faith depend largely on who propagates it. Many parties, groups, and individuals join in support of the distorted civil religion, but our chief concern here is with those who support it from within the Christian community. Earlier in this volume we touched on the two religions practiced in ancient Israel—the true worship of and service to Jehovah, and the idolatrous worship of false gods and national policies—and on Israel's wicked kings soliciting the aid and consolation of the prophetic and priestly communities. The U.S. and the ancient Hebrew nation are not, of course, analogous in every respect: America is not chosen by God to prepare the world for the first advent of a Messiah, and the two civil faiths of America are not identical to the two of the ancient Hebrews. But we can learn much from the Old Testament narratives. A potentate—whether king, emperor, president, or prime minister—must be very unresourceful and unimaginative to be unable to trot out some priest or prophet who will baptize with praise his grimiest deeds. And if he cannot secure some form of religious sanction, the ruler can at least get many churches to stick to "church affairs," or in other words to restrict religion to "religion."

John Lukacs wrote *The Passing of the Modern Age* out of deep concern for what he called "the dissolution of religion." "Almost all of the German cardinals, bishops, pastors, and priests under Hitler restricted religion to religion; they said nothing about the misdeeds of the state, not to speak of its misdeeds against non-Christians par excellence, such as the Jews."[24] No state has ever gone to war without the blessing of some official priest or preacher. One of the doughboys' favorite souvenirs from World War I was German uniform belt buckles inscribed with *"Gott mit Uns."* When faithful to its mission, the church affirms that it has been established by God and entrusted with a general competence with respect to the highest goals and purposes of life; it does not derive its authority from the state. The Nazi regime was very successful in re-

---

24. Harper and Row, 1972. This quote is from a review by Dolph Honicker, *Nashville Tennessean,* 21 November 1970.

ducing the church to an innocuous appendage of its national policy, an instrument of its own apostate civil religion.[25] When the church is true to its doctrine and mission, it is a constant threat to totalitarian states.

In the recent past, conservative and evangelical spokesmen have supplied the "higher powers that be" with their modern Amaziahs, despite the long-standing conservative tradition that the church must not "meddle" in civil affairs. During our involvement in Vietnam, the well-known Cardinal Spellman declared, "Any solution other than total victory is inconceivable";[26] and Billy Graham called Martin Luther King's simultaneous involvement in civil rights and antiwar movements an "affront to the thousands of loyal negro troops who are in Vietnam," a prolongation of the war, and a "comfort to the enemy."[27] On another occasion Graham wrote, "I have been extremely careful not to be drawn into either the moral implications or the tactical military problems of the Vietnam war."[28]

Church leaders such as Spellman and Graham must not be denied the freedom of speech. Much of the criticism of Graham from liberal churchmen undoubtedly was a product not simply of disagreement with what Graham had said but of an envy of his ability to reach and command respect among the middle-class masses. On the other hand, powerful church spokesmen must exercise great caution that their vast audiences not accept their personal moral views and judgments as the indisputable will of God. It has been chic in many circles to denigrate Billy Graham, especially after his long silence concerning Vietnam and Watergate; his close association and friendship with recent presidents was taken as uncritical endorsement of their policies. In a brief but enlightening article entitled "Can Billy Graham Survive Richard Nixon?", Richard V. Pierard asked, concerning the propriety of a ministry specifically

---

25. See a brief discussion of this in Herbert Richardson, "Civil Religion in Theological Perspective," in *American Civil Religion*, pp. 179-81. For extensive studies see Arthur Cochrane, *The Church's Confession Under Hitler* (Philadelphia: Westminster, 1962); and John S. Conway, *The Nazi Persecution of the Churches, 1933-1945* (New York: Basic, 1968).

26. Quoted in *Christian Century*, 1 February 1967, p. 133.

27. Quoted in *Christian Century*, 17 May 1967, p. 645.

28. *Christian Century*, 29 March 1967, p. 411. This was part of a letter protesting an editorial that had suggested Graham was involved in supporting the war.

to presidents, "Does this inevitably degenerate into vapid civil religion or can a prophetic witness result that will orient a state into paths of righteousness?" He answered, "I regard the latter as both possible and desirable," but he noted that Nixon exploited his relationship with Graham and the evangelist's simplistic social ethic, rugged individualism, and naive conception of America. Graham may be commended for leading millions to Christ, and, God willing, he will remain effective for many years to come. "But it is absolutely essential that these converts be taught how to live a total Christian life—one with an impact on the social, political, and economic aspects of their existence as well as the spiritual."[29]

A new day is dawning for American conservative and evangelical Christians. One of the most encouraging developments in the last several years has been a gradual but certain change in evangelical thinking about America as a nation and the proper relationship between it and Christians. No longer will we automatically identify the will of God with the political will of the nation. The voice of the majority is no longer ipso facto the voice of God. The cold-war period produced reams of sermons, tracts, and books on "godless" communism, fostering a simple Manichean world view and undergirding our own tainted national condition. More than anything else it was seeing our youth in the quagmire of Vietnam that shook the very foundations of our comfortable premises and presumptions. Too long and too explicitly we have supported the radical Right's elevation of laissez-faire capitalism and anticommunism to the same doctrinal plane as Biblical teachings on the Lord's Supper, the church, and Christ's second coming. With some important excep-

---

29. *Reformed Journal* 24 (1974): 13. Pierard concluded: "Graham and his people could be doing more in this respect than they have so far, and I am fearful that the ties with Nixon could retard further progress here."

Encouragingly, Billy Graham seems to have realized that to simply identify divine providence with the prevailing Americanism is to distort both Biblical Christianity and the noblest civil religion. After the Vietnam war he publicly expressed doubts about its moral validity and purpose. When the Watergate transcripts were released, he deplored their moral tone: " 'Thou shalt not take the name of the Lord thy God in vain' is a commandment that has not been suspended, regardless of any need to release tensions." And addressing nearly 2,500 Protestant evangelical leaders at the International Congress on World Evangelism, held in Lausanne, Switzerland, in the summer of 1974, Graham made a frank confession that must not be lost upon the millions of other evangelical Americans. It is an enormous mistake, he admitted, "to identify the Gospel with any political program or culture. I confess tonight that this has been one of my own dangers in my ministry. When I go to preach the Gospel, I go as an ambassador of the kingdom of God—not America." Quoted in *Time*, 5 August 1974, p. 48.

tions, it is true that liberal churches were the first to awaken to this exploitation of American Christianity, but some of the more impressive strides have been made in conservative and evangelical quarters. No longer is it acceptable for the minister to condemn war dissenters as both unpatriotic and sinful. The laity may lag considerably behind the leadership, but many signs point to an aroused conscience that will bring Christian witness to bear on urgent social and political issues.

In conclusion, we have seen that the ultimate foundation of a free society is cohesive, collective sentiment. This sentiment is fostered by all those agencies of the spirit and mind that gather the traditions of a nation, transmit them from generation to generation, and thereby create a continuous, treasured common life that constitutes a decent civilization. If a civilization elects to be Christian as well, it must consider itself to be under the just, righteous, and transcendent God who is revealed in the Scriptures. Without this kind of vision, to borrow an Old Testament proverb, our people perish.

The characteristic contribution of American religion to American politics has been—not perspective, wisdom, depth of insight—but the rousing of the sentiments and energies of charity, generosity, and social reform; the characteristic vices have been those of a tremendous oversimplification and sentimentalization of politics.

William Lee Miller

It is neither wise or right for a nation to disregard its own needs, and it is foolish—and may be wicked—to think that other nations will disregard theirs. But it is wicked for a nation only to regard its own interest, and foolish to believe that such is the sole motive that actuates any other nation. It should be our steady aim to raise the ethical standard of national action just as we strive to raise the ethical standard of individual action.

Theodore Roosevelt

I do not think we can conclude that it matters greatly to God whether the free trade area of the Common Market prevails in Europe, whether the British fish or do not fish in Icelandic territorial waters, or even whether Indians, or Pakistanis run Kashmir. It might matter, but it is hard for us, with our limited vision, to know.

George Kennan

Clear your mind of cant.

Samuel Johnson

chapter ten

Morality and Moralism
in American Political Life

Can you identify the following campaign speech?

Our goal in this campaign has been to stand up for the truth and speak the truth. Or, as our young people put it, to tell it like it is. Our opponents are hoping the American voters will be satisfied with deceptions, half-truths, and pious propaganda. We think the people can stand the truth and I intend to tell it. If I am elected, decency, honor, and integrity will be returned to all echelons of national government. Our party stands for principles, not politics.

In foreign policy, our goal is abolition of war. We do not shrink from this task because it is difficult. Rather, we renew our dedication to this ideal because history and the Almighty have placed this burden only upon our shoulders. It is within our capability to shape a world where all nations live peaceably, justly, and securely, and wherein man's inhumanity to man is a mere memory.

On the domestic scene, there are many goals. The ugly racism that has dogged our past can be pulled up by the roots. Prosperity is a gift for the asking by all able-bodied men and women who are willing to work for a living. Our unemployment and welfare problems will be solved when people choose personal industry over slothfulness. Our goal is the total abolition of poverty. The crime problem will be reduced when an administration that does not believe in coddling criminals is elected. If you stand for what is right and good for America, then cast your ballot for us in the November election.

Sound familiar? Actually, this is not an excerpt from any campaign speech, but its sentiments ring so familiar that we suspect we have heard it many times in the last decade or so. It would be well received by most audiences. It would receive the following headline: "Candidate X Reaffirms Goals of World Peace and Domestic Prosperity."

But suppose the same candidate had made the following appeal:

> I'm here to seek your votes as president of this great nation. Our nation is, as we all know, facing many grave problems on both the foreign and domestic fronts. I would be much less than honest if I pretended that my party and I knew the solutions to all these problems or that my opponents in this campaign were less concerned about them than ourselves. What I do ask is that you compare the record of the two parties on the issues, and it should be clear who deserves the opportunity to search for these solutions.
>
> I wish I could promise world peace for a millennium. What statesman has not dreamed of a world of blissful peace and security for all mankind? The force of this ancient dream must be harnessed in new and creative ways to diminish carnal conflict as much as we can. But there is no guarantee of peace with justice. We live in a world of conflicting ideologies, limited resources, and imperfect rulers. What I do promise is to forge a foreign policy based on the interests of all our citizens. I shall pursue policies I believe will minimize the chances of involvement in international conflict. If war seems unavoidable, I shall conduct it as justly and expeditiously as possible, giving full attention to the voices of all our citizens, both supporters and dissenters.
>
> I have no panacea for the problems of poverty, unemployment, and civil disorder, nor, it is obvious from the last four years, does my opponent. And while we are both concerned about these problems, my election will open the way for new men, new programs, and new ideas to be employed—not in totally eradicating the problems, for they are the lot of all people everywhere—but in reducing their impact on our personal lives and in raising the quality of life in our society.

The reception to this speech, of course, would be quite different. Some listeners might find it a refreshing breeze of honesty, but many others would conclude that the candidate lacks idealism and optimism. The press would headline the news story, "Candidate X Cites National Limitations," or "World Peace and Domestic Prosperity Not Possible, Says Candidate X." But why does no presidential candidate dare speak like this? Why can no American statesman declare that eternal peace will never prevail in this dispensation, or that we will never eradicate poverty and racism, without being charged with blasphemy or cynicism or both? Are not both ideas among the basic tenets of the Judeo-Christian tradition? Do our politicians really believe the venerable platitudes about government solving almost all human problems? Or are they catering to the American mind that is hopelessly, chronically optimistic, idealistic, and utopian? Are we the most high-minded people in the world or the most hypocritical?[1]

These questions are answered easily only if we look at American political practices through the eyes of a foreigner. To him, we are the most idealistic and moralistic nation in the West. We like our politics clear and simple. Our heroes wear white hats and the villains, black ones; we abhor candidates who wear gray ones. Our political process is more than an arena for resolving social conflict and formulating laws—it gives us national identity, defines our character, and pinpoints, produces, and propagates our goals, ideals, heroes, and paradigms for our fellow citizens, ourselves, and our children. As Bayless Manning put it, "In substantial measure, the American looks upon his politics as a Morality Play."[2]

Everywhere you look there is evidence supporting Manning's observation, but the best place to begin is political campaigns. Voters want a Mr. Truth or a Mr. Right. The candidate's private life is more important than his stand on the issues. The use of profanity, a divorce, or some other impropriety diminishes the candidate's hopes substantially. Many church people were more upset by Nixon's frequent vulgarities than by anything else revealed in the Watergate transcripts. And Gerald Ford may well have been correct when he said that his wife's comments indicating a "casual" attitude toward premarital affairs could cost him twenty million votes. Emotional stability is another must. Abraham Lincoln may have wept in compassion for families who lost loved ones in the Civil War, but no candidate can afford to shed tears over anything while running for high office. The one thing for which all Americans admire the Kennedys is the stoic manner in which they have borne their grief in public. When any politician's emotional composure is but slightly affected, it will not go without notice in every news medium.

1. Irving Kristol dealt with this issue in his excellent article "A Foolish American 'Ism'—Utopianism," *New York Times Magazine*, 14 November 1971, pp. 31, 93-103. Kristol gave me the idea of noting the American idealism and moralism in presidential rhetoric.

2. "The Purity Potlatch: An Essay on Conflict of Interests, American Government, and Moral Escalation," *Federal Bar Journal* 24 (1964): 243.

Americans are realistic enough to know that no one—politician, priest, or king—is morally impeccable, but they will not tolerate any hint of imperfection in public pronouncements. We look to our leaders for moral affirmations. We demand that they speak with composure, sobriety, and uncompromised morality. Should anything turn up that reflects unfavorably upon their character, we demand a denial from them and a reassurance that they know what is true and moral, and are fully committed to it. The vocabulary of our politics is rife with *God* and other value-laden terms. Rhetoric is simplified, highly connotative, dogmatic, ritualistic, formal, redundant, and platitudinous. The content is seldom descriptive and hardly objective.

The national party convention is an interesting act in the morality play. Conducted quadrennially, it brings together a most unique congregation. It involves the reaffirmation of party principles—principles that somehow become eternal principles of right and justice as opposed to the other party's principles of evil and oppression. The speeches, the special music, and the zeal of true believers (displayed in prolonged and noisy demonstrations) are intended not only to revive those in the fold but, via television, to reach out and convert the "lost." The national moral symbols are drafted into the service of party principles. A new standard-bearer is anointed and sent forth with the collective blessing to battle the enemy. And should this candidate be elected, he is immediately transformed into an actor much bigger than life, at once establishing, declaring, and embodying standards that are not of this world. We expect him to utter ultimate moral maxims on every appropriate occasion.[3] And when he dies, he is not forgotten: the guardians of our national memory soon beatify and apotheosize him, we formulate many myths about him for our moral edification, and with few exceptions we remember only the good and noble things he did as a moral agent on the great stage of life. Some might think this an uncanny way to conduct political affairs, and

---

3. See an interesting study by Paul A. Carter entitled "The Pastoral Office of the Presidency," *Theology Today* 25 (1968): 52-63. Theodore Roosevelt once declared that "the White House is a bully pulpit." TR mixed the image of Calvin with that of the cowboy, giving the presidency the moral authority of both. According to Clinton L. Rossiter, TR was always staging "the breathless drama of a Western movie, and he never left the audience in doubt that he was the 'good guy' and the other fellows—Democrats, senators, monopolists, Socialists, diplomats, nature fakers, muckrakers—the 'bad guys.'" *The American Presidency* (New York: New American Library, 1956), pp. 74, 75.

perhaps it is! Before we appraise it from the Christian perspective, we must inquire into the intricate relationship between politics and morality.

Politics and Morality

One of the most baffling and perplexing considerations for the Christian activist is the relationship between politics and morality. Which issues are moral concerns and which are simply political? At the outset let us forward the thesis that every political issue is ipso facto moral. Every political choice has moral ramifications, even those that appear to deal only with resources, property, regulation of commerce, construction of facilities, and other impersonal matters. But the ultimate concern of politics is people, and decisions affect human society for good or ill. The ultimate criterion for choosing among political options is how each option would affect human society as a whole or some group within society. One of the most important tenets of Biblical faith is that no aspect of our lives, including national and international affairs, is beyond the concern of God or exempt from the scrutiny of conscience. No nation can be truly Christian that relegates national and international affairs to the category of politics alone. To evaluate any issue of public policy apart from its moral rightness or wrongness is to abdicate the responsibility of Christian stewardship. On the other hand, Christians who are involved in the political process have a reservoir of Biblical heritage and insight upon which to draw when making decisions.

Conversely, every issue of social morality is ipso facto political. Human beings by nature are social creatures. We are unwilling and unable to live in total isolation from one another, but we also are unable to live with others without conflict. This is in large part because the supply of power and material resources is less than the individual and collective demand. Communities search for methods to resolve these conflicts, to make possible cooperation and fellowship on some level. Man is no longer simply a social being but, of necessity, a political being in the broadest sense. If conflicts are to be adjusted satisfactorily, the community must delegate authority to some individuals or groups to secure—and if necessary compel —a resolution. While we may endlessly debate what form of government is best or upon what philosophy our civil law should be based, human communities seem never to have existed apart from political institutions of some kind.

It is important to remember that political issues do not have the same degree of moral relevance. A bill to end some kind of racial discrimination has more moral ramifications than does one that determines the route of a new interstate highway through a city. The latter may well have moral overtones, especially if the new highway were to displace underprivileged, inner-city residents and fail to provide other housing.

The point should be clear. Politics and morality are insolubly married, but the relationship between the two is intricate and complex. Neither we citizens nor our chosen representatives are infinite or omniscient. We are subject to the same biases, prejudices, short-sightedness, and self-interest as are the rest of the human family. One human being can never judge another and be absolutely certain that his judgment is correct, fair, and complete, and this uncertainty is multiplied many times over in the realm of political judgments. No legislature is fully wise, fully perceptive. A bill may be widely acclaimed when it becomes law, but it may spawn unforeseen harm. The task of legislating is actually a combination of reason and faith. We trust that in the immediate and distant future our political decisions will be carefully thought out and will not be counterproductive. Fortunately for Americans, our Constitution is sufficiently vague on enough points to have required relatively few amendments. But the vast number of laws our Congress and statehouses have rescinded or replaced testifies not only to rapid social growth and moral transition but also to human shortcomings and ignorance.

The moral questions raised by great political issues are seldom if ever easy to answer. Issues like war and depression bear intensely upon the consciousness and livelihood of even the least politically motivated citizens, and we tend to see them in terms of a single moral principle. We disdain moral complexity and long for the comfort of simplicity. But several moral precepts, or at least several values and goods, may be in mutual juxtaposition. The wise and prudent leader or citizen is aware that not all principles and values can be served at once. He sometimes finds himself in a dilemma that cannot be solved with any overriding moral criterion; valid moral objections may be raised against any particular proposal. The Civil War is a case in point. We have already noted Abraham Lincoln's anguish over two objectives, both morally relevant—the preservation of the then-fragile Union and the abolition of slavery. He decided the former to be the more important goal, and while this decision was attacked by radical abolitionists, it was consistent with Lincoln's primary concern as chief executive, the protection of the national interest. There is no serious ethical flaw in his reasoning, merely because he did not seek to achieve both goals simultaneously.

Essential to sound decisions in the political sphere, as in the ecclesiastical and the educational, is a practical wisdom that includes both a commitment to great objectives and a tactical resourcefulness that cannot be grasped fully in moral terms. With the perspective of hindsight we can see that competing objectives are not far apart morally. But intelligence and prudence may dictate that we reconcile two valid morals. Certainly we should serve all moral principles at the same time whenever possible and practical. But, again, this is most difficult, and the man of wisdom is also prudent in resolving conflict; he is aware that conscientious men and women of equal moral sensitivity may differ about moral priorities, and he makes his decisions only after carefully considering the facts and perspectives others bring to bear on the issue. Politics is the art of compromise and the art of the possible.

Political Moralism

The immense difficulty in perceiving the intricate relationship between political and moral issues gives rise to another problem that has plagued Christians especially—political moralism. We have traditionally been a part of American politics. A number of our distinguished officials have approached political questions from an avowedly Christian perspective. Woodrow Wilson, who stirred idealism among millions of people at home and abroad, contended that states should adhere to New Testament principles of individual morality. When asking Congress in 1917 to declare war, Wilson declared: "We are at the beginning of an age in which it will be insisted that the same standards of conduct and responsibility for wrong done shall be observed among nations and their governments that are observed among the individual citizens of civilized states." Eisenhower's secretary of state, John Foster Dulles, condemned as "immoral" those nations whose foreign policies were conducted without regard to "principles." "The broad principles that should govern our international conduct are not obscure," Dulles stated. "They grow out of the practice by the nations of the simple things

Christ taught."[4] When Franklin Roosevelt forwarded his conception of the "four freedoms"(one of which was freedom to worship God) in an address on January 6, 1941, he appealed to the idealism of the Allied nations.

What is political moralism? Moralism is a cheap imitation of genuine morality, using moral, even Biblical, symbols and language, and even projecting moral and noble aims. "Political moralizing," wrote Gene E. Rainey, "is phrasing solutions to problems (and sometimes the problems themselves) with terms commonly associated with theology. The time-honored vocabulary of politics is rejected; as a result, 'compromise,' 'pressure,' 'persuasion,' and similar jargon are shunted aside. In addition, value judgments abound."[5] Preachers who discuss political issues frequently moralize, and this in turn influences the laity to give political issues a moralistic slant. The preacher who argues that the conversion of Communist Party leaders is the prerequisite for world peace has fallen prey to the casuistry of moralism. Moralists tend to prefer symbolic actions to substantive politics. They agitate for particular legislation or a certain foreign policy not so much to influence events on behalf of the national interest but to register publicly virtuous attitudes. For example, note the attempts of both the Right and the Left to make recognition of Communist China an instrument of ethical approval of Chinese internal affairs.

Do Americans really convert all political issues into moral issues? The evidence seems contradictory. Many have argued that Americans possess a hearty crusading spirit and are quick to jump on the bandwagon for any new and exciting cause that comes along. "The 'morality' that the American religious tradition produces has not been any cool, calm ethic of a Confucius or of wisdom literature," concluded William Lee Miller. "It has rather been passionate, zealous, full of fervor. It has been surcharged with emotion and filled with the drama of conversion and revival."[6] The history of organized religion's response in America to societal malaise has in-

---

4. The Wilson and Dulles quotes are taken from the thoughtful article by Arthur Schlesinger, Jr., "The Necessary Amorality of Foreign Affairs," *Harper's Magazine*, August 1971, pp. 72-77. Some response in religious circles to Schlesinger's article was published in the symposium "Morality and Foreign Affairs," *Theology Today* 28 (1972): 486ff.

5. "Political Extremism and Political Moralizing," *Kerygma* 1, no. 1, p. 21.

6. "American Religious and Political Attitudes," in James Ward Smith and A. Leland Jamison, eds., *Religious Perspectives in American Culture* (Princeton: Princeton University, 1961), pp. 111, 112.

cluded protracted forays against such evils as slavery, sweatshops, and demon rum, and both for and against wars.

On the other hand, there is evidence that many Americans prefer to compartmentalize their religion, politics, business, and social lives. Political issues are simply that—political issues. Many of these people may be overreacting to the excessive moralism of others. But most others must be refusing to come to grips with the moral dimensions and demands of the situation. Millions dismissed the My Lai massacre as simply "war" and the Watergate scandals as "politics as usual." People grow extremely uncomfortable when asked to appraise issues on moral grounds. Several aspirants to public office have concluded that it is hazardous to approach great national issues from a moral standpoint. In an interview shortly after his crushing defeat for the presidency in 1972, Senator George McGovern said: "I would have to warn any future presidential candidate that regardless of how clear the moral imperatives might be to him, it is highly risky to assume that drawing an issue sharply in moral terms will win majority support. It might even repel large numbers of people who don't want to be disturbed in their lethargy and apathy and who prefer not to feel conscience-stricken about what the nation is doing."[7]

Both ideas are partially correct. Americans do tend to be utopians, idealists, and moralists. On the other hand, they are quite selective in what issues they will translate into moral concerns. They prefer issues characterized by simplicity and human drama, issues connected with certain preconceived moral laws and principles (such as "rugged individualism") rather than issues with significant sociopolitical implications or with historical importance. We may generalize that Americans who challenge the status quo are more likely to speak in moralistic terms than those who defend it. In the twentieth century there has been a notable difference in what the various Protestant churches have made moral issues. Liberal Protestants have worked to end racial discrimination, to gain voting rights and open housing, and to end the Vietnam war. Conservative and fundamentalist Christians have fought pornography and sexual obscenity, horseracing, gambling, and liquor-by-the-drink. The emphasis of both groups is needed. Conservative obsession with personal piety has resulted in acquiescence in the status quo with respect to much of social morality and human rights. Liberal con-

7. From an exclusive interview in *Christian Century*, 31 January 1973, p. 122.

centration on social morality has led not only to instances of excessive involvement in partisan politics but to the neglect of matters relating to individual piety, which do indeed relate to Christian living and help set standards of public morality.

Dangers of Moralism

The American proclivity for moralism is understandable and may indeed be a sign of our society's health. Man is, as Aristotle said, a social and political animal; but man is also a moral being who cannot eschew moral judgments. Even the most self-seeking individual finds it necessary to at least pretend to others and himself that his political activity is part of a consistent, total scheme of good and value. Each of us contends (some correctly, some not) that he pursues values and goals that transcend narrow self-interest. Commitment to the good is ennobling. When we only pretend to have it we deceive ourselves, and we perpetuate this delusion with moralism. Three specific dangers of moralism merit mention.

First, political moralism is based upon and perpetuates a sense of moral superiority or, if you will, self-righteousness. Political moralists convert their stances on current issues into moral absolutes. They characterize their opponents not simply as mistaken or unwise but as immoral. Their opponents neither know nor love the truth. They alone, or their party alone, possess the truth. "So, my friends, the reason why the American people are going to reject our opponents and are going to elect us is that we fight for the truth, and the people know the truth, because the people live the truth and it (cheers and applause) . . ."[8] These are the words of candidate Richard M. Nixon at a political rally in Herald Square six days before the 1960 election. In 1972 Nixon's third opponent in a presidential election, Senator McGovern, engaged excessively in the same kind of moralism, and, right or wrong, the great majority of Americans rejected his view of political issues and morality.[9]

Moral absolutism may strike and wreak havoc at any point along the political spectrum. No candidate, no political party, and neither the Right nor the Left has a monopoly on virtue and wisdom. Since

8. Quoted in Theodore H. White, *The Making of the President, 1960* (New York: Pocket, 1961), p. 365.

9. For an interesting analysis of morality and moralism in the 1972 presidential campaign, see Rainey, "Moralizing, Politics, and the 1972 Election," *Mission* 6 (1972): 99-105.

moral men seek to justify their deeds with moral reasons, as we noted, all are continually tempted to invest their aspirations, interests, and conduct with ultimate, ethical meaning. Once they offer a partisan policy to their public with a "Thus saith the Lord," they close their minds to alternative policies. The omnipresent danger of political moralism is that it ends up in fanaticism, and the fanatic, as Mr. Dooley put it, "does what he thinks th' Lord wud do if He only knew th' facts in th' case."

During the process of moral self-aggrandizement, one loses the Christian sense of humility that is at the heart of human compassion and restraint. There is a time to be morally indignant and a time to acquiesce in human shortcomings and honest differences of opinion. Herbert Butterfield, after observing that "moral indignation corrupts the agent who possesses it and is not calculated to reform the man who is the object of it," made the necessary point: "The passing of what purports to be a moral judgment—particularly a judgment which amounts to the assertion that they are worse men than I am—is not merely irrelevant, but actually immoral and harmful." It is "really a demand for an illegitimate form of power. The attachment to it is based on its efficacy as a tactical weapon, its ability to rouse irrational fervour and extraordinary malevolence against some enemy."[10] While there is a time for moral indignation (and quite often it has been in short supply), Christians are wise to reflect on Jehovah's question to the prophet Jonah, who had attempted to run ahead of the will of God: "Doest thou well to be angry?" (Jonah 4:4 KJV). Or, as Robert Gordis put it, "moralizing is not an excess of morality, but a deficiency of morality, the lack either of intelligence or of honesty."[11]

Michael Novak reminded us of the useful distinction between moralism and moral inspiration. Political candidates, not to mention army sergeants, athletic coaches, corporation executives, college professors, parents, religious instructors, team captains, and even doctors and psychiatrists, must inspire their followers. Such moral inspiration draws upon resources already *in* others and convinces them that they are becoming more fully themselves, developing their full potential. "Conversely, moralism speaks *down* to others, exhorting them to some supposedly higher but alien self." Novak noted that McGovern's campaign for the White House

10. Quoted in Schlesinger, "Foreign Affairs," p. 74.

11. *Religion and International Responsibility* (New York: Council on Religion and International Affairs, 1959), p. 16.

failed, in large part, because the challenger gave many Americans the impression that he was preaching down to them, exhorting them to a higher but alien and impractical plateau. He no longer spoke as one of the people, he condescended to them.[12] People can live with their own moralizing, but they find it intolerable in others.

Much of our discussion of political moralism has centered in domestic politics, but moralism probably has been more rampant and certainly is more dangerous in international affairs. In the last chapter we noted the nation's proclivity toward self-righteousness. Suffice it to say here that comparatively few problems in international politics call for unequivocal ethical approval or disapproval. Whenever moralism has intruded into foreign policy, the root cause is, once again, pride. The critic who judges most foreign policy issues according to moral criteria may presume that he knows better than others what is best for other nations. Our early involvement in the Vietnamese conflict was defended on moral grounds, and after the war had dragged on for a decade it was criticized on moral grounds. The more passionately zealots believe in their cause and the more they sense that their crusade is succeeding, the more likely they are to reject compromise and seek final vindication and victory for their principles. They slough off criticism and pursue their policies with unqualified zeal.[13]

Other dangers of political moralism are its tendencies to corrupt language and to foster a view of man and society that obstructs more than it aids the resolution of problems. A basic strain of puritanical morality has been the Manichean world view, or a two-valued orientation to all problems. There is a fundamental difference between right and wrong; the right must be supported, the wrong must be suppressed, and error and evil have no rights against the truth. The only problem is that man is finite; only God is infinite, and only He can see in absolute terms what must remain to us matters of probability and contingency.

The propensity to see things as all white and all black is most evident, and perhaps most disastrous, in foreign affairs. Allies and

12. *Choosing Our King* (New York: Macmillan, 1974), p. 102.

13. J. William Fulbright has dealt with this theme in a number of his writings. See *The Arrogance of Power* (New York: Vintage, 1966) and *The Crippled Giant* (New York: Random, 1972). A history of recent American foreign policy by a Christian political scientist is John M. Swomley, Jr., *American Empire: The Political Ethics of Twentieth-Century Conquest* (New York: Macmillan, 1970). See also Henry S. Commager, "A Historian Looks at Political Morality," *Saturday Review*, 10 July 1965, pp. 16-18.

enemies cannot be gray; they must be either black or white. Once we make that distinction with confidence, then, to borrow from the title of an old book by Barry Goldwater, "Why not victory?" The cold-war years provide the most glaring evidence of this attitude. Many sermons, articles, and tracts "preached" the "gospel" of anticommunism. They were heavily documented. Renegades from the enemy were specially honored for their exposés. In hindsight we can see it would have been more rational to expose the error of the communists' moral absolutism, the danger of their official godlessness, and the emptiness of their dream of the ultimate revolution and the utopian society. Instead we identified our political and economic institutions with the good and the communists' with the evil, and then told citizens to choose between good and evil, God and the Devil. Church leaders too easily aligned themselves with the radical Right's moralistic anticommunism, and this made impossible any real openness to nations whose historical and sociological situation was entirely different from ours.[14] Frozen attitudes accounted in large measure for the frustration and agony of the Vietnam experience. "A nation that crusades for moral ideas that are not supported by national interest," declared John C. Bennett, "is likely to throw its weight around too much."[15]

Moralism also corrupts language, and the corruption of language leads to the corruption of thoughts and attitudes. Irving Kristol perceived two traditions in American public address—the prophetic-utopian tradition, which has always been more popular, and the constitutional-legal tradition, which supplied the rhetoric for official occasions like presidential messages and congressional debates and for official documents like treaties and Supreme Court decisions.[16] Utopian-moralistic rhetoric (exemplified in the hypothetical speech opening this chapter) now seems to predominate. As we become further removed chronologically from the founding fathers, our rhetoric about foreign affairs becomes more windy, lofty, and high-flown, and less sensible, realistic, and forthright. Double talk is now the accepted jargon for American politics. John Kennedy's inaugural, which committed America to "pay any price,

---

14. For further study on the churches and the radical Right, see Daniel Bell, ed., *The Radical Right* (Garden City, N.Y.: Doubleday, 1963), and Richard Hofstadter, *The Paranoid Style in American Politics* (New York: Vintage, 1967).

15. *Moral Tensions in International Affairs* (New York: Council on Religion and International Affairs, 1964), p. 15.

16. In "A Foolish American 'Ism'—Utopianism."

bear any burden, meet any hardship, support any friend, or oppose any foe in order to assure the survival and success of liberty," is an example of such loftiness. This may flatter and soothe the citizenry, but it also widens the credibility gap, making it even more difficult to bridge. Our more cautious historians must record for posterity not what our statesmen have said but, as well as it can be determined, what they have meant.

Many examples could be cited. Our youth would have much more respect for diplomatic decisions to collude with rightist governments, even military dictatorships, if they were justified in terms of defending not liberty and freedom but the current national interest. For one generation of political partisans to base their careers on a fervid anticommunism that denounces moderates on this issue as unpatriotic and traitorous, and then to visit the Chinese mainland, announce the dawn of a new diplomatic era, and call it a "journey for peace" is to turn a moralistic somersault. Finite man has no absolute assurance that what his nation does in one part of the world will not ignite tensions and conflict elsewhere. Détente with the People's Republic of China will likely be the single greatest achievement of the Nixon administration, but it should have sold the venture as an end to the extremism and hostility of the past in recognition of changing conditions in the present and in calculated hopes for peace and progress in the future. How much of the disillusionment over Vietnam was because the war had been oversold?

A third danger of political moralism, and very much related to the other two, is that it retards needed social and political progress. Moralism disguises the moralists' power base and betrays the best interests of its own constituencies. Moralism masks self-interest gone amok and serves the purposes only of special individuals and groups. The thrust of Biblical theology is clear: fallen man cannot help but sin against his fellow men; he may be able to minimize it but he cannot eliminate it. No political action is completely free from the taint of egotism, which, out of pride or self-deception, claims for the sponsor more than his due. In this sense, politics and Christian ethics are uncomfortable bedfellows. Man's quest for power over other men and resources, which is the essence of the exercise of political power, points away from the very core of Biblical faith. Politics all too easily exploits man as an object. The man of God respects man as an end in himself.

No obstacle to social justice is greater than self-righteous hardness, which encapsulates the conscience of the strong and mighty against the claims of the weak and exploited. No nationalism is more destructive than that which is hardened by spiritual pride. Nothing is more ruthless than the powerful who are absolutely certain that they alone know what is best for themselves and others and, possessing this coveted key to peace and justice, feel a God-given responsibility to impose their will on others. This has been one of the most destructive elements of twentieth-century political communism; communists have sincerely believed that they alone have the key to history and human betterment and that all opponents are obstacles to be rendered powerless or removed.

Such absolutism has been kept out of American politics by our marvelous constitutional system. But pride and self-interest are always with us, and they unconsciously influence our political decisions and our dealings with other groups. A look at the political views of some American moralizers should clarify the point. Most moralizers attempt to solve problems or answer questions not through rigorous analysis or meaningful inquiry but through simplistic moral remedies sometimes based on distorted moral principles. The resulting moral jargon, as we just noted, obfuscates the issues. Political moralizers are too passive to analyze anything meaningfully. Consider their relatively expense-free solutions to the problem of escalating crime in the sixties and seventies. To curb juvenile delinquency parents must exercise more physical discipline and send their children to Sunday school and worship services (never mind that many culturally deprived children are not certain who their parents are or that many parents do not know where or what the nearest church building is). To control adult crime we should impose stiffer jail sentences and return to capital punishment (never mind that the majority of lawbreakers are not even apprehended), and we need a larger and freer police force. Punishment is to be just that—punishment. Rehabilitation programs are generally discounted. Individualism is so rooted in American ideology that most moralists have little time to look at socio-economic conditions such as inferior housing and education, discrimination in employment, racism, and urban frustration and to consider their contributions to violent crime. After all, America is a land of great opportunity, and each person can pull himself up by the bootstraps if he will. Urban renewal and rehabilitation programs have always been a tax burden on the well-to-do. And gun control, to the moralist, is no solution at all. After all, guns do not kill people, people do.

The moralist generally abhors welfare. The introduction of the welfare state through the New Deal is both the cause and result of moral decay. The essence of the Puritan work ethic, "He who does not work should not eat," is universally valid. But the fact escapes the political moralist that the great majority of welfare recipients, at least until the recession of the mid-seventies, were children, aged people, and mothers; less than one percent were able-bodied males.[17] To the moralist, welfare reform means the abolition of welfare. Responsible individuals, churches, and local authorities can fulfill the responsibilities of society to those less fortunate and thus remove the heavy financial burden from the federal government. Besides, welfare pays poor women to have more babies and entices their men to cease looking for one of the many available jobs.

The doctrinaire moralist could continue. Modern art and sex education in public schools are part of the communist conspiracy to destroy the morals of youth and cause America to collapse into the arms of the enemy. Social security and public convalescent homes have destroyed respect for Biblically enjoined commands to honor aged parents. Network television news departments, influenced by the communists, can bring any administration to its knees. The moralist who is really concerned about property valuation, social prestige, and the like may be intelligent and moral enough to know that he should not support programs that sustain segregation in a neighborhood, but he is uncomfortable with and angry at anyone who reminds him of it. If the moralist is doing better than his neighbors through tax write-offs, tax shelters, and tax loopholes, he may know something is amiss but he does not want to be reminded that reform is based on the principles of justice and fairness. To adapt a Scripture verse for our purpose, the moralist "has a form of morality, but denies the power thereof."

In conclusion, awareness of the phenomenon of political moralism is three-fourths of the battle to eliminate it. Since Americans appropriate the symbols of morality from the Bible, we should take its injunctions more seriously. As difficult as it may be, we must apply Paul's dictum "Each esteem others better than self" and Jesus' Golden Rule more rigorously when making decisions that

---

17. Reo M. Christenson, *Challenge and Decision*, 3rd ed. (New York: Harper and Row, 1970), p. 155.

relate to the larger communities of which we are members. And before judging between political options, we should listen with special attentiveness to the views and judgments of our political enemies. Our pride and hostility blind us too frequently, especially to our opponents' strengths. We need to recall an often recited aphorism of Reinhold Niebuhr: "In my truth is bound to be some error; in his error, some truth." Are we honest and humble enough to concede that our opponents perceive more of our collective interests than we want to admit?

Our country! In her intercourse with foreign nations may she always be right; but our country, right or wrong!

Stephen Decatur

I would remind my countrymen that they are men first, and Americans at a late and convenient hour.

Henry David Thoreau

The flag is a simple symbol, half a lie and half true; more of a promise than a reality. Its respect must be elicited, not commanded; the love of what it means must be given, never forced. When the flag becomes a fetish, we're on our way to a tyranny that all patriots must resist.

Howard Moody

Patriotism is the last refuge of a scoundrel.

Samuel Johnson

The more we indulge in uncritical reverence for the supposed wisdom of the American way of life, the more odious we make it in the eyes of the world, the more we destroy our moral authority.

Reinhold Niebuhr

. . . Proclaim liberty throughout all the land unto all the inhabitants thereof. . . .

(Lev. 25:10 KJV)

chapter eleven

New Testament Christianity and the Spirit of '76

July 4, 1776—the most memorable date in American history. A fact that eludes most Americans is that the official act by which the Continental Congress separated the states from Great Britain passed on July 2. This act was a resolution that had been submitted June 7, 1776, by Richard Henry Lee on behalf of the Virginia delegation. It declared that "these United Colonies are, and of right ought to be, free and independent states, that they are absolved from all allegiance to the British Crown, and that all political connection between them and the State of Great Britain is, and ought to be, totally dissolved." The document popularly known as the Declaration of Independence was drafted by a special committee, submitted to the Congress on June 28, and, with modifications, accepted by the Congress on July 4. Its primary purpose was not so much to declare independence as to proclaim to the world the reasons for having already declared independence. It was an ex post facto justification of a radical act.[1] Nowhere in the document is the word *nation*, and the ensuing war was to secure not nationhood but independence.

---

1. Two interesting and worthwhile studies of the Declaration of Independence are Carl L. Becker, *The Declaration of Independence: A Study in the History of Political Ideas* (New York: Vintage, 1942) and Robert Ginsberg, ed., *A Casebook on the Declaration of Independence* (New York: Crowell, 1967).

The actions of the delegates to the Continental Congress culminated in the birth of a nation, and each July 4 we celebrate the birthday of this relatively young nation. It has come a long way in just two centuries. By the nation's centennial it had survived the great Constitutional crisis brought on by western expansion, the conflict between nationalism and sectionalism that culminated in bloody civil strife, and the trials of radical Reconstruction. Philadelphia was the center for celebration in 1876. The great attractions at the national fair were Alexander Graham Bell's remarkable invention, the telephone, and the massive, forty-foot-high Corliss steam engine that epitomized the America of 1876—a country moving rapidly from an agrarian society to an industrialized one, and proud of it. The engine was located in the center of Machinery Hall, surrounded like an altar by rows of glistening locomotives, Singer sewing machines, and Pullman berths. On the lighter side, a young man named Charles Hires peddled a new carbonated drink that was to become a favorite among children. He called it "root beer."

By the time our bicentennial rolled around, Americans were uncertain just where and how to celebrate it. Some worried about the commercialism and vulgarity connected with the celebration, and about the lack of a single unifying theme. But our attitudes toward the bicentennial differed in more important respects from our approach to milestones in the past. In the 1960s and early 1970s, attitudes toward the nation and patriotism began to change, particularly for young citizens. A survey of youth in 1974 quantified a dramatic drop in patriotic fervor: forty percent of noncollege youth and only nineteen percent of college youth (as compared with sixty and thirty-five, respectively, in 1969) considered patriotism "a very important value."[2] Some even hate America and what it stands for. They spell it *amerika* because of the fascism and imperialism they perceive in our system. Others are ashamed of their country. They no longer claim that it is the greatest country in which to live. Once it was considered a great honor to enlist in the armed forces and to wear a military uniform in public; seldom is this true today. The number of military schools in this country has dropped dramatically, and several of those still operating are struggling to survive. To be identified as American in a foreign land embarrasses many tourists. To a great many Americans, our

---

2. *Time*, 3 June 1974, p. 46.

nation is simply failing to live up to our historical and traditional utopian expectations.

Christian spokesmen have at times been numbered in this group of disappointed and disillusioned Americans. An excess of patriotism, they argue, has been at the root of many of our national shortcomings. The definition of *patriotism* from that flamboyant naval officer, Stephen Decatur—"my country right or wrong"—has gained too wide an acceptance. Such a definition is untenable on moral grounds; it is a vicious jingoism. But right or wrong morally, these spokesmen note, it is true that an overwhelming majority of Americans are loyal to their country no matter what happens.

Just as many Christian spokesmen argue conversely. To them we have not been patriotic enough in recent times, and this deficiency is the fundamental cause of our troubles at home and abroad. American ideals are no longer furthered, and our flag is not granted its due respect. The solution is to instill the ideals and values of Americanism in each rising generation, and to do this some special ceremonies and programs have been created. One was the "Honor America Day" religious service in Washington, D.C., on July 4, 1970; Billy Graham delivered the keynote address on "The Unfinished Dream."[3] It is appropriate for us to ask, What is patriotism? Can a Christian remain faithful to his calling and pledge allegiance to a civil state, or are the two irreconcilable and incompatible?

Patriotism Reexamined

What is patriotism? First, we should emphasize that patriotism is not merely the celebration of certain rituals or the exhibition of external symbols. Perhaps no other nation is as steeped in patriotic fervor, affirmation, and symbolism. What other nation demands a pledge of allegiance daily? Where else do they plaster automobile windows and bumpers, clothing, and decorative posters with varying representations of the flag. But, then, where else do they burn their nation's flag or mock their national anthem. One must not judge another's patriotism and devotion to his country by his participation in public rites and symbolic behavior. Not all patriotism is genuine; homage to the shibboleths and goals of a nation can be mere lip service. Jesus recognized that the man who prays the loudest and beats his breast the hardest may be the least committed. Nationalism produces its own special breed of pharisee.

---

3. The text of this address is in *Christianity Today*, 31 July 1970, pp. 20, 21.

Nor must the symbols of the fatherland become the exclusive possession of a single group or party within the nation. They belong to all the people. In our recent past the fifty stars came to signify, for many blacks, so many stations of racism. To the poor, to anti-war demonstrators, and to the other disaffected minorities the Pledge of Allegiance became the opposite of the truth—"one nation divisible, with liberty and justice for some." The flag came to represent entrenched majorities, WASPs, the Establishment, and the status quo. It did not represent the poor, blacks, Indians, war protesters, environmentalists, and dissenters in general. Citizens who displayed the flag were stereotyped as staunch supporters of the war in Vietnam. This put flag wavers constantly on the defensive. "In case you see a flag on my porch," wrote Brooks Atkinson, "don't jump to the conclusion that I think American imperialism is nobler than the imperialism of other nations."[4]

An ever-present danger is that the flag is too often associated with conflict and violence. Something about war seems to justify using the flag to support it; the literature of war is replete with waving banners, and, of course, in the national anthem the American flag is gallantly streaming "o'er the ramparts." In January 1973 the director of the U.S. Olympic Invitational Track Meet announced that "The Star-Spangled Banner" would not be played at the meet. After receiving telephone calls from irate citizens across the country, he announced that he would be "delighted to continue the custom" of playing the anthem. Then twenty New York City councilmen introduced a bill of dubious constitutionality that made it unlawful to "commence any sporting event . . . without first playing the national anthem."[5] But does it make sense to play the anthem and have armed color bearers present the flag prior to football games and boxing matches, but not before plays, movies, lectures, concerts, and poetry festivals? Is there an inherent link between sports and partiotism? It may well be that patriotic symbols have been used (and exploited) too exclusively by advocates of violence. Recall Guy de Maupassant's remark that patriotism is "the egg from which wars are hatched." The anthem and flag, being appropriate to the warlike spirit, are equally appropriate to sports, which emphasize the instinct of combat and the will to win. Even "noncontact sports" extol competition and the pursuit of victory,

---

4. "Flagwaving," *New Republic*, 14 February 1970, p. 14.

5. *Nashville Tennessean*, 19 January 1973; *Time*, 29 January 1973, p. 24.

including the individual heroism and team spirit that are evoked in wartime. But true patriots must reaffirm that the flag celebrates the common experience of all Americans. No one should use the flag to promote his own interests, causes, and beliefs.

Patriotism, then, is essentially a matter of conviction and attitude. It is no less a matter of one's heartfelt emotions. Leonard W. Doob defined *patriotism* as "the more or less conscious conviction of a person that his own welfare and that of the significant groups to which he belongs are dependent upon the preservation or expansion (or both) of the power and culture of his society."[6] Patriotism is universal since people are always socialized in groups, one of which is certain to be recognized for its own distinctive culture; and people come to associate distinctiveness and welfare with their society. Each community feels itself unique and inherently superior to the other communities in its social environment—there are always "Greeks" and "barbarians." Patriotism appears to be the inevitable companion of sentiments of solidarity in human groups. Garry Wills called patriotism "the bond of social affections." The phenomenon is nothing modern; certainly as far back as recorded history men have felt what we feel for the places and people which belong to us and to which we belong. All of our loyalties begin with the people and the places that are closest and dearest to us. And while there is something immature about a man or woman who spends all his time pining for his childhood days and home, we feel a certain sadness for a man who does not have a special place in his heart for his birthplace and home country.

True patriotism is a continuing and legitimate love affair with a set of principles, with a common vision of the good life. A man without aspirations is not a whole man. A society without a shared vision of its potential is a desolate one, lacking vitality and cohesiveness. Patriotism in America is too often a holiday phenomenon— evoked only by the flag, a tune, or an oration. But citizens whose patriotism is genuine and deep perceive on numerous occasions a connection between their nation and their blessings at home, at work, and at leisure.

We must emphasize that patriotism is not a forced conformity to a single party, faction, ideology, or manner of behavior. Nor is it blind loyalty to any group currently in power. Many holders of

---

6. *Patriotism and Nationalism* (New Haven: Yale University, 1964), p. 6.

power urge a loyalty that amounts to conformity, an uncritical and unquestioning acceptance of America as it is—the political institutions, the elected representatives and their practices, the social relationships, and the economic policies. The patriotic citizen-servant is to obey orders without question and to the letter: "Theirs is not to reason why; theirs is but to do and die." This philosophy is stated even more simply on a bumper sticker that is widely used: "America—Love It or Leave It." Taken at face value it is difficult to fault that sentiment. But American dissenters, possessing a considerable measure of native intelligence, know perfectly well what most people who exhibit such stickers mean. They mean just what the stolid-faced burghers of the Church of England would have meant had they pasted on the back of a coach-and-four, stickers that read, "England—Love It or Leave It"—"Conform, brother. Conform to what we think, or get out."

But coerced patriotism is a counterfeit, just as forced loyalty is the very antithesis of genuine loyalty. Patriotism cannot be imposed by a party or administration in power. It is a condition elicited by the quality of an individual's or a people's behavior. If we are to find true and concrete meaning in patriotism, we must root it once again in the individual's own conscience and beliefs. Allegiance and genuine affection develop in the giver (the citizenry) when merited by the receiver (the governmental authorities). This affection and allegiance must not be manipulated by unscrupulous or cowardly leaders. Patriotism in our heritage is more a commitment to a certain view of man and a way of living together than it is to a certain group of people and a piece of geography.

Patriotism must in no way be pitted against individualism. Let no one, be he president or dogcatcher, assume that he has been especially anointed to define orthodox Americanism. When the Supreme Court overturned an earlier ruling that had allowed public schools to make saluting the flag compulsory, Justice Jackson held that the freedoms of speech and conscience imply the freedom not to express oneself, either verbally or, as when saluting the national flag, symbolically. Stressing the futility of trying to compel conformity, Jackson warned that "those who begin coercive elimination of dissent soon find themselves exterminating dissenters. Compulsory unification of opinion achieves only the unanimity of the graveyard." He concluded: "If there is any fixed star in our constitutional constellation, it is that no official, high or petty, can prescribe what shall be orthodox in politics, nationalism, religion, or other matters of opinion or force citizens to confess by word or act their faith therein."[7]

Patriotism constitutes loyalty to the best of the commonwealth and may require opposition to particular policies of the government or particular institutions of society. The Christian patriot may work and pray for the defeat of a certain officeholder or his policies. While in the United States Dietrich Bonhoeffer wrote Reinhold Niebuhr that he would have to return to his German homeland, adding: "Christians in Germany will face the terrible alternative of either willing the defeat of their nation in order that Christian civilization may survive or of willing the victory of their nation and thereby destroying our civilization. I know which of these alternatives I must choose, but I cannot make that choice in security."[8] We may cringe at words like *Christian civilization,* but Bonhoeffer realized the stakes. As a Christian and a patriot, he returned to resist, and it cost him his life. Were the Christians who prayed for America to abandon its purposes and policies in Vietnam, and even for its forces to be defeated, unpatriotic? Vietnam and Nazi Germany certainly are not analogous. But at least we should love our country enough not to allow it to escape the tragic Southeast Asian experience of the past decade before it learns some difficult, searing lessons and reorders its priorities.

All of this underscores the thesis that true patriotism and political loyalty are neither incompatible nor inconsistent with Christian faith and commitment. Scripture even makes political loyalty a religious duty. Jesus instructed the Pharisees: "Render therefore unto Caesar the things which are Caesar's. . . ." (KJV). Paul wrote to the church in Rome: "Let every person be subject to the governing authorities. For there is no authority except from God, and those that exist have been instituted by God" (RSV). The apostle Peter proclaimed: "Honour all men. . . . Fear God. Honour the king" (KJV). And "the king" was the Roman emperor. Since our nation is a republic instead of a monarchy, this verse could more relevantly read, "Honor the nation."

Love of country is no less noble a virtue for Christians than for those outside the community of faith. No city or community is weaker because the members of each of its families—the father, the

---

7. West Virginia State Board of Education v. Barnette, 319 U.S. 624 (1943).

8. Quoted in Reinhold Niebuhr, "The Death of a Martyr," *Christianity and Crisis,* 25 June 1945, p. 6.

mother, the sons, the daughters, and the other kin—are knit together by special ties of respect, admiration, and love. And the family of all nations will not be more fragile or impoverished because those who populate any one nation have a special pride and affection for it and its people.

Paul is usually remembered for his dramatic conversion from militant Judaism to Christianity and for his sacrificial commitment to Christ as an apostle and a missionary. But recall that Paul spoke proudly of his Roman citizenship and cited his civil rights when they were in jeopardy. Neither did he conceal his deep affection for his own people and his pride in their achievements. One of the most inspiring and edifying chapters in the Bible is Hebrews 11, where Paul, if we may assume Pauline authorship, recounted the great deeds of national heroes, faithful and obedient men and women from all walks of life. Then he admonished Hebrew Christians: "And what of ourselves? With all these witnesses to faith around us like a cloud, we must throw off every encumbrance, every sin to which we cling, and run with resolution the race for which we are entered" (Heb. 12:1). If by recounting the great heritage of Old Testament men and women Paul could motivate first-century Christians to remain faithful to their calling, should not the Christian citizen feel encompassed by another great "cloud of witnesses" who are observing his conduct and seeking by their spirit to inspire his generation to remain committed to worthy ideals and perform great national and international tasks? If the essence of Christian living is self-denial and service to others, then patriotism for the Christian, while it guards his own liberty and freedom, can never be purely selfish.

So American Christians can be patriots and can speak with pride of the ideals and heritage that have made this country great. Will the time ever come for us to abolish what our forefathers created? Has their vision of liberty, justice for all, and happiness proved unattainable? Do the heroes, the mythoi, and the folk narratives that have bound diverse peoples together as a nation for two centuries no longer enthrall and inspire us? Does our prior allegiance to God inhibit us in our role as citizens? The answers to these questions should be obvious. Christians ought to be the best citizens and the truest patriots. One who loves God can love his country without making it into God, without succumbing to a new idolatry. And the greatness of America is not simply its realization of an ever-elusive ideal, but its unrelenting pursuit of it.

Channeling Patriotic Fervor

Political activism that is spawned by genuine patriotism will enable us to improve our contemporary society, instill pride, and look to the future with confidence. True patriotism is never concerned simply with the past or the status quo. It is unfortunate that many of our patriotic institutions and societies tend to love the past with a love approaching idolatry, tolerate the present, and fear the future and change like a plague. But patriotism is much more than a love affair with what was or is; it is a passionate attachment to what can and must be. How may Christians be patriotic? How should patriotism function and what are its proper limits? We offer four suggestions:

1. Patriotic celebrations should lead us to reflect upon and reevaluate our past and present situation in appreciation and gratitude. We may celebrate the marvelous way in which our system has worked.

Our record includes many blots, and they have been openly evaluated and chronicled in many a journal, newspaper, and book. But much in the American past justifies pride. We should not think our nation is better than other nations, but Americans have demonstrated a concern for citizens of other countries in which we can take pride. Though its motives have not always been noble, America has opened its heart and doors to the persecuted and distressed of the world. Literally millions have crossed our borders to breathe the fresh air of freedom. We have not subjugated alien peoples (except the native American Indian), and we have not exploited colonies. Except in the case of the Mexicans (in the estimation of some historians), we have been magnanimous toward our conquered foes and most generous to other peoples. Witness the outpouring of concern and benevolence in the spring of 1975 for the Vietnamese orphans and refugees who were left homeless by a war in which our nation had been deeply involved. We have shared our wealth and our faith with other peoples, responding, although at times in a piecemeal manner, to victims of floods, hurricanes, earthquakes, and other natural disasters. We have never permitted religious tyranny or class warfare. For the most part we have kept the military subordinate to civilian authority. We have generally conducted our affairs in a glass house. Because of the First Amendment's freedoms of expression, assembly, and press, not just we but the whole world learn about our most difficult, persistent problems. The story of Watergate has been told and retold around the world.

Putting our heritage in this perspective liberates us from the deceitful rhetoric of the New Left and other radicals whose critiques of American society have been in vogue during the last decade. It has been fashionable to deprecate America, to accept half-truths as the truth, and to hail communist dictatorships as "peoples' democracies" and aggressors as "liberators." Terms such as *freedom, peace,* and *justice* have been debased. Pointing to occasional denials of civil rights, police abuses, illegal dossiers, and governmental electronic eavesdropping, these self-appointed critics declare America a police state. Yet no thoughtful American believes that any president could use the police and FBI to attain and retain dictatorial powers. Most police officials perform their duties properly and in subservience to the electorate and local authorities. The police are overridden as often as they are upheld in the courts.

We are told that America is imperialistic. Since the Second World War dozens of new nations have been born, proclaiming their independence loudly and defiantly. In this revolutionary environment America has symbolized the old order. Yet the greater imperialists are the communist powers that spread their influence by violent insurgency. They prefer low-cost guerilla warfare, but the great powers have shown they are willing to resort to naked aggression, as Russia did in Hungary and Czechoslovakia. We cannot ignore Vietnam where we too were an aggressor, but neither should we forget that North Vietnam was a chief aggressor and catalyst.

America's government, critics have argued, is both repressive and racist. Like all governments ours does attempt to control and limit the flow of information to its citizens. But the court system and the First Amendment are great antidotes to political repression. When the Supreme Court upheld the rights of two of the nation's greatest and most powerful newspapers to publish the embarrassing Pentagon Papers, it confirmed that the press is still free. And our "underground press" is not underground at all, but is free to publish without official interference the most revolutionary and offensive invective the radicals can muster.

To our national disgrace, there is much substance to the charge that our nation has been racist. But it is also true that our minorities have enjoyed more rights and greater prosperity than have the minorities in other great nations. The famous *Brown* decision in

1954 launched a not-always-bloodless revolution that has opened many doors of opportunity in all professions to black people. Was it not only a few years ago when we were being chilled and discomfited by such catchwords as "black rage," "black militancy," "black separation," and "black revolution," phrases that connote a hostile race that is still alien after living in this country for three and a half centuries? But after and even during these dramatic and widely publicized clashes, and with little fanfare, black people began making rapid strides toward achieving the American dream and lifting themselves into the middle class. No longer are "black" and "subordinate" necessarily synonymous.[9]

For two centuries our people have upheld the instrumental concept of government—government is not an end in itself, but serves the interests of the nation. In recent years two presidents, a Democrat and a Republican, both with noble purposes and memorable achievements to their credit, were compelled to step down because they were unable to make the same distinction between valid and unlawful uses of power that the nation eventually did. The Vietnam war, its expansion, and its prolongation long after its original purpose was clearly beyond attainment, were "sold" to the American people by the very "best and brightest" officials, in the words of journalist Michael Halberstam. These men were generally honorable and distinguished, but they made political decisions in the light of military criteria rather than vice versa, and they devoutly believed that once the country commits itself to a venture, whether it is right or wrong, wise or foolish, then it is more important to save face than lives. "My country—right or wrong" was the prevailing philosophy.

This approach to loyalty had its sequel in Watergate, which eventually led to the nation's first presidential resignation. By their own admission, those who conceived and then covered up the many and varied acts we call Watergate had put the Nixon presidency in the place of the country. It was then "Our president—right or wrong." Nixon had appointed a committee and announced sessions to plan the forthcoming bicentennial celebration, but in the months that followed it appeared that Watergate would rain on our birthday parade. How could we celebrate the old shibboleths,

9. A journalistic report on the rising middle class may be found in a cover story in *Time*, 17 June 1974, pp. 19-28; it was condensed in *Reader's Digest*, October 1974, pp. 144-48. I am indebted to several columns by Jack Anderson for some illustrations cited in this first point.

the hallowed liberties, when each day's headline broadcasted a new mockery of and disregard for them? Now it is only a source of irony, not shame, that as we commence our third century as a nation, our two highest executive officials have been appointed rather than elected.

But neither Vietnam nor Watergate can spoil future celebrations. For the nation at large, after tasting the sour fruits and coming to grips with the deceptions and faulty premises, determined to discard error even though the flag itself (under the catchall phrase "national security") was often wrapped around it, and to correct wrong even if it embarrasses the nation and disgraces its most cherished office. And so it has. The Republic still stands, older and maturer than other regimes. We have survived two hundred years under laws we collectively established, and we the people have a voice, whether or not it always prevails. We have dealt with each major crisis by democratic methods. Where there is a change in administrations, there are no tanks in the streets, no armored trucks hauling critics to concentration camps. We have trusted the familiar and orderly processes of traditional political institutions and respected the rule of law. We have not, like so many other peoples, succumbed to the easy solutions of rank demagogues, dictators, or revolutionists. One concept that does not die in America—the division of powers—has maintained freedom with order, change with stability, dissent with unity. And a relatively free economic system —itself a model for the world—has brought for millions a decent home and a full table.

Americans of late have been chronic complainers about recession and inflation, but precious few would exchange their personal financial condition with the citizens of any other nation. No one should underestimate the strains and sacrifices faced by unemployed Americans and their families, but no other group of jobless people has been blessed with as many unemployment benefits and as much compensation. We have made gigantic strides in health, education, and welfare. College enrollment doubled between 1960 and 1970; today one in three college-age youths is in college. Urban renewal has revitalized many inner-city districts. And although the cost of health care has skyrocketed, its quality and accessibility has greatly improved, as evidenced by the increase in doctors and hospital beds, the increase in life expectancy, and the declining rate of maternal and infant mortality. Working conditions in factories are greatly improved; there are more white-collar jobs; and for most Americans the work week is shorter, annual vacations are longer, retirement is earlier, and the pension is larger than it was for their ancestors.

2. True patriotism leads Christians to renew their loyalty to America's great ideals, concepts, and institutions, to rise above any commitment to men, factions, and parties. Commitment to ideals is what the American experiment is all about—a commitment to a life together that will enhance the worth and invite the participation of each citizen. This is a great ideal, to be sure, and it has not been fully realized. "The land of the free and the home of the brave" is not a headline, but a hope and a challenge. "Liberty and justice for all" is not a boast, but a desire and a goal.

One problem we Americans have is to take our precious rights and liberties for granted. Perhaps the reason is that "the water is not appreciated until the well runs dry." This reminder should not be dismissed like a July 4 proclamation or an American Legion speech. Russian dissident and writer Mikhail Agursky offered another analogy to make the same point:

> A man who has been accustomed to breathing fresh air all his life does not notice it, and never realizes what a blessing it is. He thinks of it only occasionally when meeting in a stuffy room, but knows that he need only open the window for the air to become fresh again. A man who has grown up in a democratic society and who takes the basic freedoms as much for granted as the air he breathes is in much the same position. People who have grown up under democracy do not value it highly enough.[10]

Agursky noted that democracies are becoming less and less stable because "the influence of religious values [has] declined" and "these societies have lost the basic, valuable first principles of democracy."[11]

One way to enhance our sense of loyalty is to expand our knowledge of our heritage. As our black citizens reached for their legitimate place in our society, it became generally recognized that it is necessary to develop ethnic pride and self-esteem. Thus the burgeoning of college curricula, new books, biographies, plays, and poetry written to enrich black culture and to inform all Americans of the blacks' rich heritage. Many who have agitated for black studies have opposed American studies for all students, black and white, but the principle that knowledge of one's culture and heri-

---

10. In Alexander Solzhenitsyn et al., *From Under the Rubble* (Boston: Little and Brown, 1974), pp. 75, 76.

11. Ibid., pp. 79, 80.

tage renews one's appreciation for and commitment to it operates no less in one instance than in the other.

Two documents require continual study and appreciation. One is the Declaration of Independence—the most widely known and influential secular document in the history of mankind. Formulated during a great debate over the rights of men, the necessity and feasibility of revolution, and the obligations of the state and her subjects, this Declaration has been invoked whenever and wherever these issues are raised. As long as men and societies long for freedom, these issues will not, indeed cannot, die. No wonder that historian Henry Commager asserted that the Declaration of Independence has some claim to be the "most subversive document in modern history." If they are taken seriously, its principles—all men are created equal; all have a right to life, liberty, and pursuit of happiness; the chief function of government is to secure these rights for all the governed; and if the government cannot or will not do this, it may be overthrown and replaced—are explosive. The Declaration of Independence is more than a faded parchment in our national archives. It is radically relevant and contemporary. Are not its principles and arguments still valid today? This document is worthy of careful study by those who would understand human events and human ideals.

A document that is equally worthy is the Constitution. The Constitution has never failed us, though during times of national crisis we have often failed to adhere to its spirit. William Gladstone, the great British statesman and prime minister, once described the American Constitution as "the most wonderful work ever struck off at a given time by the brain and purpose of man." Christians may hesitate to accept this evaluation, but we must admit that our Constitution has withstood the most decisive of all tests—time. Written during the Philadelphia Convention of 1787, it is now the oldest written constitution in the world. But its brilliance and relevance for our time do not lie merely in its mechanism for balancing political power and its allocation of sovereignty in terms of federalism. The first ten amendments, or the Bill of Rights, have made America a land of freedom and opportunity. Because we are so frequently tempted to deny or short-cut these liberties, we must reread the Bill of Rights in the light of contemporary challenges. The entire Constitution and the Declaration can be read in a brief sitting.

3. True patriotism leads us to renew our appreciation for all

our human and natural resources. If it is unpatriotic to desecrate the flag, which is a symbol of the country, is it not also unpatriotic to desecrate the countryside itself—to pollute, despoil, and ravage the air, land, and water? Such degradation of the environment makes the "pursuit of happiness" and the promotion of the general welfare ragged indeed.

A number of this nation's superpatriots have openly detested the abuse of the flag. Of course the Supreme Court has found it an onerous task to determine orthodox ways the flag may be used as a symbol. Few protested when prowar advocates used the flag for a lapel button or a bumper sticker, but however antiwar advocates used the flag was generally suspect. Yet the superpatriots who get so concerned about the misuse of the flag are hardly concerned at all about the exploitation and prostitution of our land and its natural resources for private capital gain. But these resources are part of what the flag stands for. The symbol is cherished more than the real thing! Why is not the colossal waste that characterizes so many defense contracts and so much of our life style unpatriotic? True patriotism also will work to expose and terminate any exploitation of minority groups, the poor, the young, the old, and other disadvantaged and powerless people. We have made many positive and encouraging strides in this area in the last decade, but we must make many more.

4. Christians may channel patriotic fervor into developing new and competent leaders from all echelons of society and all walks of life. As we have emphasized, patriotism does not exist for its own sake. The ultimate goal should be to train and inspire bright, young leaders for the future. A renowned student of democracy pointed out that the "effectiveness of democracy depends first and foremost on the efficiency and skill of its leadership."[12]

Perhaps no need seems more pressing now than the one for more competent leadership. "There is a very obvious dearth of people who seem able to supply convincing answers, or even point to directions toward solutions," said Harvard's president, Derek Bok.[13] The problem is not only America's. Abroad there is also a sense of diminished vision, of global problems overwhelming the capacity of leaders. The birth of our nation was attended and facilitated by

---

12. Giovanni Sartori, "Democracy," in *International Encyclopedia of the Social Sciences*, (New York: Macmillan and Free Press, 1968), 4:119.

13. Quoted in *Time*, 15 July 1974, p. 21.

a group of extraordinarily gifted young leaders—Franklin, Jefferson, Washington, Hamilton, Madison, and Adams, to name a few. If a ragtag collection of dispersed colonials could produce such outstanding leaders, what should 210 million Americans be able to produce? The bumper sticker "Impeach Someone" says it all. Why is the outlook so bleak?

There are several explanations. Institutions and the burgeoning masses they were intended to serve are changing in ways their leaders do not always grasp. Leaders are increasingly exposed by the mass media to the scrutiny of the public at large, too often making politicians into celebrities. In contrast to the colonial period, a political career is no longer the most distinguished career. When the assassinations of the 1960s introduced an unprecedented measure of terror into American politics, many of the better leaders exhausted themselves in protest or left politics to the mediocre. During the mid-twentieth century we demanded more services from the government than it can deliver. Another problem is that the nation keeps searching for that single leader on a white horse who can rescue the people from the throes of every problem. This emphasis on personal charisma rather than on quiet expertise makes the populace even more susceptible to the empty promises of a demagogue. It took more than a single leader to bring America to birth; and after the series of economic and political shock waves we have undergone in recent years, it will take more than one man on a white horse to unite us again, rekindle pristine idealism, and restore confidence. The great leader is neither a folk hero nor a manager, but perhaps a little of both. He "leads" but is not so far ahead that he is out of touch with the masses. He carefully negotiates to fill the void that separates the real from the ideal. To him rhetoric is no substitute for record, appearances for substance, charisma for character. He does not fear public scrutiny; he invites constructive criticism; and because taking an oath of office does not endow him with omniscience and moral perfection, he is willing to admit his mistakes and begin again. And, finally, he does not compromise his integrity for the highest bidder. One of the chief duties of leadership, and the one that most leaders of democracies today fail to perform, is to look toward the future. Too often decisions and votes are based on narrow interests and short-range priorities.

Now beginning a third century of independence, we have no simple magic formula for producing the leaders who will cope with problems that cannot now even be imagined. It is easy, and perhaps it is the only logical thing to do, to trust God's providence. The great leader Moses emerged during the darkest hour of the young Hebrew nation. In United States history the only leaders whose roles in profound crises were at all similar to Moses' were Lincoln and Franklin Roosevelt. But the plagues of medieval Europe and the strife in the Mideast and Ireland during the 1970s did not produce a single great leader.

We must search for leaders in all walks of life and all strata of society. Our educational institutions must continue to train people for all areas of public service; our problems are too complex to be solved only by professional politicians. Our leaders must be persons of unquestioned integrity, persons who are simply not for sale at any price. They must be humane, dedicated to the goals and values that have made our nation great. They must have an enlightened vision of what the nation can become, and they must be able to articulate this vision so as to inspire trust and enthusiasm. The church must assume a large share of the responsibility for training this kind of leadership. Watergate alone has reinforced the familiar but ignored idea that the exercise of power divorced from ethics and genuine morality sows the seeds of national disaster. No other single institution in this land is better equipped—constitutionally, historically, and authoritatively—to train our youth to make political decisions and exercise corporate power in light of authentic Christian morality and humane values. Christian leaders must not shirk this grave responsibility.

As patriotic citizens, the very least we can offer is our active trust. It is true that there can be no leaders if there are no followers. We must keep well informed, for ignorance and apathy can destroy any democracy. We must pay serious attention to the issues, for otherwise leaders will not consider our wishes or take us into their confidence. We must forego the temptation to appraise a candidate on the basis of the brief, image-making commercials that constantly bombard us at election time. And we must not reduce great issues into the clichés and platitudes that an apathetic or impatient public almost forces its leaders to utter. There are encouraging signs that we are learning to be good followers and are more prepared than ever to be dealt with fairly and frankly, even if it requires some sacrifice to live with that fairness and frankness.

If our democratic system is to continue to work for us, we must work—and the "we" includes many people, not just the elite. The primary responsibility for progress toward a more decent, humane —even Christian, if you will—society belongs to the people, not the government. While our problems differ from those of the early patriots two hundred years ago, they are no less grave. And we will face now-unimaginable problems as we move into the twenty-first century, when the world will be changed by new patterns of population and new relationships between that population and the natural environment, political structure, and military might. Much work remains to be initiated. Whether we act alone or in groups, Christian citizens can make a unique contribution. Patriotism provides the motivation for such activism and is a marvelous organizing force within society. Christians may indeed participate fully in patriotic celebrations and do their part to enlarge the spirit of '76.

part four

America:
A Christian Nation?

Blessed is the nation whose God is the Lord. . . .
(Ps. 33:12 KJV)

A responsible society is one where freedom is the freedom of men who acknowledge responsibility to justice and public order, and where those who hold political authority or economic power are responsible for its exercise to God and the people whose welfare is affected by it.

World Council of Churches (1948)

We are a religious people whose institutions presuppose a Supreme Being.

William O. Douglas

Righteousness exalteth a nation: but sin is a reproach to any people.
(Prov. 14:34 KJV)

chapter twelve

Are There Canons to Define
a Christian Nation?

Is America a Christian nation? If not is it a pagan nation? Or is it better described as more-or-less Christian? But, then, how "Christian" is it?

These are questions of great gravity, and we dare not avoid them because they are not easily answered. Until recently it would not have been difficult to obtain a confident, affirmative response to the first question. That the United States is a Christian nation has been assumed almost universally, but it has been an unexamined assumption. Robert T. Handy pointed out that Americans traditionally have perceived their country as a Christian nation and that our many churches have thought it their duty to create and then sustain this special status.[1] The concept of Christian America was a shared vision. Now this concept is being questioned in different quarters, and no longer are we so confident that the United States is Christian. Many believe that, while there may be no such thing as a Christian nation, America is the closest thing to it. But many others are downright uncomfortable with any such generalization about the American character.

In part 4 of this book, we focus on the question, Is America a

---

1. *A Christian America* (New York: Oxford University, 1971), p. vii.

Christian nation? To answer it we must define terms and forward standards for measuring societies. Are there canons for measuring the character of a nation? If no clear canons or standards exist, we cannot determine whether America or any other nation is Christian. Our purpose here is to examine some of the traditional criteria used to determine a Christian nation, to measure our nation by these criteria, and, if these canons prove inadequate, to formulate new ones based on Biblical teachings.

The Founding of This Nation

America is a Christian nation, it is argued, by virtue of the reasons for its founding. The earliest colonies were settled by Europeans, mainly Englishmen, who were yearning for the fresh air of religious freedom. On this continent they cast aside the yoke of religious intolerance and persecution and, unfettered by neighbor or government, worshiped and served God according to the dictates of their individual consciences. They so appreciated this spirit of freedom that they gratefully extended it to everyone. Our founding fathers, themselves God-fearing and righteous men, later guaranteed this religious freedom to all posterity in the First Amendment of our Constitution, which prohibited the fledgling national government's interference with the individual's free exercise of his religious faith. And throughout our history throngs of people have renounced their citizenship in other lands and come to our shores in search of that same religious tolerance and freedom.

This view of America's founding is a popular one and has been told often in American pulpits, plus or minus a few details. It is a persuasive view because it is not totally devoid of truth. Much like the ancient Hebrews, especially the Pharisees of Jesus' day, Americans take pride in the great accomplishments of their ancestors. But even if this view of the founding of our nation were totally correct, this would not *in and of itself* make the United States a Christian nation today.

Was America founded as a Christian nation? Our founding fathers took for granted a certain religious orientation, to be certain. They did not intend to establish a state hostile or antagonistic to religious institutions and customs. The government, they believed, should be tolerant of and accommodate all religious groups and institutions. In this environment sects proliferated. But the "Christian America" our founders created was not the result of some deliberate, theological design for the New World, but a by-product of political theories on the relationship between church and state, as we shall note again.

What motivated large numbers of Europeans to pull up stakes and make the treacherous voyage across the Atlantic to begin anew? The idea that all of them were in search of religious freedom is a myth. Though religion motivated some people in all the colonization enterprises, as a rule its most significant manifestation was their attempts to convert whatever heathen they encountered. At one time or another, it is acknowledged, Roman Catholics, Quakers, Huguenots, Moravians, Mennonites, mystics, and pietists emigrated from England, France, and Central Europe because they had been unable to order their lives as they wished. Maryland had a strong religious orientation, but no settlement outside of New England was motivated solely by the quest for religious freedom and religious community. Outside of Massachusetts the new settlers who were interested in religious freedom, except for Quakers in Rhode Island and Pennsylvania, contented themselves with the measure of religious freedom they were granted, only rarely attempting to influence the political life of the community. Even religious conviction was not all that brought the Puritans and Pilgrims to the new land; also compelling were their all-pervasive faith in the righteousness of their cause and course, and their rigid adherence to certain principles of ecclesiastical organization and civil government that gave Massachusetts a certain strength and character. Other motivations of early colonists were the lure of treasure and booty, the search for new capital investments, the desire to enlarge personal estates and acquire new land in the wilderness, and the quest for a higher standard of living in a land with boundless untilled soil and wildlife.[2]

The beliefs and behavior of the founding fathers have been researched by many students of Americanism. (By the term *founding fathers* we generally refer not to the early colonists but to those who signed the Declaration of Independence, to the fifty-five men who wrote the Constitution, and to those others whose actions and words also helped found a new and separate nation.) These men were truly an exceptional elite—"rich and well born," talented, educated, creative, and resourceful—hardly representative of the four million Americans in the new nation. These men were dis-

---

2. Charles M. Andrews, *Our Earliest Colonial Settlements* (Ithaca: Cornell University, 1933), p. 3.

tinguished both in economic status and in government experience.[3]

That political leaders such as Franklin, Jefferson, and Washington should be so highly esteemed by ministers in conservative and evangelical churches today is somewhat ironic, for if they were living today and advocating the same religious convictions and life style, many of these same ministers would feel bound to disfellowship them. Some, Franklin and Jefferson not excluded, were less than morally impeccable in their sexual behavior. Many were Deistic, believing that God effects His providence only through natural, immutable laws, that the Bible is the best but not a perfect or even consistent revelation of His nature, and that Jesus Christ was an ideal man whose system was as complete as any man could devise. Franklin's motion for prayer at the Constitutional Convention is often cited as an index to his spiritual life, and there is no reason to doubt his sincerity; the fact that the motion was defeated, however, is not widely circulated. A few weeks before he died, Franklin wrote Ezra Stiles, president of Yale University, and set forth his creed:

> I believe in one God . . . that he governs it [the universe] by His providence . . . that the soul of man is immortal. . . . As to Jesus of Nazareth, my opinion of whom you particularly desire, I think the system of morals and his religion, as he left them to us, the best the world ever saw or is likely to see; but I apprehend it has received various corrupt changes, and I have, with most of the present dissenters in England, some doubts as to his divinity. . . . I see no harm, however, in its being believed, if that belief has the good consequence, as probably it has, of making his doctrines more respected and better observed.[4]

Like Washington, Jefferson did not permit himself to be drawn into controversy over his religious beliefs or behavior. He considered himself a Christian but shunned institutional affiliations. His suspected agnosticism received considerable public airing, and he was not completely oblivious to this fact. He considered the essence of religion to be not theological doctrine but morality. In fact, he accepted the Christian system not because of its theology but in

3. Recommended reading on the founding fathers is "The Founding Fathers: The Nation's First Elite," in Thomas R. Dye and L. Harmon Zeigler, *The Irony of Democracy* (North Scituate, Mass.: Duxbury, 1975), pp. 31-65; and Seymour Martin Lipset, *The First New Nation* (Garden City, N.Y.: Doubleday-Anchor, 1963).

4. Much of this letter is published in Norman Cousins, *In God We Trust* (New York: Harper, 1958), pp. 18, 19. This volume is an excellent collection of the religious views and writings of the nation's founders.

spite of it. "Of the divergent tendencies in traditional Christianity, we cannot be surprised that the Jeffersonians found piety or the abstract love of God uncongenial, and morality or the ordering of men's social relations most meaningful," wrote Daniel J. Boorstin. "When the Jeffersonian came to the traditional subject matter of religion, he showed a similar disposition to humanize his God into a beneficent being, and to make the primary quality of religion the exposition and inculcation of that benevolence."[5]

While it is interesting to read maxims much like those of Proverbs in Franklin's *Poor Richard's Almanac* and statements from Washington about the importance of the Bible, we must realize that these men lived and wrote during the Age of Reason, one of the most irreligious periods of our history. The Enlightenment glorified man, not God. Few if any of the founding fathers we revere the most were evangelical Christians who cared much for either personal salvation or a personal relationship with God. Thomas Paine, author of *Common Sense,* was an avowed atheist. Jefferson's brief quotes about the value of the Bible have served for years as ideal church bulletin fillers, but, as we have noted, Jefferson did not believe the Bible to be divinely inspired. "The Jefferson Bible," as it is popularly known, was Jefferson's attempt, in his words, "to pick out the diamonds from the dunghills" in the New Testament. His *Life and Morals of Jesus of Nazareth* pieced together the "genuine" portions of the Gospels—namely, those that reveal the morals of Jesus and that lack the "inferior" theological accretions. Anything Jefferson found unreasonable, such as the virgin birth, miracles, and the resurrection, was deleted. Recall also that these colonial political theorists did not, indeed could not, base their case for armed revolution on Biblical principles. England was the "ordained" power. Christians today might easily imagine themselves siding with the patriots, but conscientious Christians during the Revolution found the issue a very vexatious one; there was, perhaps, more Biblical justification for siding with the Loyalists than with the rebels.

Those American colonists who sought religious freedom in the New World were perhaps the least willing to extend this freedom

5. Daniel J. Boorstin, *The Lost World of Thomas Jefferson* (Boston: Beacon, 1948), pp. 151, 152. A good essay on TJ's religious views is David Little, "The Origins of Perplexity: Civil Religion and Moral Belief in the Thought of Thomas Jefferson," in Russell E. Richey and Donald G. Jones, eds., *American Civil Religion* (New York: Harper and Row, 1974), pp. 185-210.

to others. The Puritans persecuted the Quakers, whose beliefs were similar in many ways to their own, "legally" banishing the Friends from Massachusetts in 1658 on pain of death. Quakers fleeing from England also were warned not to land on the shores of Virginia, where the Church of England prevailed. In Virginia all sorts of restrictions and penalties were leveled at not only Quakers but also Baptists and Catholics. Offenders were censored and banned from public office, and repeated offenders could be jailed. In 1700 Quaker Pennsylvania required by law all citizens to attend church on Sunday or prove they had been reading the Bible. Offenders were subject to fines. Prejudice against Catholics ran high in most of the colonies at one time or another. One of the ironies of American history is that most of the religiously oppressive measures that thousands of settlers had come to this continent to escape were then adopted in this land.

Against this historical backdrop we can see the real contributions to "Christian America" of our founding fathers. While not all of them acknowledged a formal faith or maintained religious affiliations, their view of man and political society had a deeply religious foundation. They believed that man's religious convictions are his private concern and that his right to hold them should be guaranteed by the state. From Virginia's experience, both Madison and Jefferson discovered that religious monopoly and religious oppression are not far apart and that all institutions, no matter how small, and all people, no matter how unpopular, should be guaranteed their freedom. No state government has any business determining the religion of its citizens. If any group or individual is to be free, all must be free. And the freedom to worship and believe what one's conscience dictates is also the freedom *not* to worship and *not* to believe.

The High Preference for Christianity

Those who argue that the United States is a Christian nation also point to the majority's preference for the Christian faith. Among all the so-called Christian nations of the West, the United States perhaps has a higher percentage of Christian church members, greater budgets, more missionaries, more Christian service and involvement, and more people attending worship services and church functions than any other nation. No other nation matches America in religious expenditures. More Bibles and religious literature are sold here than in any other country. The other religions of the world, whether Islam, Hinduism, Shinto, or whatever, pose no threat whatever to Christianity's dominance and popularity in America. Not only do more Americans convert to Christianity, but relatively few Americans know anything of the history and contributions of the world's other major religions.

This is powerful evidence, but again the question arises: Does the great popularity of Christianity in and of itself render our nation Christian? For anyone remotely familiar with Christian doctrine, the answer is obvious (cf. Matt. 7:21). Numbers and popularity alone do not represent strength and true vitality. Leading churchmen, sociologists, and other responsible observers have for some time questioned the depth of the religious commitment of American church members. "Quite simply, between science and psychology, modern man has lost his soul, and his Christian faith," stated Clare Booth Luce. "The churches have themselves bought too many of the materialistic values of our success-oriented society. There has been a collapse of faith among churchmen themselves."[6] In the next chapter we will look at some secular substitutes for genuine Christianity in America.

Even if polls and statistics present an accurate picture of American religious commitment, the report is less than heartening. Overall, polls show that church attendance has leveled off or even declined between 1958 and the early seventies, with attendance somewhat higher for Roman Catholics than for Protestants. The American citizens who worship God in a church or synagogue at least one hour each week are a small minority indeed, and undoubtedly only a fraction of these engage in regular family devotionals or personal prayer. And how many of those who do attend worship with some degree of regularity know much about Christian doctrine or make a conscious effort to apply Christian principles to everyday problems? Membership in the churches of the United States showed a net loss of 179,425 persons in 1974, with the liberal Protestant denominations losing the most.[7] While the percentage of loss may not seem significant, it is the first loss in nearly three decades. But the greatest disappointment is the finding of a recent Gallup poll: people do not think that religion can answer the prob-

---

6. In "What's Happening to America's Values? A Conversation with Clare Booth Luce," *Reader's Digest*, October 1974, p. 214; excerpted from *U.S. News and World Report*, 24 June 1974.

7. See *Yearbook of American and Canadian Churches* (Nashville: Abingdon, 1975); and "The Pulpit Squeeze," *Time*, 30 June 1975, p. 52.

lems of our day. In 1957 eighty percent believed religion can provide answers; today only sixty-two percent believe it.[8]

Despite these figures we must not conclude that the church wields any less influence on the public at large than it did during the euphoric fifties and sixties. It may well be that the "fat" is leaving and the "muscle and sinew" is developing. Churches today are undoubtedly less of a cultural phenomenon than a decade or so ago. Our only point here is that the popularity and proliferation of Christian bodies and institutions in America do not ipso facto make this a Christian nation.

Ceremonial Allusions and Symbolism

Another argument forwarded by those who call America a Christian nation is that our nation is replete with ceremonial allusions, statements of allegiance and commitment, outward trappings, and public symbolism, all of which display a near-unanimous commitment to and affection for the principles of the Christian religion. We list this argument separately although the public symbolism and trappings are but an outgrowth of the popularity of the Christian religion in America that we cited in the preceding paragraphs.

"We are a religious people whose institutions presuppose a Supreme Being," declared Justice William O. Douglas in *Zorach* v. *Clauson* (1952). Though Douglas might not make such a statement now, or at least not without further clarifying it, there is considerable evidence to support it. Churches are tax-exempt.[9] Our coins are engraved with "In God we trust." Oaths in court and at inauguration ceremonies are usually taken with one hand placed on a Bible. The armed services, including their academies, provide chaplains and worship services. Chaplains serve the national Congress and state legislatures. Financial assistance is given veterans training for the ministry. Astronauts have read the Bible in outer space. Invocations are offered before many sporting events.

Humans and the societies they compose use and manipulate symbols, so religious symbolism in American public life should not surprise us. Of course it does raise the ire of fastidious and militant atheists such as Madalyn Murray O'Hair, the woman who succeeded in getting the Supreme Court to rule on mandatory prayer in public schools. If Mrs. O'Hair had her way, "In God we trust" would

---

8. *Nashville Tennessean,* 9 March 1975.

9. Walz v. Tax Commission, 397 U.S. 664 (1970).

be removed from coins and the Bible would no longer be read in public assemblages. She gains little respect for the cause of atheism by such protests. Indeed she would most likely win more respect for it by objecting to public displays of religious sentiment not because they violate the Constitutional separation of church and state, but because they are mechanical, routine, and insincere, and consequently of little spiritual value. Surely the separation doctrine was never intended to remove incidental expressions of public faith, be they Christian or whatever. Pure and total separation is probably impossible. Even strong advocates of religious liberty and of the separation of church and state have argued that the state should acknowledge publicly the religious commitment of the majority of its citizens, particularly if that commitment is a vital support of liberty itself. But even in the unlikely event that the Court ordered all vestiges of Christianity and other religions removed from public life, this would not necessarily make America any less a Christian nation. A nation is Christian by virtue not of symbols and public ceremonies alone but of the character of its citizens— their convictions and commitments, their attitudes, their interpersonal relations, their institutions, and their behavior in general. Public style can never be a substitute for substance.

Christian Laws and Public Policy

The United States is a Christian nation, it is urged, because its laws and public policy are based in at least a general way on the Holy Scriptures. The law in America has a moral as well as a political element. Christian people can use it to further the will of God: "Righteousness exalteth a nation. . . ." (Prov. 14:34). Again, this argument contains a smattering of truth, but it constitutes an overgeneralization that too few Chrisians have analyzed carefully. The issue is an imporant one. What is or should be the relationship between the law and Christianity in American society? Should the law, either in whole or in part, be based on the dictates of the Christian faith? This argument in support of "Christian America" offers the opportunity to answer these important questions in some detail.

A central concern here is the definition of *law*. To define it is almost like defining life itself, for how can we distinguish law from ethics, norms, religion, customs, philosophy, and social science? Law contains all of these elements, but it also possesses a unique characteristic—it is sanctioned exclusively by organized political govern-

227

ment. Law is a public, institutionalized mechanism for resolving controversies and ordering relationships within a political society. By defining what citizens expect of one another, law makes possible a public order, and since it enables a person to predict the future and confidently contract with others to carry out his purposes, it facilitates cooperation.[10] But when we come to the crucial relationship between law and morality, we are confronted by a problem that is not easily resolved. Two polar positions that Christians and citizens in general must avoid are represented by the catchwords "There oughta' be a law!" and "You can't legislate morality!"

The first extreme position is that the law of the land must be patterned after the social ethics of the Bible. It makes the Bible a blueprint for public law and policy. Once we accomplish this, we have a Christian state. This would make our form of government the closest in the modern world to a theocracy.

Desirable as this may seem to many Christians, it is impractical and unworkable in our pluralistic, secular society. The moral principles of the New Testament were intended, in the final analysis, for Christ's disciples, saints who have separated themselves from the world and consecrated their lives to God and His service. The ethical dictates of the New Testament are not readily met by one who is unconverted. And the state can neither command nor punish certain hopes, aspirations, affections, and devotions. For example, in 1940 the Supreme Court upheld a Minersville, Pennsylvania, law that required the children of Walter Gobitis, devout Jehovah's Witnesses, to salute the American flag in the public school or be punished. Believing that saluting the flag constitutes idolatry, the Gobitis children disobeyed both their teachers and the law. Although backed by its highest court, the nation could not elicit from these little children the affections for their country that the Minersville law was intended to elicit. (Of course the Supreme Court later reversed its decision of 1940.)

Another example is the ethical commands of the Sermon on the Mount. While the guidelines that Jesus drew on this occasion are of some use to all individuals, in the final analysis they make sense only for disciples of Christ who live in a hostile social environment and await final vindication in an afterlife. Harold O. J. Brown stated the point well: "The Christian has no real leverage by which

---

10. For an excellent discussion of the nature and applications of law in the United States and the Western democracies, see Henry J. Abraham, *The Judicial Process*, 2nd ed. (New York: Oxford University, 1968).

to demand or expect Christian moral standards from those who do not believe the premises of Christianity. From this perspective, Christian ethics are only for Christians."[11]

Just as the law and public policy cannot be concerned with correct beliefs and attitudes, neither can it be concerned with sin, that is, not with sin *as sin*. It is not the duty of the state to prevent or punish sin (again we refer to sin as sin). The positive law and governmental institutions do, indeed must, concern themselves with overt behavior related to good order, peace, justice, freedom, and community welfare. Whatever threatens these conditions must be proscribed, perhaps even severely punished. The purpose of the law is not to make a man good or righteous, or even decent and respectable; it is to require him when dealing with others to meet minimal standards of justice and to protect him from injustice. The state does not punish the lawbreaker because he has sinned—although indeed in the sight of God he is accountable for sin—but because he has threatened the community's sense of order, justice, and decency.[12]

The second polar position is that the laws of the state should be totally devoid of moral premises and content. Morality should be taught by the family, the church, and other private institutions, but not by the political state.

The greatest problem with this position is its untenable presupposition that moral premises and content can be separated from law and public policy. But it is impossible to speak of human rights, order, community, and justice amorally. (We discussed this issue in chapter 10.) The law necessarily reflects moral ends, choices, and values. Would anyone argue that the Supreme Court's decisions concerning capital punishment and abortion were solely *political?* And what about judicial and legislative decisions concerning obscenity and pornography? Advocates of stricter censorship, to cite one example, insist that such laws need not be understood as an effort to distract men's interest from the carnal or sensual aspects

---

11. *The Protest of a Troubled Protestant* (Grand Rapids: Zondervan, 1970), p. 74. I am indebted to Brown's thought-provoking volume for several ideas in this chapter.

12. Sidney Hook has an excellent discussion of this point in "The Irrelevance of Sin," chap. 2 in his *Religion in a Free Society* (Lincoln: University of Nebraska, 1967), pp. 27-41. Hook emphasized this point by using the Old Testament narrative of Jehovah commanding Abraham to sacrifice his son Isaac. Had Abraham refused to obey God, he would have been a sinner; had he obeyed, he would, in a modern democratic state, have been tried for a criminal offense.

of life and center them on the more noble and spiritual aspects. Censorship would not try to direct thoughts *anywhere*, but would try to control some of those forces in our modern mass society that lower moral standards and, ultimately, debase moral character. If these forces are restrained, truly worthy thoughts and ideals are much more likely to emerge and develop.

This view of the moral purpose of law is not new. It is rooted in Aristotelian philosophy. Aristotle believed that men do not form political societies simply to preserve life, liberty, and security, but to promote the whole range of human needs, both the material (or "lower") as well as the moral (or "higher") needs. Legislators are to train citizens in good habits. Certainly society is to preserve life, but its highest end is to develop in citizens those qualities and capacities that are uniquely human. Those who debase these qualities or abuse these capacities receive correction and guidance from the political community through the legal process.

A number of contemporary political philosophers advocate this classical view. To Walter Berns, public and private morality depend on citizens having a certain character, and consequently "the formation of character is the principal duty of government."[13] Harry M. Clor concurred. Both he and Berns argued that laws against vices like pornography, obscenity, gambling, prostitution, and public indecency—frequently referred to as "crimes without victims"—must not be lifted. The preventive and coercive functions of these restrictions are supplemented, and perhaps superseded, by their hortatory and educative functions.[14] Vice laws proclaim that the organized community draws a line between art and pornography, between decent and indecent, between what is permissible and what is not. Some may indeed step over the line, but at least they and everyone else are fully aware that a line exists, and this awareness cannot but affect positively the moral attitudes and values of most people. Even if these laws cannot be enforced evenly or effectively, so long as they reflect the majority view they should remain on the statute books. Oliver Wendell Holmes, Jr., once a professor at the Harvard Law School, addressed himself to this

---

13. Walter Berns, *Freedom, Virtue, and the First Amendment* (Westport, Conn.: Greenwood, 1957), p. 246.

14. For a discussion of this point and a contemporary critique of John Stuart Mill, see Patrick Devlin, *The Enforcement of Morals* (London: Oxford University, 1959); see also H. L. A. Hart, *Law, Liberty, and Morality* (Stanford: Stanford University, 1965).

point. "The first requirement of a sound body of law," he asserted, "is that it should correspond with the actual feelings and demands of the community, whether right or wrong. If people would gratify the passion of revenge outside the law, if the law did not help them, the law has no choice but to satisfy the craving itself, and thus avoid the greater evil of private retribution."[15]

Can morality be legislated? Strictly speaking it cannot. The law cannot make one love, respect, or be kind to another, but it can and should restrain such immoralities as injustice and cruelty. No law can secure respect and brotherly love for those of different race or national origin. But legislatures have passed and the courts upheld laws prohibiting discrimination in the fields of employment, education, voting rights, housing, and public accommodations; the special interests of one person were not allowed to limit the civil rights of others. It is a sad commentary on the conscience of "Christian America" that the *Brown* decision of the Supreme Court in 1954 probably did more to evoke from the majority of whites a decent Christian attitude toward blacks than had several decades of sermons.

In summary, somewhere between the clichés "There oughta' be a law" and "You can't legislate morality" is a happy medium. There is a time to legislate and a time not to legislate, and knowing the difference between the two is for Christian political activists the better part of wisdom. A word of warning is in order. As we noted in chapter 5, the cultivation of moral values and insights is indeed a part of the Christian life, and the churches and church leaders should address themselves to the issues of our times prophetically. This is a contribution to moral awareness that probably no other institution will make. Legal rules are not self-sustaining; they require a theoretical base, be it Constitutional, moral, or whatever. Moral values should be informed by religious insight that necessarily helps to shape the moral choices of the community at large. All too frequently, unfortunately, Christian pressure groups have not acknowledged the limitations of law and have supported unwise laws.

The Prohibition Amendment is one example. It was pushed through Congress by a propagandizing, vocal minority while the majority was generally opposed, or at least passive and indifferent, to it. The Prohibition Amendment was the greatest short-term leg-

---

15. *The Common Law* (1881), pp. 41, 42.

islative success of our Protestant churches, but in the long run it was an abysmal failure. Fundamentalist and conservative Protestants were imposing their moral convictions on Roman Catholics, Jews, and liberal Protestants, not to mention the unaffiliated. But the law's ability to regulate the day-by-day behavior of individual citizens is not unlimited. No church or Christian pressure group should seek legal sanction for its own moral conceptions unless it can translate them into moral values and social policies appropriate to the purposes of the entire secular community.

Christians must trust not some new law or amendment, helpful as it may be, but the leavening quality of Christian character in all human relationships and institutions. In more recent times Christians have banded together and agitated for more censorship, for prohibition of liquor by the drink, and for banning the teaching of evolution from public schools. Other Christian groups have advocated vociferously amendments to the Constitution that would return prayer and Bible reading to public schools, ban busing for racial integration, and ban abortion. Well intended as these movements are, advocates must not forget that a new law will be obeyed only if its demands are not too far above the moral level of the community as a whole. Since law is the creature of a society's prevailing morality, Christians cannot expect it to embody their higher ethical ideals. Christians should honor and obey the law and work for realistic improvements, but they must not endow it with an aura of sanctity it does not merit.

The battle of the mid-seventies concerning the Equal Rights Amendment provides a final illustration. The majority of conservative Christian activists have opposed this amendment, claiming that the very survival of the home and the nuclear family is at stake. The battle has been so emotional, so intense, that each side often has misrepresented the other.[16] The strongest argument of

16. Of great concern should be the barrage of overgeneralizations, prophecies of doom, and appeals to fear used to defeat the ERA. If the ERA is ratified, critics contend, churches will be required to ordain women as ministers and church officers or lose tax-exempt status, and this will destroy the separation of church and state. Women will lose the right to be mothers and wives. They will be drafted to fight alongside men, labor laws protecting women will be eliminated, public restrooms will be sexually integrated, and homosexual marriages will become legal. The central fallacy of many of these claims is their assumption that one can know for certain how a new law will be interpreted by the federal courts. Few if any American institutions are as unpredictable as our Supreme Court. A clause or amendment in our Constitution may be interpreted in one way, for one interest, for several decades, and then interpreted another

Christian opponents of the ERA is that there already is adequate legal machinery, in both judicial precedents and statutory law, to remedy any remaining sexual discrimination. As responsible and concerned followers of Christ, we must deplore the moral laxity and the debunking of traditional Christian doctrine and principles that have led to widespread pornography, public nudity on the stages and the beaches, pointless explicitness in mass media, co-ed dorms, increasing rape incidents, and other such trends. These are what undermine the sanctity of the home and threaten its survival, not a Constitutional amendment. Can we not see that defeating the ERA amendment is going to do very little to reverse the trend toward immorality? To illustrate, if the nation is moving toward sexually integrated restrooms, stopping the ERA will not terminate that movement. The victory for either the proponents or opponents of the ERA will be largely symbolic. Granted, symbolic victories are worth something, but should the amendment be defeated, Christians who opposed it might be tempted to relax their vigil.

To conclude this warning, Christians need not apologize for involvement in the political process. This process is one valid, powerful means of effecting the will of God in secular society. But the time and energy we spend on this must be realistic, and, most important, to influence those outside our community of faith our arguments must be fair, intelligent, informed, and reasonable. Christians must acknowledge the limits of law and political institutions to compel a large, pluralistic society to conform to a single system of ethics. Rather than joining pressure groups (most congressmen find it easy simply to dispose of correspondence from such groups anyway) that support or oppose a single law through well-financed campaigns, the Christian should exercise a leavening influence for moral goodness through disciplined involvement in the widest possible range of societal activities, institutions, and communities.

---

way for several more generations. A study of the various court decisions based on the Fourteenth Amendment is evidence enough on this point.

The Supreme Court is not as detached from the currents of contemporary thinking and moral standards as some suppose. Law and its interpretation reflect the general moral standards of society. If the Court is to thrive, as Wallace Mendelson has said so well, it "must respect the social sources that determine elections and other major political settlements. No court can long withstand the morals of its era." It is the "child of its time." *Justices Black and Frankfurter: Conflict in the Court*, 2nd ed. (Chicago: University of Chicago, 1967), pp. 75, 76. See also Robert A. Dahl, "Decision-Making in a Democracy: The Supreme Court as a National Policy-Maker," *Journal of Public Law* 279 (1957).

Whither Now, American Christians?

We have examined four related but distinct arguments that Christians sometimes offer to support the concept of "Christian America." We have noted that while the founding fathers possessed deep religious convictions, it was not their purpose to found a Christian nation as the Puritans had founded a Christian colony. We have argued that religious symbolism in public life cannot turn a secular state into a spiritual one and that the Bible should not be used as a blueprint for public law in a secular society. Only in the second claim—America leads the West in religious activity of all kinds—do we find anything approaching credible evidence that this nation is indeed Christian. But the obvious hypocrisy and superficiality lurking behind many of these statistics force us to conclude that the idea of a Christian America is unfounded, impractical, and by historical standards antiquated. Brown put it succinctly and accurately: we should call America "a pagan nation, inhabited by a minority of committed Christians."[17]

What is the appropriate Christian response? We could pine for a community in which everyone shares the same racial stock and national origin, worships the same God, and believes in the deity of Christ and the inspiration of Scripture, but the futility of this response is obvious. For better or worse we live in a nation of people of different origin, race, life styles, allegiances, and religions. Ours is a pluralistic society, and committed, evangelical disciples of Christ are truly in the minority. Lest we despair, recall from both Biblical and secular history that the character of a nation is not necessarily determined by the majority of its people— a deeply committed minority is quite sufficient. Does any alternative system of values in this nation enjoy the commitment and the dedicated dissemination that Christianity does? If God spared an entire nation because of the dedication of one woman named Esther, if He spared multitudes because of the prayers of one man named Moses, if God would have spared Sodom for ten righteous Sodomites, then will not the Almighty spare this great nation because of the leavening influence of some truly converted people? Christians today who find their situation difficult and nearly overwhelming should realize that their plight is not unprecedented. New Testament Christianity did not emerge in circumstances as hospitable as those in America today, yet the early church was vigorous and dy-

---

17. *Protest of a Troubled Protestant*, p. 73.

namic. So revolutionary was its impact that several observers said the apostles had turned the world upside down (Acts 17:6). Ironically, the more the Christian church and the political authorities accommodated each other, the more the cutting edge of primitive Christianity was blunted.

Another look at the Scriptures should convince us of an important fact. As we noted in chapter 1, the idea of a specially consecrated nation goes back to ancient Israel. But in Biblical theology, a group of people cannot choose to become God's special people; He must choose them.[18] The people of God are called from the world into a special community in which they are blessed by God and benefited by Christ's death (cf. I Peter 1:1; 2:10). But nowhere in the New Testament does God direct His children to found a special nation and locate in a certain geographical place, not even in the old Promised Land of Canaan. The overriding concern of New Testament authors was that the saints would remain steadfast in the face of illegal and "official" persecution, and that whenever they were dispersed, they would spread the good news of salvation through Christ. Nothing in the New Testament leads Christian disciples to expect any legal status or special place in society. Perhaps the legal status and protection afforded American Christians has made many of them indifferent and apathetic instead of committed disciples. Cross bearing is not the same for Christians in America as it has been for those in the totalitarian states of the twentieth century. The time has arrived when American Christians are a minority in a political society that is officially non-Christian and, in reality, may even be anti-Christian. At least now we can share in the plight of brothers and sisters in Christ in other cultures and other centuries.

Can New Canons Be Established?

The preceding analysis does not mean that the Bible has no message for nations today. Hezekiah affirmed of Jehovah, ". . . thou alone art God of all the kingdoms of the earth. . . ." (II Kings 19:15). The Psalmist declared, "Happy is the nation whose God is the Lord. . . ." (33:12). The wise man of ancient days exhorted, "Righteousness raises a people to honour; to do wrong is a disgrace to any nation" (Prov. 14:34). When giving the parable of the last great judgment, Jesus began: "When the Son of Man comes

---

18. Ibid., p. 80.

in his glory and all the angels with him, he will sit in state on his throne, with all the nations gathered before him" (Matt. 25:31, 32).

Are these Scriptures relevant to America or any other nation today? If indeed they are, we can derive from the Bible three general canons by which we can measure how Christian a nation is. At the outset we may eliminate the objection that no government—certainly none governing a large population—has lived up to these principles and that none ever will. Ethical principles are canons by which one judges achievement and national character. At the personal level we do not abandon standards of love, honesty, or justice because no one is perfectly loving, honest, or just. Nations, like individuals, must be judged not only by their ideals but by the extent to which they realize their ideals.

1. The responsible state respects the worth and value of the individual. This canon is based on a doctrine that is embedded on virtually every page of Scripture—God loves *all* men. God demonstrated this outgoing love in the incarnation, in God's becoming man in Christ. God's impartial love should evoke in man a brotherly love for all whom God has created in His image, and this love is the only foundation for a decent society. Can one expect such love in a pluralistic, populous society? Is this goal too high? Perhaps. But we can translate this dictate of Christian discipleship to mean that each citizen must respect the rights of others, treating each other citizen as an equal. This mutual respect and good will must go beyond an enlightened self-interest wherein people respect the rights of others only when it is to their own advantage to do so. Stated in minimal terms, a responsible society is one in which man is never made a mere means for economic or political ends. He is respected as an end in himself. Man is not made for the government, but government for man. The conscience of each individual is fully respected and free. It may be too much to expect ordinary citizens to love their enemies (Matt. 5:44), but they must respect the views of their opponents and enemies and allow them to seek public acceptance of their views, no matter how unpopular and reprehensible.[19]

---

19. When the Senate was considering in 1971 whether to expand the investigative powers of the Subversive Activities Control Board, Senator Sam Ervin, fearing it would lead to more "witch-hunting," told the Senate why he could not vote yes: "I hate the thoughts of Black Panthers. I hate the thoughts of the Weathermen's faction of the Students for a Democratic Society. I hate the thoughts of fascists. I hate the thoughts of totalitarians. I hate the thoughts of people who adopt violence as a policy. But those people have the same right

Just as citizens must respect all individuals, the state must be concerned for the welfare of every man and woman. We have referred already to the fact that Christ Himself concentrated His ministry on the neediest people, the people whom respectable society despised or overlooked. Society must be no less concerned for those who are powerless and neglected than for the high and mighty. As Judge Jerome Frank observed, "The test of the moral quality of a civilization is its treatment of the weak and powerless."[20] "The worst citizen no less than the best," wrote Justice Hugo L. Black of a defiant racist in a dissenting opinion, "is entitled to equal protection of the laws of his state and of his nation."[21] "It is a fair summary of history to say that safeguards of liberty have been forged in controversies involving not very nice people," concluded Justice Felix Frankfurter.[22]

2. The responsible state places transcendent values over materialism and other purely human philosophies. This canon is based on the Biblical teachings that God is the ultimate Sovereign over all nations, that all material things will perish eventually with this imperfect earthly system, and that man is more than merely mortal. The responsible state does not enthrone materialistic philosophies and values in God's place, nor does it make man serve technological progress. Its faith is not ultimately in armaments. "In God we trust" is more than just a slogan—it is a reality. Citizens resist absolutizing any human philosophy, institution, or political regime, refusing to endow human goals and means with a sanctity they do not merit. Those who are mandated to exercise power realize their responsibility to God and to the people who have bestowed their trust on them. Even in a democracy public officials must maintain a transcendent frame of reference, and trust in God leads naturally to a concern for bettering man and enriching his spirit. Cultural and educational values are not perpetually neglected. The responsible church does not sell itself to the mis-

---

to freedom of speech, subject to a very slight qualification, that I have. I love the Constitution so much that I am willing to stand on the floor of the Senate and fight for their right to think the thoughts and speak the words that I hate. If we ever reach the condition in this country that we attempt to have free speech for everybody except those whose ideas we hate, not only free speech but freedom itself are out in our society." Quoted in Robert Sherrill, *Why They Call It Politics*, 2nd ed. (New York: Harcourt Brace Jovanovich, 1974), p. 155.

20. United States v. Murphy, 22 F. 2d 698 (1955).

21. Bell v. Maryland, 378 U.S. 226 (1964).

22. United States v. Rabinowitz, 339 U.S. 56 (1950).

placed values and human philosophies of the unregenerate world. Church members remind the nation at large that man is immortal and that all human schemes, ideologies, partisanship, and enmity are transcended by man's ultimate relationship, his meaning for existence, and his destiny.

In the responsible society both the rulers and the ruled acknowledge a "higher law" or "natural law" upon which our "inalienable rights" are based. Rights are to be codified and safeguarded by the state, but the source of these rights is not the state, but God. These rights are so important that without them no decent and humane society could exist.

3. The responsible state creates a decent and humane community, a social order based on justice, order, and responsibility. Such a community is no accident. It requires the conscious, concerted effort of the vast majority of citizens. The responsible nation-state protects citizens against the pretensions and transgressions of others. It allows as many as possible to help make the decisions that will affect their lives, allowing them access to the information they need. The nation's leaders are concerned about public morality, about the ways in which citizens entertain themselves or use their leisure time.

To maintain the responsible state authorities may be constrained to exercise all the power at their disposal. Safeguards in the Constitution require zealous protection.[23] Many sincere citizen-activists believe that strong national power is irreconcilable with civil liberties and decent community life. It is true that raw political power can undermine these concepts, as it has so frequently in totalitarian states, but the indiscriminate fear of power may increase the power of fear. Just as often as power has been abused in history, it has been used to undergird civil liberties and the sense of

---

23. The interesting thing is that millions of Americans pay lip service to the great freedoms guaranteed by the Bill of Rights but vote against measures that make these rights and liberties concrete. To them, there are still a few people besides criminals who should have no right to speak, vote, or live where they wish. A referendum in the sixties in California was instructive concerning open housing.

Millions of other Americans may not even pay lip service to civil rights and liberties. Several polls have shown that many people would vote against the First Amendment if given the opportunity. Students in a business law class found elected officials do not know basic legal rights. They drew up a petition based on the Sixth Amendment and asked 271 state senators to sign it; 111 refused, some saying the provisions were illegal. The governor did sign it. *Time,* 29 April 1974, p. 10.

community.[24] The need for laws and for their fair and impartial enforcement is underscored by the Biblical doctrine of the dual nature of man. All men are created in the image of God and are capable of a perfect, or complete, life filled with such Christian graces as love, goodness, benevolence, joy, perseverence, and temperance. At the same time, sin is universal and deep, making all human groups self-centered and proud. Responsible national leaders know that sin is pervasive, that groups can tolerate more injustices than individuals can,[25] that a utopia is impossible, that all men are capable of hate and cruelty, and that a genuine community cannot survive when immorality is not restrained.

The Last, Best Hope of the Earth

The particular genius of a responsible nation is that it seeks to translate these three canons into concrete public policy and law. We concede that Christian political activists will agree far more easily to these canons, couched in the most general terms, than they will to any specific policies proposed to realize these canons more fully in the United States. We concede without embarrassment that non-Christians frequently do as much or more to establish and further the qualities of a responsible nation than do Christians. We also must confess that the morality of non-Christians often puts Christians to shame; the daily life style of an occasional atheist or agnostic comes closer than does that of many Christians to fulfilling the Christian moral code. It is faulty theology to argue the unique-

---

24. "Once we free ourselves of the bogey that whatever the state and its bureaucracy do is wrong and contrary to freedom, and whatever others do is efficient and synonymous with freedom, we can squarely face the true issue. Reduced to a single phrase, the issue is that in our modern world everything is political, the state is everywhere, and public responsibility is interwoven in the whole fabric of society. Freedom consists not in denying this interpenetration but in defining its legitimate uses in all spheres, setting limits and deciding the pattern of penetration and, last but not least, in safeguarding public responsibility and shared control over decisions. From this follows the importance of institutional control for a strategy of reform in a democratically planned society, and the need for a theory of power based on democratic principles." Karl Mannheim, *Freedom, Power, and Democratic Planning* (New York: Oxford University, 1950), pp. 44, 45.

25. Emil Brunner used theological language to offer a pregnant consideration: "We never see the real meaning of 'original sin,' we never perceive the depth and universality of evil, or what evil means in the depths common to us all, until we are *obliged* to do something in our official capacity—for the sake of order, and therefore the sake of love—which apart from our 'office,' would be absolutely wrong." *The Divine Imperative* (London: Lutterworth, 1937), p. 227.

ness and superiority of Christianity on the basis that only it produces moral men, for, as W. Adams Brown put it, "the sense of God's presence, which is the crown of the religious life, reaches over into the sphere of ethics and glorifies it."[26] The moral ethics of Christ are good and beneficial for all, even if not all adherents are aware that these ethics are the ethics of Christ. And yet, true New Testament Christianity illuminates the path to a responsible nation as does no other philosophy or ideology.

The three canons we cited do more than simply describe a quasi-Christian nation: they are the basis for an ideal democratic nation. Apart from them a viable democracy is impossible. J. Paul Williams argued that "democracy must become an object of religious dedication. Americans must come to look on the democratic ideal (not necessarily the American practice of it) as the Will of God or, if they prefer, the Law of Nature. . . . Governmental agencies must teach the democratic ideal as religion."[27] Should Christians concur?

This question is important, but hopefully an extended response is unnecessary here in view of the preceding chapters. We emphasized that the flourishing of Christian faith and the effectiveness of Christian witness is not contingent upon, and indeed may be blunted by, a hospitable legal and social environment. The New Testament writers even expected the state to be hostile. But Christians need not apologize for a vigilant defense of democracy, for there are many valid reasons, both ethical and political, for saying that democracy is the superior form of government. Democratic societies are less likely than others to neglect or overlook the good of any group or individual. Democracy places greater faith in man as a rational being than do other systems, encouraging him to help formulate the policies through which genuine community is realized and consequently helping to develop man's practical intelligence and moral virtue. Without minimizing the value of order, democracy offers more scope to the people's freedom and creative genius than does any other form of government. Democracy gives political expression to a basic tenet of Christianity—that every man has dignity and worth, not because of anything inherent in his nature but because he is created in the image of God. We may conclude that the goals of democracy are at least as much in har-

---

26. Quoted in Kyle Haselden, *Morality and the Mass Media* (Nashville: Broadman, 1968), p. 186.

27. *What Americans Believe and How They Worship* (New York: Harper and Row, 1962), p. 488.

mony with the spirit and intent of genuine Christianity as are the goals of any other form of government.

In closing, we recall the ideas of our founding fathers and of Abraham Lincoln. Democracy is an ideal that presupposes man's capacity to govern and improve himself. Democracy is a way, a path, not a static system. "All men are created equal" is a moral, not a factual, proposition. Its realization depends upon each new generation. In the final analysis, Lincoln thought, "the people" can be trusted because they are not easily or long deceived. Truth eventually will emerge, especially when opinions are allowed to conflict. With the founding fathers, Lincoln knew that democracy in America is an experiment, but it is a worthy experiment, Lincoln reasoned, for "no man is good enough to govern another man without that other's consent." Throughout our history this grand experiment has led to an expansion of all manner of civil rights and liberties. But at times, especially during the Civil War, the experiment appeared doomed. Lincoln, however, never exploited his few public appearances during the Civil War to give a doctrinaire defense of the Union cause; instead he appraised the conflict as part of the great experiment that "embraces more than the fate of these United States" and that is "testing whether that nation or any nation so conceived and so dedicated can long endure."[28] Lincoln would insist not that democracy be taught as a religion, but that for nations to achieve their full destiny under God, democracy is "the last, best hope of the earth."

---

28. See the excellent discussion of Lincoln's views on democracy and the Civil War in Sidney E. Mead, *The Lively Experiment* (New York: Harper and Row, 1963), pp. 72-89.

Never put off until tomorrow the fun you can have today.

Aldous Huxley

I mention all this because, as a matter of fact, the movies were really the family religion at Douglastown. . . . My grandfather's favorite place of worship was the Capitol theatre, in New York. When the Roxy theatre was built, he transferred his allegiance to that huge pile of solidified caramel, and later on there was no shrine that so stirred his devotion as the Music Hall.

Thomas Merton

Professional football has emerged as a new religion which supplements—and in some cases even supplants—the older religious expressions of Judaism and Christianity.

A. James Rudin

We are living in a culture that is remarkably secular. Religion just doesn't play the role it used to play, and this is particularly true for people under forty. When a very strong religious bond is missing there are few other things that can hold a culture together.

Richard Hofstadter

You say, "How rich I am! And how well I have done! I have everything I want." In fact, though you do not know it, you are the most pitiful wretch, poor, blind and naked.

Jesus to Laodiceans (Rev. 3:17)

These are the words of the Lord: Stop at the cross-roads; look for the ancient paths; ask, "Where is the way that leads to what is good?" Then take that way, and you will find rest for yourselves.

(Jer. 6:16)

chapter thirteen

Secular Surrogates
for Authentic Faith

The responsible society in Biblical perspective, as we have seen, is characterized by decency, humaneness, justice, and order. Such a society is created when enough of its citizens daily practice, either consciously or unwittingly, the moral guidelines and dictates of the Christian faith. Both Franklin and Jefferson concurred that what the various denominations and sects of colonial times taught and motivated their adherents to do served to undergird the general moral standards of society.

For theologians and philosophers to describe in detail a just and humane political state is plainly insufficient. The philosophers and political theorists in ancient Greece and Rome, such as Plato, Aristotle, and Cicero, expatiated at length upon the characteristics of a just and peaceful society, and yet the great political empires of which they were citizens eventually collapsed because of confusion over what course to undertake and a lack of will to undertake the right one. Nations emerge, flourish, and fall. Babylon, Assyria, Greece, Medo-Persia, Egypt, and Rome are but some of the better-known nations that students now encounter only in historical volumes. The distinguished historian Arnold Toynbee reminded us that great civilizations usually commit suicide. According to Toynbee, the Greek's deification of man and human power was a central cause of the passing of their great civilization.[1]

Is American civilization in its last years? Is American society decadent? Or are we as a nation at the crossroads during the next year or so, as Billy Graham has preached during the last quarter century? Any prophecy about the American future should be suspect. There is probably considerable evidence to support several irreconcilable generalizations about our national character and destiny. The doomsdayers and prophets of gloom have long been with us. On the other hand, we must not say that the American civilization is invulnerable either to internal decay or external aggression. Christian political activists cannot afford to discount or ignore evidence that certain qualities of a responsible society are imperiled.

If, as we have argued, a great society in modern times can decay and fall, and if God's commandments still offer the profoundest wisdom that we can bring to bear on the modern political world, then it is important for us to inquire into the religious behavior of American citizens. Does American religious behavior reinforce the renewal of the Republic? What kind of values are being furthered in this society?

Since the colonial days Americans have been incurably religious. Their varieties of religious experience and behavior have been numerous. Herein we use the term *religion* in as broad a sense as possible, including all the ways in which people seek ultimate meaning and value in life. Religion bestows values and a sense of identity, usually within a community. Despite the high preference for the Christian faith, millions of Americans have added to their Christian commitment, secular supplements. Eventually these supplements—alternative communities and value-systems—supercede and even supplant authentic Christian faith. So deceptive is this process that too many are not aware of it. They cling doggedly to the conception they are faithful Christians despite their compromises with the world and various secular value-systems. Hence, millions of Americans profess Christianity and operate with secular values. They are Puritan in style and secular in substance.

This dualism in American character is nothing new. Alexis de Tocqueville, that most perceptive observer of the American scene during the 1830s, discerned this paradox: Americans are alternately

---

1. See *Civilization on Trial* (New York: Oxford University, 1948).

a people of intense materialism and intense spiritualism. A few years ago Reinhold Niebuhr suggested that this paradox is very much with us; contemporary America is "at once the most religious and the most secular of Western nations. . . . We are 'religious' in the sense that religious communities enjoy the devotion and engage the active loyalty of more laymen than in any nation in the Western world. We are 'secular' in the sense that we pursue the immediate goals of life, without asking too many ultimate questions about the meaning of life and without being too disrupted by the tragedies and antinomies of life."[2]

To the extent that Americans substitute secular surrogates for authentic Christian faith, they may indeed be undermining rather than undergirding a responsible society. Our purpose here is to identify six such surrogates that have made deep inroads into the systems of belief and values of professing Christians in America. We will leave others undiscussed (e.g., a man's work—he may expect salvation solely by adherence to the Puritan work ethic), and we do not suggest that the following are of equal importance.

Civil Religion

Civil religion is the common faith uniting the American people, different from but operating alongside of (and in its apostate version competing with) the Christian and Jewish faiths. It makes the nation the object of highest loyalty, and it inculcates the values of Americanism. Established institutions and opinions, the status quo, become the highest good. Since civil religion was the special subject of part 3 of this volume, we need not discuss its role in American society here.

Culture Religion

We have already spoken of cultural religion (in chap. 8) in two ways: religious expressions that do not claim to be Biblical or Christian and the "common religion" or "general faith" of most Christian denominations. The former constitutes a secular surrogate that is a substantial threat to authentic Christian faith.

---

2. *Pious and Secular America* (New York: Scribners, 1958), pp. 1, 2. Patrick Moynihan put it this way: "The crisis of the time is not political, it is in essence religious. It is a crisis of large numbers of intensely moral, even godly, people who no longer hope for God. Hence, the quest for divinity assumes a secular form, but with an intensity of conviction that is genuinely new to our politics." "Politics as the Art of the Impossible," Commencement address at Notre Dame University, 1 June 1969.

No astute observer can overlook the proliferation of doctrines, value-systems, and experiences that may be labeled "culture religion." Since the mid-sixties more and more Americans have found religious meaning in such things as crusades for social justice, encounter groups, technological achievements, and sensuous experience and other forms of group therapy. To scores of "liberated" and uninhibited couples, Esalen-like institutes became churches for the ultimate in experience and meaning. The use of illegal drugs is common in not a few "religious" groups. At times Ouija boards have outsold that traditional American favorite, Monopoly. Millions know their zodiacal sign and read the daily horoscope with a serious religiosity. William Blatty's best-selling *The Exorcist* and the popular film version of it, as well as the several cheap films on related themes, encouraged serious interest in and, in some quarters, worship of the Devil. In the academic world, Eastern religions, metaphysics, Transcendental Meditation, psychodrama, and T-groups have all attracted cadres of serious disciples. This frenzied search for person-changing experiences does little to strengthen basic Christian commitment. Instead it demonstrates a vacuum in the lives of many Americans, especially of youth. It is symptomatic of a crisis in human relations and ultimate values that goes to the very core of the spiritual dimension in life. The church must perceive that this "religious" phenomenon represents a vacuum in the lives of many people and that Christians frequently have failed to communicate to the world that commitment to Christ is no tame, humdrum, sheltered routine, but the most challenging and exciting adventure that human experience could ever realize.

Mass Media

The term *media* connotes a variety of channels used to provide and communicate information and opinion, to advertise, and to entertain. We may not be aware of how much the mass media pervade our daily lives. America is a nation of "media freaks." We read sixty-five million daily newspapers, plus millions more weekly newspapers and magazines. More than sixty million homes have at least one television set, often two or three. More Americans have television in their homes than have indoor plumbing or telephones. There are more radios in America than people—almost fifty percent more, or more than 300 million. Including film, books, and stereos in the category of media, total media consumption per person averages some fifty hours per week, exceeding every other activity but sleeping.[3]

At first thought it may seem strange that mass media is considered a threat to authentic faith. Methods of mass media are so new and recently developed when compared with historic, primitive Christian faith. And yet mass media, particularly the movies and television, may be preempting many of religion's functions, providing for twentieth-century Americans what worship provided for their ancestors. A person may regularly view a particular program, for example, similarly to the way a committed Christian regularly attends church worship. Coming back to the program week after week might assure a viewer that his own life is as consistent as the program he watches. The opening minute or two of music and scenes are identical each week and possess the quality of ritual. For the elderly and the lonely, television gives meaning to life. "I'm an old man and all alone, and the TV brings people and music and talk into my life," said one American quoted in *The People Look at Television*. "Maybe without TV I would be ready to die; but this TV gives me life. It gives me what to look forward to—that tomorrow, if I live, I'll watch this and that program."[4]

Not only do people watch shows with almost religious regularity, but they invest a great deal of emotion and empathy in them. They strongly identify with the heroes and heroines of film and television. Each weekday, for example, millions of housewives become emotionally engrossed in one or more soap operas. When they miss a segment, they contact another regular viewer to brief them on what transpired. How surprised ministers would be if church members listened with as much emotion to sermons, and if those who missed a sermon expended as much energy to learn his topic and how he developed it! One traditional role for religion has been to provide courage and hope in the face of tragedy. This is one area, it may be argued, in which television and movies are replacing worship. The media does depict cruel realism, including death and violence, but it reduces all of this to mere fantasy by constantly interrupting it with commercial messages. What intensely concerns us one moment—the reality of suffering, for example—becomes unreal and artificial for us the next as we listen to a discussion of

3. Don R. Pember, *Mass Media in America* (Chicago: Science Research, 1974), p. 2.

4. Gary A. Steiner, *The People Look at Television: A Study of Audience Attitudes* (New York: Knopf, 1963). Quoted in *Look*, 7 September 1971, p. 49.

body odor. In this sense television is an addiction that, much like drugs and alcohol, enables a person to escape in some degree the loneliness, meaninglessness and cruelty of real life.

We can cite statistics on how mass media pervade our daily lives, but most Americans remain unaware of just how pervasive the media are. Our daily routines and habits, our perceptions of ourselves, our society and the world, our systems of values and ethics—all of these are influenced significantly by the invisible environment formed by the media. The church is in no position to compete with the business and entertainment worlds in using the media to present and promote itself. The practical effect is that the mass media are the most effective educators in America. Not the local congregation, not the community school, and perhaps not even the home possess the potential of the mass media for shaping the morality and values of American youth. For millions the media play the roles of preacher, teacher, parent, public official, doctor, counselor, and companion. By the time the average child enters the first grade, Nicholas Johnson pointed out, he has received more hours of instruction from television than he will receive from professors during four years of college.[5] Motion pictures may have declined somewhat in percentage of viewers since the 1930s and 1940s, but they retain immense potential for influencing audiences, especially the young; seventy-five percent of moviegoers are under thirty.

With the mass media influencing most Americans so pervasively, it is incumbent upon responsible Christian citizens to discern the values and attitudes and ethics that the media are inculcating. The media, and television particularly, are mirrors of our society. What do they tell us about ourselves? In what direction are they pointing us? The answers are not always encouraging.

From television we see a society composed primarily of white, Anglo-Saxon Protestants, although in recent times ethnic groups have earned considerably more representation in family shows. From situation comedies we conclude that maturing children are much smarter than their bigoted parents and that little children are often raised by only one parent. From situation comedies and detective series we see a society in which all problems, no matter how far-reaching or tragic, are always solved—quickly, usually in an hour or a half-hour. In many detective series and movies, heroes

---

5. "What Do We Do About Television?" *Saturday Review,* 11 July 1970, p. 14.

and villains are stereotypes. The hero may have little capacity for love or compassion, but he is clearly in the "right." The villain is often a one-dimensional character whose motives are seldom analyzed, and as long as he is a "bad guy," it does not matter what treatment befalls him. In most westerns any method of bringing a man to justice is acceptable. Advertisements, the most costly films we produce, show people to whom material success is the ultimate criterion for greatness, who are more concerned about irregularity and hemorrhoids than the world's starving multitudes, and who have serious and continuing discussions about detergents, coffee, underarm perspiration, breath odor, and headache remedies. Except for soap operas, in which no one is normal unless he is grappling with a divorce, abortion, adulterous affair, or mental disorder, television pictures Americans with few daily vexations, or as David Susskind once quipped, "a happy people seeking happy solutions to happy problems." To Emmy-winning writer Loring Mandel, television tells us:

> That America is traditionally anti-intellectual. A lie. That the Good Man is the Man Who Ultimately Goes Along. A lie. That beneficence is inherent in business. A lie. That love is good, sex is better, and that passion doesn't exist. That any means are justifiable. That passivity is wise. That intensity is a spectator sport. That people bleed only from the corner of their mouths, and that instant regeneration of human tissue is a fact of violence. And by the purposeful omission of material that is relevant to our contemporary situation the entertainment programmers make reality more foreign to us. By expressing simplistic solutions to all problems, they rob us of the tools of decision. The truth is not in them.[6]

We have emphasized that human life is valued highly in the responsible society; each person is unique and irreplaceable, created in the image of God. Not so in the mass media! Violence in the media has always been a solution to many dilemmas, but certainly television and movie entertainment has never been so violent. In 1955 "action-adventure programs" (a long-time euphemism for "shoot-'em-ups") accounted for less than twenty percent of prime-time offerings. By 1975 the figure had soared to sixty percent, propelled by no fewer than twenty-four crime series. It has been estimated that today's average fifteen-year-old has witnessed on television more than thirteen thousand killings.[7] It would be the

---

6. *New York Times*, 25 March 1970.
7. *Newsweek*, 10 March 1975, p. 81. A cover story on crime in America in *Time*, 30 June 1975, named television violence as one major cause of violent crime.

height of folly to argue that all this violence has no impact on the value-system and psyche of impressionable youth. Television's prevailing message for adults may be less aggression than fear. Vulnerable people, such as singles, the elderly, and women, may well dramatically overestimate the danger of violence in real life.[8] The impact of fear, dehumanization, aggression, and even barbarity cannot be measured statistically as can the impact of advertisements. Christian critics should not ask that movies and television be purged of all violence. Its portrayal is as old as Greek tragedies and Biblical narratives, and it is as essential to drama as is love. What is reprehensible and, by Christian ethics and values, unacceptable, is the use of violence to increase profits without regard for subliminal consequences or societal standards of decency.

A final observation. The mass media in America may unintentionally undermine the traditional values upon which the responsible society is based when they give considerable attention to certain minority groups and their views. Of course any considered and responsible opinion deserves the right to compete in the marketplace of ideas. But at times it seems that any eccentric group, any outspoken dissenter, or any iconoclastic critic can get more time in the media than can majority groups. This may sound like the typical establishmentarian overgeneralization, but it deserves consideration. In the late sixties revolutionaries and anarchists gained publicity and attention they could not have obtained any other way.[9] In more recent times moral anarchists of all kinds have appeared on two- or three-hour specials and late-night talk shows. While such personalities and their views render a show more interesting to sophisticated and open-minded viewers, there is the omnipresent danger that when we give unmerited public attention to life styles and opinions that undermine the responsible society, we create the impression that these minority views are actually majority views.

---

8. There has been much debate on the effects of television violence on viewers. The research is reviewed in Steven H. Chaffee and Michael J. Petrick, *Using the Mass Media* (New York: McGraw-Hill, 1975), pp. 175-90.

9. Successful figures like Jerry Rubin, Abbie Hoffman, Eldridge Cleaver, and Rap Brown have made hundreds of thousands of dollars from best-selling books, interviews, movie rights, and lecture fees. Campus forums feature members of the New Left, old-style communists, anarchists, and Maoists; lecture fees have exceeded $2,000. Perhaps these "celebrities" are creatures of the media; their revolutionary life styles provide good show business. Hoffman said: "It's embarrassing. You try to overthrow the government and you end up on the bestseller list." Quoted in *Parade*, 5 July 1970, p. 7.

This is not a call for governmental censorship or harassment, but for both producers and viewers to make responsible decisions.

We must not conclude without acknowledging both an emerging maturity on the part of television and movies in dealing with certain themes, and the potential of the media to expand the awareness and sensitize the consciences of Christians. The outside world may be brought into the living rooms and dens of virtually all Americans. Good drama is available, even if in only a minority of shows. The mass media can inform the Christian political activist and inspire him to seek just solutions to problems at home and abroad. For example, "Hunger in America," a remarkable CBS documentary, informed a vast audience that many Americans were starving to death in our land of plenty, and it demonstrated the power of television to mobilize the nation on an issue; congressional hearings and legislation followed in the wake of this report. For another example, the media brought home to the nation the hazards of smoking. The important thing is for responsible Christians to sort out the overwhelming quantities of media stimuli, separating the worthwhile from the worthless, the informing and inspiring from the trivial, and even the truths from the untruths.

Hedonism and Materialism

Many Americans are willing to substitute for authentic Christian faith two philosophies that may be discussed together—hedonism and materialism. Many people who essentially follow one of these human philosophies also follow the other. Both share a basic premise that is the antithesis to the letter and spirit of New Testament Christianity—man is to live first and foremost for himself. What makes both of these secular surrogates so dangerous is their deceptiveness. It is easy for their adherents to rationalize. Perhaps millions of American Christians have been able to accommodate a self-serving life style based on hedonism or materialism with their conception of what the Christian life ought to be. Too often the church, even the preaching ministry, has bought the morally bankrupt value-systems of these counterfeit religions. Neither philosophy is new. He who practices either one has not learned to master himself.

Hedonism holds that the pursuit of pleasure is life's highest purpose.[10] Pleasure is pursued for its own sake. So serious may be the

---

10. A useful study of hedonism and its effects is William S. Banowsky, *It's a Playboy World* (Old Tappan, N.J.: Revell, 1969), pp. 35-52.

pursuit that hedonism is properly labeled a "religion." Discipline is largely irrelevant. As few restraints as possible are imposed, and there are no absolute prohibitions. *Hedonism* connotes for many an uninhibited, "swinging" sex life, but the philosophy of hedonism applies to all kinds of interpersonal relations. Everyone is free to "do his own thing" without the pangs of conscience. No definition of *hedonism* is more succinct than the slogan "If it feels good, do it!"

Though hedonism is as old as human history, it seems to have gained masses of converts since World War II in the Western world, and particularly in America. Jobs were plentiful, automation gave both men and women more leisure time, and there were simply more material goods with which to enjoy life. Consequently preoccupation with this philosophy is not limited to a minority of social extremists and publicity-seeking moral anarchists. But what have been the fruits of modern hedonism? There is little argument that the changes initiated since 1960 in public dress style, the mass media (both print and electronic), and public entertainment are little less than radical. What about attitudes and behavior? Perhaps *revolution* in this important area of ethics is an overworked and imprecise term, but who would deny that the changes, especially among our youth, have been substantial? William Barclay offered one impressionistic reaction: "Thirty years ago no one ever really questioned the Christian ethic. Thirty years ago no one ever doubted that divorce was disgraceful; that illegitimate babies were a disaster; that chastity was a good thing; that an honest day's work was part of the duty of any respectable and responsible man; that honesty ought to be part of life. But today, for the first time in history, the whole Christian ethic is under attack. It is not only the theology that people want to abandon—it is the ethic as well."[11]

More objective analysis confirms the trends that gravely concern dedicated students of the Scriptures like Barclay. A Gallup Poll reported in mid-1975 revealed that a large majority of both college freshmen and seniors say it is not wrong for people to have sexual relations before marriage, although seniors are about twice as likely as freshmen to say this.[12] The same poll showed that eighty-three percent of those with a college background drink alcoholic beverages, and about half of those polled believe that use of marijuana

---

11. *Ethics in a Permissive Society* (New York: Harper and Row, 1971), p. 13.
12. *Nashville Tennessean,* 18 May 1975.

should be legalized. Other researchers have turned up similar statistics on American sexual attitudes and behavior. The number of premarital pregnancies is as high as ever despite accessibility of contraceptive devices. Professors Melvin Zelnik and John F. Kantner of Johns Hopkins University completed a study showing widespread casual sex among teenagers. The researchers discovered that for every ten babies born live to United States teenagers, six were conceived out of wedlock; forty-one percent of white teenagers who get pregnant out of wedlock solve their problem with an abortion.[13] Obviously, attitudes on abortion have changed. Before 1967 practically all states prohibited it except when the life of the mother was endangered. But on January 23, 1973, the Supreme Court, basing its decision on the implied Constitutional right of privacy, struck down state laws and granted unrestricted right for abortion during the first three months of pregnancy. Statistics released in mid-1975 by the National Academy of Sciences' Institute of Medicine showed that only one-fourth of legal abortions were obtained by married women, and that the total number of abortions had increased to 615,800 by 1973 and was still on the increase.[14] Attitudes on divorce are apparently undergoing some change as the divorce rate continues to climb. Despite the removal of most inhibitions in our society and the easy availability of all kinds of verbal and visual stimuli, true love seems to be running less smoothly than ever before. Many otherwise sober-minded sociologists and philosophers insist that marriage and the nuclear family is a virtually obsolete life style today.

These moral and social changes in contemporary America, careful analysis reveals, must not be attributed exclusively to our citizens' embracing rampant hedonism. Socio-economic factors play a major role. For example, premarital sex is greater among black youth than white, but the rate of abortion at least for teenagers is significantly higher among whites. Also, the divorce rate among non-whites is almost double that among whites. But the greatest single factor in moral decline has been a wide acceptance of the hedonism advocated by pop practitioners and propagandists such as Hugh Hefner and Helen Gurley Brown. Too often the church has offered aid and succor to practicing hedonists. Unitarians in the Dallas suburb of Richardson had been "sharing" experiences Sunday

13. *Nashville Tennessean,* 5 August 1974.

14. *National Observer,* 7 June 1975.

mornings with such folk as a witch and two lesbians, so that few church members were surprised when Diane King, an exotic dancer at a Dallas night club, stripped in church to her G-string. They criticized the performance not for being immoral but for degrading womanhood.[15] Obviously this event is atypical. More typically, large denominational bodies have passed decrees denying the normative character of Biblical dictates concerning sexual morality; ministers and church leaders have refused to address moral problems unequivocally; church members have been overly tolerant.

The philosophy of hedonism is reinforced by another old philosophy that has had great impact on modern life—experientialism.[16] Experientialism emphasizes experiencing as much of life as possible. Even measurable religion means experiential religion. This seems more scientific, and the principle has been applied to other areas of life. Vicarious experience is helpful but generally insufficient. For example, an explicit "porno flick" or *Penthouse* and *Playgirl* are important supplements but inadequate substitutes for firsthand sexual experience. The ultimate experience, declare sex mechanics like Masters and Johnson, can be, indeed must be, experienced by all. In the search for ultimate experience, few kinds of behavior are barred. Prostitution, mate swapping, orgies, heavy drugs, and certainly all kinds of homosexual activity—none is condemned! After all, who has the right to say that his is the only valid and gratifying experience? Sin for virtue's sake; it may save your marriage.

This is hedonism in its extreme form and is practiced only by a minority of citizens, one may counter. Hopefully this disclaimer is correct. But this extreme form of hedonism is promoted widely in magazines like *Playboy, Penthouse,* and *Cosmopolitan,* and in best-selling books like those of Alex Comfort (*Joy, More Joy*) and Xaviera Hollander (*Happy Hooker*). One can search most of these magazines and books in vain for a concern for God's will, religion in general, moral character, responsibility to others, and personal accountability. God and His will have been deleted from moral experience, and the will of man is supreme. So persuasive is this indoctrination that many youth are licentious only because they feel they must to be accepted. One report from the college

---

15. *Newsweek,* 2 June 1975, pp. 46, 49; *National Observer,* 7 June 1975.

16. I am indebted to an excellent discussion of experientialism in Rousas J. Rushdoony, *The Politics of Pornography* (New Rochelle, N.Y.: Arlington, 1974), pp. 84-103.

scene, aptly titled "The Embarrassed Virgins," cited a "saturated sexual atmosphere" and noted that "some psychiatrists believe that youngsters are afraid of what they so insistently demand; they really want less rather than more freedom."[17]

Pure and undefiled hedonism (as well as materialism) can lead to moral suicide, both individually and societally. Perhaps the term *suicide* is not just a figure of speech. Statistics in the mid-seventies reveal an increase among young people of suicide; it is the second leading cause of death among youth. Not a few responsible thinkers attribute these grim statistics to a life style that claimed to promote self-knowledge and openness, honesty and caring, while promoting "guiltless sex," widespread use of drugs, psychological therapies, a new female consciousness.[18] Unbridled hedonism means cultural suicide as well. "Excessive concern with the gratification of sensual desires, or extreme forms of self-gratifications, weakens the higher faculties upon which self-control and social responsibility depend," declared Harry M. Clor. "And excessive preoccupation with sensual gratification results in the withdrawal of energies or interests from social concerns and their concentration upon selfish concerns."[19] A nation of thoroughgoing sensualists would never be able to respond to a call such as Churchill's for national sacrifice even if they wished, insisted Clor, for they would be unable to forego immediate satisfaction for long-range ends. Is this analysis reactionary? It is interesting that the morning after the Viet Cong took over Saigon, the new Revolutionary Government of South Vietnam warned that "anyone acting like Americans or participating in such American-style activities as opening night clubs, brothels, or other places of entertainment will be punished."[20]

Just as hedonism proclaims that man is made for pleasure rather than pleasure for man, materialism proclaims that man is created to serve material ends rather than material things to serve man. Few doctrines are any clearer in the Scriptures than man's proper relationship to his material possessions. God does not measure a man's greatness by the possessions he accumulates. Nothing can ensnare a person's soul faster than a love for wealth and worldly goods. Few things present as great a barrier to full and committed

---

17. *Time,* 9 July 1973, p. 64.

18. "Survival Tactics," *National Observer,* 10 May 1975.

19. *Obscenity and Public Morality* (Chicago: University of Chicago, 1969), p. 187.

20. *Newsweek,* 12 May 1975, p. 47; and *Time,* 12 May 1975, p. 10.

discipleship. The parables of Jesus and certain events in His lifetime drive home this point. "Man cannot live on bread alone," Jesus declared, "he lives on every word that God utters" (Matt. 4:4). Jesus also cautioned, "Beware! Be on your guard against greed of every kind, for even when a man has more than enough, his wealth does not give him life" (Luke 12:15).

Perhaps no other aspect of the American character is more obvious to and despised by foreigners than our materialism. On the office wall of Monty Hall, emcee of ABC's "Let's Make a Deal," is a sign that reads, "You can learn more about America by watching one half hour of 'Let's Make a Deal' than you can from watching Walter Cronkite for a month." Perhaps the sign is correct. There are more game shows than soap operas on American television. Contestants are screened for their ability to act uncontrollably excited, nearly delirious, about winning money and prizes. In one screen test a man suffered a heart attack trying to stuff his grocery cart with free food before the buzzer sounded.[21] In July 1975 a woman was hospitalized in Danville, Illinois, after being knocked down and trampled in a department store by several shoppers dashing for money-filled balloons being released from the ceiling.[22] Perhaps this evidence is atypical, but Americans might be the most greedy people on earth.

With only six to seven percent of the world's population, we produce nearly one-third of all the world's goods and services. Americans own more automobiles, television sets, air conditioners, refrigerators, automatic washers and driers, stereophonic equipment, other electric appliances and gadgets, paper, and chemicals, and have better food, clothing, and housing than any other nation, more in fact, than several other nations combined. Americans waste more fuel, energy, and natural resources than several other nations use. If all major nations had demanded an equal yield of the world's natural resources, these resources would long ago have been totally depleted. Of late, many Americans have been both frustrated and angered by smaller nations that are no longer willing to sell us their natural resources so cheaply, making our lives more comfortable.

Materialism is one of the most deceitful of the secular surrogates for Christian faith. Jesus admonished, "Do not store up for your-

---

21. *Newsweek*, 7 July 1975, pp. 38, 39.

22. *Nashville Tennessean*, 5 July 1975.

selves treasure on earth, where it grows rusty and moth-eaten, and thieves break in to steal it" (Matt. 6:19), but this teaching is paid little more than lip service by most Americans. What is the position of Biblical literalists on that Scripture? In the same sermon Jesus warned, ". . . You cannot serve God and Money" (Matt. 6:24), but Americans just do not believe it and even boast of their high standard of living. Biblical admonitions against greed also are virtually lost upon many American Christians. The almighty dollar is both status in a status-conscious if classless society, and the essence of life. Americans also are fierce competitors, and the best reward is financial gain. Might Jesus evaluate Americans much as He did the self-confident and complacent Laodiceans, who thought they were wealthy and needed nothing but in actuality were "poor, blind, and naked" (Rev. 3:17)?

We have already mentioned the mass media as a secular substitute, and it also gives impetus to the materialistic impulse, especially though not exclusively in its advertising. Toynbee wrote that he disliked Western civilization because of the advertising that flourishes in it, advertising that is the "fine art of taking advantage of human silliness. It rams unwanted goods down surfeited throats when two-thirds of all human beings now alive are in desperate need of the bare necessities of life. This is an ugly aspect of the affluent society."[23] John Kenneth Galbraith coined the phrase "synthesizer of wants" for media advertising. It can stimulate demand for objects and gadgets of which consumers have never heard and for which they have never felt any need. Markets can be created overnight if the appeal is right. Advertising may persuade men and women that to entice the opposite sex they need a new fragrance, new mouthwash, new toothpaste, or new deodorant. Consumers are instructed that they need a second or even third car. No similar dynamic force promotes the unmerchantable services of the state—public health, urban renewal, education, disease prevention, or the tax revenue services needed to make these services possible. And yet the demand for new services and products makes these governmental services all the more needed. The result: a deterioration of our physical environment and of the quality of public and private life.

Perhaps the archetype of hedonism and its vast if not always

---

23. "Why I Dislike Western Civilization," *New York Times Magazine*, 10 May 1964, p. 30.

exorbitantly profitable empire of books, gadgets, clubs, mansions, and ocean resorts, is *Playboy*. It advocates a life style that is at odds with Christian ideals. If the life of Christ ("Foxes have holes, and the birds of the air have nests; but the Son of man has nowhere to lay his head"), Christ's dictum to the rich young ruler ("Sell what you possess and give to the poor"), and the early church's example of self-denial and sharing with others mean anything today, they mean that the Christian cannot embrace the life style of the Playboy.

When one peruses the ads and pictorial features, his overall impression is materialism unbounded. The average young man probably will never be able to purchase, or even rent, a yacht. The "Playboy pads" frequently featured are too expensive for all but a very small percentage of people today. With the world becoming more and more overpopulated, with our precious resources, including land itself, dwindling away, with less wealth to share and inflation eating away at what we do have, the majority of readers do not have the resources for the Epicurean life style depicted by *Playboy* and its advertisers. Until a young man reaches the pinnacle of financial success, he must forego the finest living accommodations, automobiles imported from Europe, expensive motorcycles, dunebuggies, electronic gadgets, the latest clothing fashions, and the best foods and liquors. If he reads *Playboy*, he may feel cheated.

This indictment of *Playboy*, of course, could be applied to many other magazines and other media, but *Playboy* seems more richly to deserve it. We refer to a statement made earlier in another context: we are to love people and use things, not vice versa, even if persons do not object to being "thingified." The warning of the apostle Paul is not to be taken lightly: "Those who want to be rich fall into temptations and snares and many foolish harmful desires which plunge men into ruin and perdition. The love of money is the root of all evil things, and there are some who in reaching for it have wandered from the faith. . . ." (I Tim. 6:9, 10).

Life in an affluent society is not totally inimical to Christian maturity and service, and in the final chapter of this section we will outline a Christian response to relative affluence and abundance. Suffice it to say here that American Christians must not be "conned" into wasting money and time. We must distinguish between three things—what we need, what we want, and what the forces of Madison Avenue attempt to bully us into demanding.

Professional Football

A standard joke takes for granted that all red-blooded American males spend the first day of each year intensely watching football games. We should not be surprised by the thesis, forwarded in recent years, that "professional football has emerged as a new religion which supplements—and in some cases even supplants—the older religious expressions of Judaism and Christianity."[24] We might first suspect that the social philosophers and theologians who say this are speaking tongue-in-cheek, but further inquiry assures us they are not. Richard T. Hughes argued that the civil religion lost much of its sanctity and authority during the sixties when the Supreme Court removed prayer and Bible reading from public schools, and that taking "the place of the public school as expositor of the civil religion is professional football."[25]

Nearly all who agree with this thesis are highly critical of this new role for the sport. They see it as a degenerate and apostate version of civil religion. At best, "pro football performs the culture-sanctifying role of a socio-cultural religion by effectively embodying traditional, middle-class American values and symbolizing them each week during the fall and winter months for millions who sympathetically participate in its rites."[26] At worst, it sows the seeds of the destruction of our Republic by introducing children and young adults to intentional brutality, aggressive competition, greed for profit, male chauvinism, the language of war, and disciplined conformity to the status quo. One of the most flagrant attacks upon the place of football in contemporary American society has come from Eugene Bianchi, a religion professor, in an essay entitled "Pigskin Piety."[27] Bianchi is justifiably troubled by the "wedding of violence and lucre," by having players "bought and sold like chattel, in keeping with their gladiatorial prowess," and by turning the coach into a "campus deity." In his zeal to indict football he offered several sweeping and unfounded generalizations. Among them: "The absolute authority of the super-coach does not con-

---

24. A. James Rudin, "America's New Religion," *Christian Century*, 5 April 1972, p. 384.

25. "The New Expression of the American Civil Religion," *Mission* 6 (1973): 292.

26. Ibid.

27. The article is published in *Christianity and Crisis*, 21 February 1972, pp. 31-34; see Bianchi's follow-up article, "The Superbowl Culture of Male Violence,' *Christian Century*, 18 September 1974, pp. 842-45.

tribute to character-building in the players, but rather to their infantilization and the stunting of their development as self-directed persons." Again: "Collegiate and especially professional football reveal the fascist streak in our society. . . . It is the new opium of the people for conditioning them to cling uncritically to the status quo. The game is entertainment for persons who surrender their initiative and self-determination to the managers of law and order. For all its excitement, football is a political tranquilizer, a distraction from vital issues of self and societal development."[28]

Such generalizations cloud the issue, and there is evidence to refute them. Still the question remains: Is professional football a new civil or culture religion for Americans? Fundamentally, the answer is both yes and no. What we are dealing with essentially is football as a metaphor for Biblical religion. And, admittedly, it is intriguing to extend that metaphor *reductio ad absurdum*.

Just as Sunday has been the traditional day of worship for Christians since the time of the New Testament, so Sunday is the special day for professional football. In fact, pro football competes quite favorably with Christian churches. The stadium may be viewed as a great shrine or cathedral, where devotees wait all night to make their offerings at the gate and be ushered to the choice pews. (How shocked ministers and elders would be if church members waited all night outside the church building to be assured of a front-row seat at a worship service!) Pro football draws more spectators, counting home viewers, than the churches draw worshipers. The "football faithful" are not ushered to velvet-cushioned pews in air-conditioned comfort. They walk great distances from a parking lot where they may have paid five dollars to leave their automobile, pay eight to fifteen dollars for admission, brave rain, sleet, snow, and obnoxious fans, sit on a hard, perhaps splintered seat, and take in as much of the 2½ hours of action as possible. The teams come on the field, each suited in distinctive uniforms (religious garb), and this cues cheerleaders to lead the throng of thousands in the liturgy of traditional and hallowed chants. The game is usually opened by a prayer. It does not matter if the one who prays is Protestant, Catholic, or Jew; his invocation is a mere formality, and his words receive little attention unless he is irreverent, like the minister who referred to God as "the great coach in the skies." The prayer unashamedly links God, country,

---

28. All quotes are from Bianchi's original article.

and good sportsmanship. The national anthem is played. The time for the kickoff has arrived. The home team has prepared for this moment. All players, both rookies (novices) and veterans (ordained clergy), have trained in secluded and security-protected camps (monasteries). The coaches (the hierarchy) are convinced that their commandments have been scrupulously obeyed—no smoking, hard drinks, drugs, or late hours. A team chaplain may have already conducted a private devotional in the locker room. The combat commences. The goal is total victory, for the winners will have been more virtuous than the losers. The quarterback and defensive captain intone mysterious nomenclature and specialized incantations that direct and edify their teammates but that remain "Greek" to most laymen. Television commentators attempt to explain this lingo to viewers, but language and communication are problems inherent in religious systems. The players seek victory by executing their coach's philosophy. He is the priest. Each one has his own "theology," and the theology of the great high priests, such as the late Vince Lombardi and Don Shula, is adopted or adapted by other coaches. Half-time offers a twenty-minute respite for players and fans alike. It may be the occasion for a more direct homage to the civil faith—marching groups and bands and floats (at times with the help of Air Force planes flying intricate formations) present a show with a patriotic theme. The troups may form a massive representation of the continental U.S., the American flag, or a battleship to the crackling sound of fireworks. After their business meeting the players return to action. If the home team is victorious, the saints may depart chanting "We're number one." If it is not, there is a doctrine for consolation: "It's not whether you win or lose, but how you play the game," and the Monday morning papers provide the statistics for a clear insight into that issue. Further, the priest may reassure the fans, setbacks (reproaches, persecutions) only help train and chastise the players, renewing their desire to secure that final goal—a national championship on "Super Sunday."[29]

It would be possible to make of any popular sport an extended

---

29. Apparently there is no limit to how far such a metaphor can be extended. David Evans found a parallel for each part of a worship service (such as prelude, call to worship, hymn, prayer, responsive reading, offering, announcements, and benediction) in every professional football game. "God Is My Quarterback: Theology and Football in America," *Theology Today* 25 (1971): 309ff.

analogy and label it "religion." Rather than serving an expressly religious function, pro football may even have passed its peak of popularity, as witnessed by the rise of old participant sports like tennis and by the waves of public indifference to the drawn-out NFL players strike in the summer of 1974 and to the now-defunct World Football League. A safer conclusion is that sports in general is vitally and intricately related to both civil and spiritual-private religion in America, and that relationship merits clarification. Three conclusions about this relationship may safely be drawn.

First, sports has a tremendous potential for imparting and improving desirable character traits in young men and women. During their formative years, Americans learn that the highest rewards, the greatest glory, and the deepest satisfaction come to those who play the hardest within the rules. Foreign observer Roger Caillois contended there is "a truly reciprocal relationship between a society and the games it plays," and he chose golf, not football, as his model. "It is not without significance that the Anglo-Saxon sport, par excellence, is golf, a game in which the player at any time has the opportunity to cheat at will, but in which the game loses all interest from that point on. It should not be surprising that this may be correlated with the attitude of the taxpaper to the treasury and the citizen to the state."[30] General habits and life style learned in youth are carried over into adulthood, and the development of self-discipline, team cooperation, and leadership traits are undoubtedly the greatest contributions sports make to the development of Christian character. The rules of the game are made the rules of life. However trite and mushy this sounds, it is yet to be refuted.

It is not true, however, that participation in sports ipso facto guarantees showers of spiritual blessings and benefits. "There are probably more really committed Christians in sports, both collegiate and professional," Billy Graham declared, "than in any other occupation in America."[31] The evangelist may be correct. Perhaps no American has done more than he to drape around sports the aura of religiosity. His use of professional athletes and beauty queens during his mass evangelism campaigns has its obvious moral—One can be talented and popular without compromising Christian prin-

---

30. Quoted in Phillip Hammond's essay in Donald R. Cutler, ed., *The Religious Situation, 1968* (Boston: Beacon, 1968), p. 387.

31. Quoted in "Are Sports Good for the Soul?" *Newsweek*, 11 January 1971, p. 51.

ciples.[32] But it may inadvertently communicate two other messages: (1) Success will come to those who profess Christian faith; and (2) competition per se, in the public limelight, builds Christian character. In fact there is evidence to the contrary. For every Bobby Richardson or Roger Staubach who will stand before a stadium audience of thousands and witness to what Christ means to him, there is a Joe Namath who will tell a national network talk-show audience of millions what a life of "swinging" and few restraints means to him. At best, obedience to impartially enforced rules is given primacy over winning itself. At worst, winning at any price leads to contempt for rules and their enforcement, making them obstacles to be circumvented whenever necessary.[33] And it is obvious that greed and materialism have infected the ranks of both professional athletes and team owners.

Second, to whatever extent professional sports functions as a civil religion in contemporary society, it has secured renewed acceptance for two related doctrines—victory and team loyalty are necessary. Neither of these beliefs is new to the national faith. The emphasis on victory especially has long been an American trait. Americans have been reluctant to get into most wars in our history, but once involved, the public consensus has been "Win it or get out!" Was not General Douglas MacArthur's most memorable statement, "There is no substitute for victory"? But never before has winning and team loyalty been given such priority in the American civil religion.[34] A venerated saint is the late Vince Lombardi, the former coach of the Green Bay Packers. It is not too much of an overstate-

32. Recall that in January 1971 Billy Graham was the first clergyman ever to be a grand marshall of the Rose Bowl parade, later taking a seat of honor for the game between Ohio State and Stanford. The cover story on Graham, "The Preaching and the Power," *Newsweek*, 20 July 1970, p. 51, discussed his regular display of "All-American athletes and demure beauty-contest winners as the kind of healthy citizens that young, born-again Christians can turn out to be.'

33. As a former debate coach, I have observed that the same ethical difficulties plague intercollegiate forensic competition. For aspiring lawyers, ministers, statesmen, and other public persuaders, there is no better extracurricular training in logical analysis, use of evidence, and refutation than debate. But pressure from debate coaches to win leads many college competitors to engage in unethical tactics, such as fabricating or altering evidence, juggling statistics, and engaging in consciously specious reasoning.

34. The dangers in the doctrine of "winism" are discussed in Adrian C. Kanaar, "Moral Issues in Sports," in Claude E. Frazier, ed., *Is It Moral to Modify Man?* (Springfield, Ill.: Thomas, 1973), pp. 270-313; and "The Value System of a Faithless People," *Christian Century*, 29 May 1974, pp. 579, 580.

ment to state that, for awhile, he was quoted in American churches and college chapels almost as much as the apostle Paul. And the most memorable of his sayings is "Winning isn't the most important thing—it's the *only* thing."

One of the clear and disturbing points of the very popular movie *Patton* is that the decorated general was largely indifferent to the moral dilemmas of warfare; once a strategic decision had been made, the important thing was persistent team commitment until total victory had been secured. War was the thrilling challenge of making these strategic and courageous decisions and then executing them. That film was a favorite in Nixon's White House. Is it unfair to wonder about a psychological connection between the conflict ideology of George Patton and Vince Lombardi and the rhetoric of Richard Nixon, long hailed as "the nation's number-one sports fan," on the Indochina conflict? In his most important speech on the war in Vietnam, delivered over nationwide television on November 3, 1969, President Nixon declared that immediate withdrawal would be a defeat and concluded: "For the United States, this first defeat in our nation's history would result in a collapse of confidence in American leadership, not only in Asia but throughout the world. . . . Let us be united against defeat." He expressed the same idea in his network address of April 30, 1970, in which he explained his decision to invade Cambodia. Nixon was not the first president to worry about losing a war. As Hugh Sidey noted, President Lyndon B. Johnson could not conceive of courage and wisdom apart from a victory of force. Johnson told the press: "I'm not going to be the first President to lose a war. . . . Boys, it is just like the Alamo. Somebody should have by God helped those Texans. I'm going to Viet Nam. . . . Come home with the coonskin on the wall."[35]

As Christians we were largely incompetent to measure the accuracy of the president's military calculations and goals. But his basic message was clear: America, having never lost a war, cannot afford to lose one now, and anyone who believes differently is a heretic, an apostate from the American civil faith. But to the great credit of Christian leaders, both conservative and liberal, they seriously questioned the premise that America must always win. And when secular optimism about the value and goals of the U.S. commitment to Vietnam was weakening, some responsible spokes-

---

35. Quoted by Hugh Sidey in *Time,* 12 May 1975, p. 28.

men of the American civil religion, both inside and outside communities of Biblical faith, were saying that America does indeed "lose" by calling citizens throughout the land to regard victory as a higher national virtue and honor than morality. Winning for its own sake has not traditionally been a Christian virtue, and this tenet, to the extent that it is still there, must be removed from the national religion. For it is precisely when men and women can learn to live together as citizens not just of a national community but of a larger community, and when they abandon the fatuous dream of their nation always "winning" over others, that they turn to Jesus Christ and perhaps are miraculously granted the power not to win on the terms of some president, emperor, or king, but to be the chrysalis of a new society that will emerge from the disintegration of the present.

The third and final link between sports and religion needs little explanation—sports provide numerous analogies to godly living. Sports have provided lingo for both religion and politics. President Nixon consistently used the language of sports in moral pep talks. He announced "huddles" with his advisers to plan an "economic game plan." Nixon's code name was "Quarterback." Many a young man's first talk or sermon has been on "the game of life"; whether the metaphor is baseball, football, basketball, or tennis, the game is fiercely played to achieve the ultimate goal of heaven.

Of course sports and religion have long been mixed. The Pythian games were related to the oracles of Apollo and his shrine at Delphi. The Olympic games were played in honor of Zeus. Pagan games were exercises in holiness to honor the gods and celebrate peace. And while the apostle Paul rejected the pagan interpretations and implications of the games, he may well have been an avid spectator. In his epistles he employed athletic metaphors: Christians wrestle with powers of darkness; Paul buffeted his body, fought the good fight, and finished the course (cf. Eph. 6:12; I Cor. 9:24-27; II Tim. 4:7).

Sometimes a simple act on the playing field, watched by an observant world, advances Christian principles more than a spate of books or many series of sermons on Christian living. Sports ideally bring together on the same field or court athletes of different racial, ethnic, and economic backgrounds who learn to live and play together in order to achieve a shared goal. While this picture is an ideal one, there is much in it that is true. A case in point is

Roger Kahn's *The Boys of Summer*,[36] a delightful study in what might be called "the Sociological Dodgers." Kahn conveyed the excitement of the great Dodger teams of the late forties and early fifties, but he also dealt specifically with the backdrop of racial attitudes. "No one made speeches on the Rights of Man. No one sang 'Let my people go.' But without pretense or visible fear these men marched unevenly against the sin of bigotry."[37] Kahn claimed that the Jackie Robinson Dodgers did as much to combat American racism and create hope as did the landmark *Brown* v. *Topeka* decision. He may well be right.

In summary, while lessons from professional football—better yet, from sports in general—supplement both the religious and civil faiths, they must not supplant either. After all, our founding fathers and national heroes are not about to be replaced by Joe Namath, Hank Aaron, Mark Spitz, and Billie Jean King. The national shrines of Washington draw more tourists than the baseball and football halls of fame combined. Where in the famous quotes and quips of professional athletes and coaches is there a confession of commitment on a par with Nathan Hale's "I regret I have but one life to give for my country"? And who can name the burial site of a single sainted ball player? But if there is imminent danger that sports are replacing the traditional faith of Christianity and Judaism, the fault is not with sports, it is with professing Christians who opt for a secular life style, who place comfort, leisure, television, and tranquility above complete commitment and activism.

Decent, hard-working people in America have been crying of late, "What's wrong? Everything seems to be coming loose at the seams! There is so much violence, crime, corruption, and perversion in the world today." The evils of our time are but by-products of man's estrangement from God. The religious hunger of Americans today is as acute as ever, and perhaps more so. But too many of our fellow citizens have been content to substitute a secular life style and value system for genuine religious faith and experience. They have been too satisfied with life on the periphery to risk the radical life of self-denial and service to others, the central doctrine of Christian faith. Concern for the physical has eclipsed concern for the spiritual. Undoubtedly, too, the church has often

---

36. Harper and Row, 1972.

37. *Christian Century*, 5 April 1972, p. 384.

failed to offer the kinds of experiences and moral applications that satisfy this universal hunger. If the church fails to evoke vital worship and fellowship in the local congregation, it misses its opportunity to make a difference in the lives of men and women.

In the final analysis, the responsibility for a rich and wholesome Christian life falls upon the individual disciple. The Christian who faithfully provides for the spiritual man will find that the whole gamut of life becomes more beautiful and meaningful. "In Christ's name, we implore you, be reconciled to God" (II Cor. 5:20).

Power tends to expand indefinitely, and will transcend all barriers, abroad and at home, until met by superior forces. . . . Among all the causes which degrade and demoralize men, power is the most constant and the most active. . . . I cannot accept . . . that we are to judge Pope and King unlike other men, with a favorable presumption that they did no wrong. If there is any presumpion it is the other way against holders of power, increasing as the power increases. Historic responsibility has to make up for the want of legal responsibility. Power tends to corrupt and absolute power corrupts absolutely. Great men are almost always bad men, even when they exercise influence and not authority: still more when you superadd the tendency or the certainty of corruption by authority. There is no worse heresy than that the office sanctifies the holder of it.

Lord Acton

If you once forfeit the confidence of your fellow citizens, you can never regain their respect and esteem. It is true that you may fool all the people some of the time; you can even fool some of the people all of the time; but you can't fool all of the people all of the time.

Abraham Lincoln

There is nothing covered up that will not be uncovered, nothing hidden that will not be made known. You may take it, then, that everything you have said in the dark will be heard in broad daylight, and what you have whispered behind closed doors will be shouted from the house-tops.

Jesus (Luke 12:2, 3)

The tendency is for an administration to run out of steam after the first four years and then to coast and to usually coast downhill.

Richard M. Nixon (1972)

chapter fourteen

The Enigma of Watergate

June 17, 1972—a day American historians will long remember as truly a "day of infamy." Some may well record it as the official date when the American public's idealism and its unwavering faith in her institutions and officials died. Death arrived after a lingering coma deepened by an expanding presidency, a resurgence of political violence, the quagmire of Vietnam, racial conflicts, a spiraling crime rate, urban riots, the streets of Chicago, My Lai, and Kent State. On June 17, 1972, five men were apprehended inside the Democratic campaign headquarters (located in the Watergate Hotel complex) and arrested for theft and bugging. Senator George McGovern attempted to exploit this issue, but most of the electorate dismissed the whole matter as "just politics." The story mustered little initial interest. The *Washington Post* assigned two of its lesser known reporters to it. But soon after Nixon's second inauguration, startling charges and details began to surface bit by bit but with almost blitzing speed. Through the televised Senate Watergate hearings, Americans soon learned that the Watergate break-in was only the tip of an iceberg. Submerged were seemingly innumerable allegations of subterfuge, illegalities, and improprieties—so much below the surface that most observers concur with Senator Howard Baker that all the events of the Nixon years will not and, with much destruction of records and evidence, cannot be known. For awhile Americans could not believe it; then they could not ignore it and were angry about it; and then they receded into what columnist James Reston called a "protective feeble cynicism." The fall of 1973 brought the appointment and dismissal of Special Prosecutor Archibald Cox. The "Saturday night massacre," as the national press called it, probably constituted the single most devastating decision of Richard Nixon in the cover-up. With his back against the wall by the following spring, the president edited and released the transcripts of White House tapes, which immediately became a national best seller. By July 1974 the House Judiciary Committee had concluded televised hearings by approving articles of impeachment against Nixon. The president soon lost a Supreme Court appeal, a "smoking gun" piece of evidence surfaced, and while he was somewhere over the heart of America in Air Force One on August 9, 1974, Nixon's term of office came to an abortive end. Many citizens breathed a sigh of relief.

The Watergate revelations created a new crisis in American politics. Some will counter that *crisis* is too strong a term, and indeed terms like *unprecedented, super,* and *crisis* are vastly overworked in America. But except for during the Civil War, when has the nation been as confused, disillusioned, and cynical about its political system and its officials? Was not Attorney General William Saxbe correct when he opined, "We now live under what I believe historians will conclude is the greatest cloud in our history"? Many indices point to this crisis. National polls reported at the end of 1973 that Americans believe their garbagemen to be more veracious than their political representatives. A congressionally sponsored poll discovered as far back as September 1973 that fifty-three percent of Americans felt there was "something deeply wrong in America today," and even more people felt that "people running the country don't really care what happens to you." In response to the query "What are our biggest problems?", inflation was first with sixty-four percent; lack of integrity in government was second with forty-three percent; crime was next with seventeen percent; and thirteen other possibilities received less than fifteen percent.[1] A poll of political scientists revealed that disillusionment

1. This poll, conducted by Louis Harris for the Senate subcommittee on intergovernmental relations, is reported in *Newsweek,* 10 December 1973, pp. 40, 45, 48. It shows that alienation cuts across class, racial, and regional lines, and documents that public trust in the leaders of most American institutions—from commercial to religious to military—has decreased significantly since 1966.

with politics is running wide and deep; amost all the professors believed that a "crisis in confidence" would continue for several years and that Watergate reduced both the power and especially the prestige of the presidency.[2] A Louis Harris poll found "that of sixteen major areas of establishment pursuit, not a single one can evoke a majority of the public which can accord it 'a great deal of confidence.'"[3]

Polls since 1973 show little restoration of public confidence. Few in public life are trusted anymore. Certainly the official statements of corporation heads and board chairmen, particularly in the oil industry, are suspect. We have lost confidence in our military leaders. After the Rockefeller Commission Report of 1975, we lost what remaining trust we had in the Central Intelligence Agency. We have lost confidence in our diplomats. We have lost confidence in our money. We have lost confidence in our television service-man and our automobile mechanic. We have lost confidence in our educational institutions. And undoubtedly we have lost confidence in God, the churches, and morality. We have lost confidence in marriage and the family. Finally, we have lost confidence in experience itself; the best campaign pitch today is to claim to be a complete amateur. A spate of current books reveals the bankruptcy of trust in government—David Broder's *The Party's Over: The Failure of Politics in America;* David Wise's best-selling *The Politics of Lying;* David Lieberman's *How the Government Breaks the Law;* Louis Harris's *The Anguish of Change;* David Loth's *Public Plunder: A History of Graft in America;* and John B. Anderson's *Vision and Betrayal in America.*

All along, the issue has been larger than Watergate, and it has been fraught with moral ambiguities. Richard Nixon's improper tax returns became public when an employee of the Internal Revenue Service leaked them to the press; the employee, by failing to respect the confidentiality of individual returns, committed an

2. This poll was conducted for *U.S. News and World Report* and reported in the 3 December 1973 issue. A plurality believed that the scandals reflect a serious decline in political ethics in America, but many contended that politicians are generally more honest and responsible than ever before and that, in the words of one, "Nixon s people are a throwback to the past." In fact, the political scientists expressed great faith in the American system—more than is sometimes heard from the "man on the street."

3. *The Anguish of Change* (New York: Norton, 1973), p. 13. See also a report on the "disillusioned Americans" in *Time*, 15 July 1974, p. 23.

illegal act, but was it unethical? Senator Sam Ervin projected an image during the televised hearings of a doting grandfather and a country lawyer who quotes Scripture better than statutes, but many recalled his vote against a similar investigation of Bobby Baker during the Johnson administration and against important civil rights legislation. Some recalled that Congressman Peter Rodino voted to seat Adam Clayton Powell even though he was a fugitive from justice from his own state of New York. Was this ethical consistency? And it was reported that sixteen of the thirty-eight members of the House Judiciary Committee considering impeachment had received contributions from the same dairy lobbies who had contributed surreptitiously to Nixon's reelection. Americans were disillusioned when they read the Pentagon Papers, but many felt that Nixon's misconduct was no worse than Daniel Ellsberg's, who leaked the secret documents to the press. Watergate was an occasion for some conservative citizens to remind liberal Democrats of Chappaquiddick and to flaunt the slogan "Nobody drowned at Watergate." Americans traditionally have regarded political deviousness as an ineradicable part of the system, as, for example, the sayings of Will Rogers demonstrate. "There is no more independence in politics than there is in jail," Rogers once said. But never before have as many Americans been as repulsed by corruption and immorality, and voters registered their disgust in the mid-term national elections of 1974.

Regrettably, the church did not speak early and specifically to this issue. Many church leaders spoke little and late.[4] Some were the most adamant defenders of the Nixon administration, as though one man and his aides embodied the entire institution of the American presidency. Some saw only the issue of partisan politics and counterattacked the Democrats. Others urged their followers to mail stones to congressmen suspected of supporting impeachment. Congressman Anderson, an active layman in the Evangelical Free Church, noted: "It does strike me as ironic that those who seem to be trying to defend the Word of God most vigorously are the same individuals who contribute to presidential idolatry and

---

4. It is interesting that for a long time there seemed to be a dearth in church periodicals and papers of serious comment about this political corruption. Writers occasionally lamented the declining trust in public leaders, but comments specifically on Watergate—until the transcripts were released—were usually only innocuous tidbits, such as the mention of "Watergate" in the Bible (cf. Neh. 8:1).

seem unconcerned as to whether or not the laws and Constitution have been violated."[5]

No space will be taken here to refute the charge that Christian concern over political corruption is getting the church too ensconced in politics. As we argued earlier in this volume, no political action can be divorced absolutely from its moral implications since it seeks to change or preserve the status quo in one way or the other. Morality is not simply the business of political idealists. As Jeb Magruder implied, morality is our compass, and if we do not use it, we will lose more than our bearings, we will lose our society. Christians no less than anyone else should support the process of justice, renew their respect for the law, and preserve the constitutional system itself. To evaluate how "Christian" America is, or just how responsible it is, one must come to grips with this issue.

A final note in beginning. We are not concerned with chronicling the Watergate "shenanigans" (Who gave the sealed envelope to whom? What caused the 18½-minute gap on one tape? Exactly who edited the tape manuscripts? Which phone was used for that call?) Plenty of books now available do just this. We are concerned with larger questions: What are the theological issues at stake? How did we allow it to happen? Are only the direct participants to blame, or are we all responsible to some degree? Is the whole thing a passing aberration? What are the Biblical lessons that Christians must learn from these events? These questions are not easily answered, but we dare not avoid them.

They All Do It—or Do They?

The first thing Christians should realize before attempting to place Watergate in Christian perspective is that corruption and other unethical behavior have long been part of American politics. Precious few Watergate developments were totally unprecedented. While this has been called an age of permissiveness, it would be exceedingly difficult to prove that the public officials of bygone generations were any more devoted to truth, any less prone to abuse power, and any more open and honest in all their dealings. (Walter Lippmann once reminded us that we cannot write a history of political corruption in America; at best we can write only a history of the political corruption that has been exposed.)

First, let us iterate the judgment that the vast majority of public

---

5. *Vision and Betrayal in America* (Waco, Tex.: Word, 1975), p. 114.

officials have been and continue to be honorable in their dealings. In political life the good outweighs the evil (presuming that evil is something more than incompetence and inefficiency). In 1517 Niccolò Machiavelli wrote *The Prince* for the benefit of the ruling Florentine house of the Medici. Machiavelli, a product of the Renaissance, made the possession of power the ultimate goal of personal and political endeavor. His book was a treatise on how to get, hold, and increase power; other qualities of leadership are relevant only to the extent that they contribute to the desired goal, namely, domination of persons and events. This end justifies any means. Any tactic in pursuit of power is legitimate. To the credit of American politicians, they have not adopted Machiavelli's doctrine. No congressman would urge his colleagues to use it for a handbook. This is not to say that Machiavelli's ideas have not been practiced but that most Americans prefer leaders of good will and integrity. Our contemporary ethical values undoubtedly are more sensitive and advanced than those in vogue during the Renaissance.

On the other hand, we have not always had the legal apparatus and administrative controls that restrain corruption today. The most eloquent senator of the early national period, Daniel Webster, was once "on the take" from Nicholas Biddle and his second Bank of the U.S. Webster once complained to Biddle, "My retainer has not been renewed, or refreshed as usual. If it be wished that my relation to the Bank should be continued it may be well to send me the usual retainers." Biddle also distributed favors to three vice presidents, eminent cabinet members, and several of the country's leading editors.[6] Lincoln's sympathetic biographer, Carl Sandburg, related that not only was there demoralizing graft in virtually every department of government during the Civil War, but Lincoln at times put men in positions where he knew they would both enrich themselves and corrupt others in order to obtain what might be considered beneficent ends. The period during and just following a great war has always been subject to excesses and corruption of all kinds. Recall the corruption of the Grant and Harding administrations. And bribery has been alleged in every administration from Truman to Nixon, though the bribe may have been nothing more than a mink coat. The situation is different now. Controls have been established, and modern administrative techniques

---

6. Paul H. Douglas, *Ethics in Government* (Cambridge: Harvard University, 1952), p. 15.

have evolved. The spoils system is virtually eliminated, and the civil service has developed a professional style of operation. By now, governmental machinery, at least at the national level, copes much better than that of private business with the problem of the dishonest employee.[7] And throughout our history there has been less corruption in Washington than at the state and local levels.

Historians and political philosophers are certain to rank Watergate as the worst of presidential misdeeds, but that is not to say that they will regard the early seventies as any more corrupt than earlier times. Many of the Watergate episodes constituted repressive behavior that is typical of ruling classes in what they, at least, perceive to be crises. (One must recall the mass unrest in the 1960s and the mass demonstrations and civil disobedience employed by the antiwar and civil rights movements.) But "official" repression is not unprecedented—the Alien and Sedition Acts in the administration of John Adams; the suspension of due process rights by Abraham Lincoln during the war; the roundup of suspected Bolsheviks in the administration of Woodrow Wilson; the incarceration of thousands of Japanese-Americans after Pearl Harbor by Franklin Roosevelt; the persecution of suspected Communists and "fellow travelers" during the Truman and Eisenhower Administrations. Assertions that the "plumbers'" tactics were unique or unprecedented are partisan or naive. Extensive wiretapping, monitoring of mail, using paid informants and provocateurs, keeping track of suspected subversives, making "surreptitious entries," infiltrating radical organizations—these have been long-standing tactics of federal security agencies.

As for dirty campaign tricks, they were not unheard of until the 1970s either. Tricks, spying, insinuations, smearing, and forged documents are as old as presidential campaigns. In 1928 Al Smith was smeared with fake photographs; and Herbert Hoover, by rearranging phrases from his speeches to make them say what he did not. In 1952 opponents of Eisenhower in Michigan stuffed mailboxes on the night before the election with brochures announcing that the popular general had died suddenly. In 1960 John Kennedy spoke of a "missile gap." When questioned about it after taking office, the late president dismissed the whole issue as campaign rhetoric. In that same close election there was a reasonable question as to whether votes were actually stolen in Texas and Illinois; no

---

7. See "Corruption in the United States," *Time,* 31 December 1973, pp. 16, 17.

investigation ensued. In 1964 Barry Goldwater's opponents depicted him as a man with an itchy finger near the atomic bomb button.

In our study of morality and moralism in American political life, we commented that American politics is one big morality play. An election campaign becomes a moral crusade whatever else it may be. The opposition, especially if it is the administration in power, must be portrayed as a motley collection of scoundrels and self-serving men. It is not enough to show they are inefficient or inert; they must be morally delinquent. Virtue-rattling, like bomb-rattling, tends to escalate. If one candidate produces a list of all financial contributors to his campaign, his opponents had better produce their lists. When in 1952 Richard Nixon was accused of maintaining a private "slush fund" for personal spending, candidate Eisenhower did not at first defend him but told the press his running mate must come "clean as a hound's tooth," a homely standard that produced the "Checkers" speech. Stevenson then reported a list of *his* personal assets.[8] Each election campaign raises the ante a little more. When higher standards are formulated and then met, the political opposition feels compelled to exploit isolated instances of impropriety so that they appear as new examples of massive, pervasive, hidden corruption. Standards may be raised to the level where old deeds can be reinterpreted as moral delinquency. The change in ethical standards over a series of election campaigns makes yesterday's peccadillo, today's enormity.[9]

This theory applies to Watergate in only a limited way. This scandal was in some ways the worst our nation has experienced. In other ways, Nixon-baiters in the press and in both parties were petty in their criticisms of certain aspects of the first family's behavior, and they failed to take into account historical precedents for the kinds of major corruption they deplored. For Christian ethicists, this realization can deflate an exaggerated righteous indignation.

The Real Watergate Issue: Power

The chief theological issues of Watergate are pride and idolatry

8. The story of the 1952 campaign and the corruption issue is told in several sources, but one adequate narrative is Eric Goldman, *The Crucial Decade—and After: America, 1945-1960* (New York: Vintage, 1960), pp. 226-36.

9. I am indebted to a single source for this idea of moral escalation: Bayless Manning, "The Purity Potlatch," *Federal Bar Journal* 24 (1964): 243-49.

—the worship of self and of other false gods. Unlike the Teapot Dome and so many other political scandals, the false god of Watergate was not money or property. Nor was it merely prestige, though prestige was a nice by-product, to be sure. In this case the false god was personal power—power for the central occupant of the White House and power for his cadre of bumbling advisers, PR men, advertising agents, and confidants who in pre-Watergate days were virtually faceless and nameless and whose own power both emanated from and depended on *his* personal power. The exercise of political power involves authority, sovereignty, and the right to control one's own destiny and perhaps that of millions of others. The mantle of power produces in some a deep sense of humility and responsibility;[10] it produces in others arrogance and an obsession with one's lofty position, sometimes accompanied by desperate tactics to prevent any erosion of that power. Watergate is simply another illustration of the latter. In the study of man, it is a footnote documenting the persistent pressure to make one's own self and one's in-group the very center of existence, to abuse the power one gains, and to become haughty. This kind of pride is nothing new; it is original sin. And it is certainly not a problem unique to the American presidency; statistics show that only half of the Supreme Court justices relinquish their office voluntarily.[11]

Pride and the lust for political power in a democracy lead to three separate but closely related conditions that devastate both the power holders and their subjects:

1. A distorted sense of values and virtues. Those who worship the false god of power exalt themselves and their extension, the tiny in-group sharing their power. Why were plans for political espionage drafted? And after they were bungled, why were they quickly covered? The answer is simple—keeping the incumbent in office was the most important if not the *only* value. The highly

---

10. At the time of this writing, Harry S. Truman is enjoying a resurgence of popularity among old and young alike. Truman uttered one of his finest (if not most eloquent) statements, and undoubtedly his sincerest, after learning of FDR's sudden death: "I don't know whether you fellows [members of the press corps] ever had a load of hay or a bull fall on you. But last night the moon, the stars, and all the planets fell on me. If you fellows ever pray, pray for me." Jonathan Daniels, *The Man of Independence* (Philadelphia: Lippincott, 1950), p. 268.

11. Henry J. Abraham, *The Judicial Process*, 2nd ed. (New York: Oxford University, 1968), p. 43. At the time of this writing, Indira Gandhi seems to be another example of a ruler who will circumvent the law in order to retain political power.

legitimate concern for "national security" became subordinate to "Nixon security." In fact they so entwined the two "securities" that Nixon's henchmen may well have believed that the success of the president was essential to the prosperity and even the security of the Republic. Perpetuation of their regime at nearly all costs came to be a higher political virtue than the perpetuation of the regime through the normal democratic processes. It is a matter of *party* in the narrowest sense over *principle* in the highest sense. The guilty Nixon aides were more dedicated to perpetuating themselves than to serving the people of the United States. The people of the United States existed for the administration. This doctrine is essentially a revival of the "Führer," or "leader," principle of Nazi Germany.

If this sounds like too much of a generalization, one need only glance at the testimony of principal witnesses in the Watergate hearings. When confronted with what former Attorney General John Mitchell himself termed the "White House horrors," he told the nation, "I still believe that the most important thing to this country was the reelection of Richard Nixon, and I was not about to countenance anything [specifically, exposure of the Watergate cover-up] that would stand in the way of that reelection." Herbert L. Porter, an official of CREEP who had already confessed to perjury in the cover-up, continued: "I have been guilty of a deep sense of loyalty to the President of the United States. . . . I was appealed to on that basis." And then there is Jeb Magruder, deputy director of CREEP who secretly offered to take the rap for Watergate because he "honestly thought" that if Mitchell and others were implicated, Nixon's "reelection would probably be negated." The admitted policy follows the "Führer principle"; justice is obstructed, the crime is covered, the voting public is deceived, and the leader is kept in power at all necessary costs. Perhaps the most published remark was Charles Colson's that he would walk over his own grandmother if it were necessary to keep Richard Nixon in power. We might recall with profit the poignant lament of Cardinal Wolsey, quoted by Senator Ervin to Porter: "Had I but served my God with half the zeal I served my King, he would not in mine age have left me naked to mine enemies."

2. An undermining of Constitutional principles and democratic rights. We refer here to agents consciously perpetrating and furthering the leader principle. All regimes rest upon some combination of consent and coercion; even the most totalitarian government

must have some degree of public support, if only acquiescence, in order to exist. The lust for political power leads to divers methods of influencing public opinion. This is not necessarily wrong; a primary commitment to eternal principles does not preclude personal loyalties. But the democratic system is threatened when legitimate methods of control are supplemented by first improper and then illegal ones. We might say that the transgressions of the Nixon "palace guard" were more amoral than immoral and are all the more pernicious for that. Here were power-intoxicated technocrats who were dedicated to getting the job done but who did not want to make decisions in an ethical context because they were convinced they were not themselves profiting financially.

Problem: The president's saturation bombing in Indochina is strongly protested. *Solution:* The CREEP sends thousands of bogus telegrams to Nixon supporting the bombing.

Problem: The administration loses an important Supreme Court decision concerning the Pentagon Papers (leaked to the press by Daniel Ellsberg), and publication cannot be legally halted. *Solution:* Break into the office of Dr. Lewis Fielding, Ellsberg's psychiatrist, and steal information that might discredit Ellsberg in his pending trial. Never mind the violation of Dr. Fielding's civil rights, not to mention the "confidentiality" (in this case between doctor and patient) that our president so doggedly defended in his battle to withhold his tape-recorded conversations from the court.

Problem: Certain Democratic candidates threaten the president's reelection. *Solution:* In the case of Edward Kennedy, "doctor" State Department documents to implicate his brother in the death of Vietnam's President Diem. In the cases of Senators Humphrey and Jackson, steal stationery from Edmund Muskie and distribute a letter accusing his Democratic colleagues of sexual misconduct.

It is no defense to urge that these practices constituted a relatively minor infringement upon civil liberties that did not materially affect the election. The encroachment on human freedom that is today a trickling stream may all too soon become a raging torrent.

The campaign to control public opinion takes, at least from the Christian perspective, another dangerous direction—the prostitution and corruption of language. The exploitation of human language for partisan political purposes is nothing new, of course, but it seems to have been carried to its greatest lengths by the Nixon administration. The previous two administrations that escalated and perpetuated the "undeclared war" in Vietnam had desensitized the public mind with the novocain of "defoliation" for systematic destruction of crops and forests; "pacification" and "peace keeping" for the expulsion of all natives and destruction of all remaining life; "interdiction," "protective reaction strikes," and "air support" for carpet bombing. Fans of George Orwell were not surprised by the doublethink: we expand the war to contain it; we destroy the village to save it: Vietnamization in reality was Americanization. It was only natural that in the Watergate hearings, breaking and entering were called "intelligence-gathering operations"; burglars, "plumbers"; and administration-sponsored crime, "White House horrors." Terms like these—and "dirty tricks," "laundered money," "puffing," "stroking," "inoperative," "misspoke," "telephone anomalies"—all perform the same function in the public imagination and perception: they separate words from truth. Months before the Watergate story broke, William Stringfellow, noted ethicist and theologian, declared that the corruption of language is "the species of violence most militant in the present American circumstances." "That violence is babel: the inversion of language, verbal inflation, defamation, euphemism and coded phrases, rhetorical wantonness, redundancy, such profusion in speech and sound that comprehension is impaired, jargon, noise, nonsense, incoherence, hyperbole, libel, rumor, a chaos of voices and tongues, falsehood."[12]

Christians may cry "shame" at the obvious manipulation of language for partisan and illegal purposes in connection with Vietnam and Watergate and yet be oblivious to other uses of language to mask moral decay. In a guest column for *Newsweek,* Jane Otten raised the problem of finding a "bon mot" to describe one's unmarried child's having set up housekeeping with a close friend of the opposite sex.[13] How nonchalantly Christians acquiesce in the nomenclature of the mass media: *adultery* is having an affair or "being intimate"; *pornography* is "adult entertainment"; *lust* is "fantasy"; *revelry* and *lasciviousness* may be "exotic dancing." And the number of euphemisms for *drunkenness* are too numerous to list here. There is nothing new about these sins. What is both new

---

12. "Must the Stones Cry Out?" *Christianity and Crisis,* 30 October 1972, p. 235. In his classic essay "Politics and the English Language," George Orwell noted: "If thought corrupts language, language can also corrupt thought. . . . Political chaos is connected with the decay of language, and . . . one can probably bring about some improvement by starting at the verbal end."

13. "Living in Syntax," *Newsweek,* 30 December 1974, p. 9.

and terrifying is the attempt to purge language of moral connotations and thus thought of moral judgment. "Shame on you! You who call evil good and good evil, who turn darkness into light and light into darkness" (Isa. 5:20).

3. The covering of a widening circle of errors in a desperate attempt to prevent any erosion of power. That men who idolize power act indiscreetly or illegally when that power is threatened is evident. And the person who commits one indiscretion or illegal act to keep the in-group in power can with even fewer conscience pangs justify the next such act.

The Watergate actors would have profited from more reading of the Bible, which many professed to have studied devoutly in earlier days. One popular Old Testament story that comes to mind involves David and Bathsheba (II Sam. 11). One restless evening King David gets out of bed, walks upon the roof of the "executive mansion," and spots a beautiful woman bathing. He calls for her, and the result of their sinful liaison is an undesired pregnancy. The king is in a squeeze, not only as the political leader of a powerful nation but more importantly as the moral leader of God's chosen people. The king is more concerned to mollify public opinion than to repent and ask God's forgiveness, for indeed the law requires that the adulterer be stoned. David believes his power and moral authority depend upon his successfully covering up his deed. He asks his right-hand man, Joab (an equivalent to Haldeman or Ehrlichman?) to send Bathsheba's husband, Uriah the Hittite, home from the battlefield. When David confers with Uriah, he demands of him how Joab is doing, how the people are doing, and how the war is going ("The President began asking me a number of leading questions, which made me think that the conversation was being taped"). Obviously the king's real purpose is not to inquire about the war; after all, he has his own intelligence system. David wants to "feel out" Uriah. David commands Uriah to go home, and following him is "a mess of meat from the king." Here is a clear case of bribery. But Uriah is a man of principle who refuses to be compromised even by the king himself; Uriah refuses to be diverted from his commitment to victory. David then coaxes Uriah to remain an extra day and, at a banquet, gets him intoxicated. But, again, David's scheming is foiled by his subject's principles. In desperation the king orders Uriah to the front lines of the hottest battle, an order enshrouded in the deepest secrecy. The cover-up is finally accomplished, or so David thinks. When word of Uriah's death is delivered to the king by unsuspecting messengers, he offers cold comfort: "Do not let this thing distress you—there is no knowing where the sword will strike" ("Both our parties have been guilty of such tactics. The campaign excesses have occurred on all sides.").

The parallel between King David and Richard Nixon must not be overextended. We are concerned only with what motivated the mistakes of each. Only an envious or cruel-hearted person could feel no sympathy for the former president. After suffering personal setbacks and being pronounced dead politically in 1962, Nixon won the office he had so coveted. It is a mistake to conclude he was the devil incarnate or that not an ounce of decency was left in him. Nor can we conclude he was power-mad. If we concede his sincerity, he once entertained a glorious vision of what this nation could become and of the significant role he might play in its destiny. But somewhere along the line be became confused, permitting the collected bitterness of a long and rigorous public life and his obsession with the exaggerated influence of his enemies to blind him to the abuse of his own official power. But the lesson from the Bible is clear, and Watergate is only one of many illustrations of it. Men who idolize pride and power easily resort to irrational and radical behavior to retain that power, and one misdirected step can easily escalate into many others.[14] As one after another of the individuals who participated in Watergate was judged or pleaded guilty, we saw in action an inexorable spiritual law: "Make no mistake about this: God is not to be fooled; a man reaps what he sows. If he sows seed in the field of his lower nature, he will reap from it a harvest of corruption. . . ." (Gal. 6:7, 8). Or as Rudyard Kipling phrased it in his poem about Tomlinson's ghost: "For the sin ye do by two and two you must pay for one by one." We may

14. A sizable group of hard-core Nixon supporters maintained that Nixon had no knowledge whatsoever of the planning and cover-up of the scandalous acts employed to keep him in power. This theory was plausible if the president could have been totally deceived by his closest and most trusted advisers and assistants. To many this was unlikely but possible. Another story in the Old Testament involving David shows how a top official's aides may deceive him. David loved his rebellious son, Absalom, and wanted him spared. An unnamed witness saw Absalom trapped in the thick of an oak tree but refused to kill him. David's close adviser, Joab, who offered a reward to anyone who would kill Absalom, asked the man why he had spared Absalom. The man explained his fear that, had he killed Absalom, Joab would not have admitted to the king his part in the plot. Joab did not argue. He simply took three darts and killed Absalom himself (see II Sam. 18:1-17).

be grateful that in a constitutional system the people may employ forms of law to check the abuse of public power.

Rationalization About Ends and Means

Watergate is but another illustration of mortal man's persistent tendency to rationalize sin and to confuse ends and means. No one would deny for a moment that the reelection of the incumbent president was a valid and legitimate end. Despite all the dissent from war protesters and from liberals who found his policies out of line with their ideologies, Richard Nixon was truly the candidate of the great "silent majority," and there is good reason to believe he could have defeated any Democratic candidate. No one can deny the right of a campaign staff to make a probable victory as certain as possible. This certainly includes the gathering of extensive information and the development and execution of a strategy designed to make "our man" look as good as possible and "their man" as undesirable as possible. The real issue here is what means may be used to accomplish this goal.

A great deal of the religious comment that has been offered on this issue has drawn, perhaps very effectively, a moral link connecting the social upheaval of the sixties (including the antiwar movement, the direct action of Martin Luther King, Jr., and draft resistance), the Chappaquiddick tragedy, the Daniel Ellsberg case, and Watergate. These commentators have taken their lead from President Nixon himself. In his April 30, 1973, address, Nixon seemed to blame the advisers "whose zeal exceeded their judgment, and who may have done wrong in a cause they deeply believed to be right." In his address of August 15, 1973, he asked Americans to "look to Watergate in a longer perspective."

> We can see that its abuses resulted from the assumption by those involved that their cause placed them beyond the reach of those rules that apply to other persons and that hold a free society together. That attitude can never be tolerated in our country. However, it did not suddenly develop in 1972. It became fashionable in the 1960s, as individuals and groups increasingly asserted the right to take the law into their own hands, insisting that their purposes represented a higher morality. Then, their attitude was praised in the press, and even from some of our pulpits, as evidence of a new idealism. . . . That same attitude brought a rising spiral of violence and fear, of riots and arson and bombing, all in the name of peace and in the name of justice.

In his appearance before the Watergate committee, Jeb Stuart

Magruder forwarded the same logic, making a calculated reference to his former college ethics teacher, William Sloane Coffin. While humbly confessing his personal guilt in planning and covering certain acts, Magruder cited Coffin's situation ethics and antiwar activities as the philosophical basis and inspiration for his own illegal involvement. "I saw people I was very close to breaking the law without any regard for any other person's pattern of behavior or belief." Magruder further recalled Coffin advocating that "students burn their draft cards and . . . have mass demonstrations."

Two questions emerge at this point. First, does the prevalence of crime, corruption, and unethical behavior justify more of the same? Can ethicists and moralists condemn any individual life style or misdeed that, though wrong in itself, is accepted and practiced by society at large? Are moral appeals irrelevant in the modern world? There is much reason to believe that the philosophy is widespread that if a behavior is prevalent, it is excusable.[15] For centuries the seventh and tenth commandments controlled sexual behavior in marriage. Though the commandments were not universally obeyed, they were standards to which conscientious men and women repaired. In 1948 Alfred Kinsey published statistics showing that marital infidelity was much greater than ever suspected. There emerged a kind of "majoritarian ethic"—if most Americans are unfaithful, unfaithfulness is acceptable. Why uphold the old morality? If some desire the Scriptures to retain a modicum of authority, then change the meaning of *fornication* to "excessive promiscuity."

For all practical purposes, millions deem moral appeals largely irrelevant. In a carefully controlled study of college students' attitudes, it was discovered that the threat of sanctions (disciplinary action) reduce cheating on examinations somewhat, and moral appeals, none at all. When sanctions were removed and morality appealed to, cheating increased, with cheaters showing no sense of guilt and their peers showing no disapproval.[16] Another study showed that most young executives would do just what many members of Nixon's campaign staff did: join the cover-up. In a random survey of 328 businessmen after Watergate, almost sixty percent

15. For this line of reasoning and the example to follow, I am indebted to Vermont Royster, "Watergate and Public Morals," *American Scholar* 43 (1974): 249-59; reprinted in *National Observer*, 30 March 1974.

16. The study was conducted by Charles R. Tittle and Alan R. Rowe at Florida Atlantic University and is reported and discussed in Royster, "Watergate and Public Morals."

agreed that to prove their loyalty they would go along with their bosses even if it meant lying and deceiving; two-thirds said that all managers are pressured to compromise personal standards to achieve company goals.[17] The corporation chairman of Gulf Oil once declared, "There is no universal ethical absolute. What is immoral to some is perfectly correct to others." In commenting on this statement, *Time* noted that American corporations go along with this policy and it has exploded into scandal—"outright bribery to thinly disguised payoffs to politicians are the accepted way of getting just about anything done, from obtaining routine licenses to killing unfavorable tax legislation."[18] Must we now change our national motto from *"E pluribus unum"* to *"Omnes idem faciunt"* —"Everybody's doing it?"

A second question is, Does a worthy end justify *any* means? The Nixon aides seemed to answer affirmatively, although there must have been some place where they, too, would have drawn the line. If the common burglary and suspension of civil rights could be justified to keep one man in power, then so could the cover-up, and the cover-up of the cover-up. We may find this philosophy reprehensible, but there can be no doubt that it is widespread in the United States. The philosophy's more serious adherents gain ideological support from both secular and religious dogma; in the case of the latter we merely cite Joseph Fletcher's widely influential book, *Situation Ethics*. Many Americans still profess belief in moral absolutes, but in practice they will set aside any law or standard when they deem it necessary to realize a "higher" goal. This is true of church members and the unaffiliated, Democrats and Republicans, young and old, management and labor, black and white. The goals have been both victory in and withdrawal from Vietnam, more and fewer civil rights, and a host of lesser issues. Even the academic community has at times silently acquiesced in, if not tacitly approved of, civil disorder, bombings, breaking and entering to destroy draft records, and public obscenity. Few critics on the left have a clear enough record to qualify them to condemn an administration on the right. Regrettably, it took Watergate to

---

17. The study was conducted by University of Georgia professor Archie B. Carroll; published in *Business Horizons,* Spring 1975; and reported in *Newsweek,* 12 May 1975, pp. 81, 82. Many test subjects consider today's business ethics far superior to those of earlier periods. See an interesting special report, "How Clean Is Business?" *Newsweek,* 1 September 1975, pp. 50-54.

18. "The American Way?" *Time,* 2 June 1975, p. 64.

demonstrate that each person's "doing his own thing" can eventually destroy a decent society. At one time in Israel, when it had no king, "every man did what was right in his own eyes" (Judg. 21:25), and the result was moral and political anarchy.

Is not the plight of the United States similar? Each annual crime report of the seventies has shown a grim increase. "Adults are confused and at a loss," declared one psychiatrist. "They don't know what standards to set for their children or themselves. The bells that used to ring in your head to say no aren't ringing anymore."[19] Urbanologist Edward Banfield saw the "slippery morality" that emerged from the 1960s as a chief cause of the high crime rate in this decade. This "morality" granted to disadvantaged groups "a kind of quasi-right to have their offenses against the law extenuated, or even to have them regarded as political acts reflecting a morality 'higher' than obedience to the law."[20] One professor of psychiatry and law concluded, "There have been an increasing criminalization of politics and a politicalization of criminals. It's reached the point where there are no criminals in San Quentin anymore. They're all freedom fighters."[21] With disillusionment setting in and with fewer and fewer Americans looking to the churches, schools, or Washington for moral direction, we ask, Is this the kind of society we want?

We have argued the thesis that our nation has experienced a disastrous siege of direct action labeled "civil disobedience." The Watergate actors were not the first to display a misguided form of moral zeal. Our history is dotted with crusaders, like some of our early revolutionaries, John Brown, and perhaps Lee Harvey Oswald and Lynette Fromme, who identify their beliefs with ultimate truth and then feel free to defy any law promoting them. Phinehas in the Old Testament is an example of self-absolutizing zeal.

But is it ever right to disobey the law? Here we need not repeat the discussion in chapter 6 in which we upheld a moral right to disobey laws in what must be, at least for American citizens, atypical circumstances. Did Nixon, Magruder, and the White House legal staff really believe that their illegal activity could be lumped together with that of civil rights and antiwar activists? Or was this some sort of forensic jugglery concocted to relieve the pressure on the administration from an already distraught and confused public?

---

19. Quoted in a cover story on crime, *Time,* 30 June 1975, p. 17.
20. Ibid.
21. Ibid.

Disobedience that is morally justified must aim at repealing an unjust law; ideally, the dissenter disobeys the unjust law itself. But most important, it is essential that both the public and the government know what the dissenter is doing. If he commits his illegal action clandestinely and then feverishly covers it up, the public conscience cannot be sensitized to the moral issue and the law's constitutionality cannot be tested. Whether their actions were right or wrong in the sight of God, many members of the civil rights and peace movements followed the noblest tradition of civil disobedience, with the former openly and symbolically disobeying unjust laws that perpetuated official racism and the latter protesting a war they believed to be both immorally conducted and constitutionally illegal. To equate public symbolic acts designed to bring the law into harmony with higher justice, with secretive acts designed only to keep one man in office is unthinkable![22] The passive mind prefers to lump all these acts together. Watergate challenges Christians to sharpen their insights and consciences and to believe firmly in an ethical standard rooted in a higher authority than that of an elective office.

Outward Virtue and Inner Corruption

Watergate vividly exposes the sharp contrast between the outward virtue and the inner corruption of individuals and in-groups, and it is also a discomfiting indicator of the state of public morality in America. When he faced the public, Nixon proclaimed for the silent majority noble ideals and old-fashioned individual virtues. He was the moralizer, the faithful son of Quaker parents, who was duty bound to use the White House pulpit to summon the people back to their ethical and religious idealism. He used the vocabulary of theology—faith, trust, belief, and spirit—almost as much as that of football and baseball, but he applied this terminology not to God or Christianity but to his own nation and, more dangerously, to his personal policies and visions. While seeking the presidency in 1968, Nixon was apparently convinced that the individual citizens of this nation were being led down a path of individual moral

22. Commenting on Magruder, his former student, Coffin stated: "However pathetic our antiwar efforts were, we were trying to keep the nation under law or under God, while Jeb and his cohorts were trying to keep it under Nixon." *Time*, 25 June 1973, p. 13. See John C. Bennett, "Watergate and Civil Disobedience," *Christianity and Crisis*, 25 June 1973, p. 118; and John A. Huffman, Jr., "Biblical Lessons of Watergate," *Christianity Today*, 10 March 1974, pp. 10-12.

degradation. (This is not in any way to imply that his diagnosis was incorrect or hypocritical; perhaps the torrents of degradation were too great for one man, even in the highest office of the land, to halt.) With little measurable effect he acted on these premises early. His administration openly repudiated and castigated the findings and recommendations of congressional commissions on drug abuse and obscenity; supporters of these well-documented studies were labeled "permissive" or even radical. Administration recommendations for reforming the welfare system appealed to the long-established individual virtues of work, thriftiness, and sobriety. Nixon's position on abortion reflected his "personal belief in the sanctity of human life," but when it came to capital punishment, this belief was eclipsed by his desire to curb serious crime. And as for crime in America, no administration has spoken out as eloquently against courts coddling criminals and for law and order than did Nixon's. The war on crime was to be waged "without mercy."

An irrelevant question is whether the spokesmen for the Nixon administration were sincere about saving the lives of human embryos, winning the fight against crime, and keeping filth off our newsstands. There needs to be more public concern about these things, as well as a widespread renewal of individual responsibility and virtue. But we must be cautious about two other matters.

First, concern about individual piety must not preclude concern for broader issues in social ethics. To cite one example, the Nixon administration adamantly refused to recognize officially the pleas of churchmen and other conscience-stricken citizens on behalf of the victims of the 1972 Christmas carpet bombing of North Vietnam. And what about the secret bombing of Cambodia? Is it of no Christian concern that President Nixon had no legal authority to order 3,630 B-52 raids and drop more than 100,000 tons of bombs on Cambodia, all the while (as in the televised address of April 30, 1970) reassuring the American people, whose tax money underwrote these missions, that we were respecting the neutrality of a friendly nation.

Second, public style and image must not be substituted for substance. The men who became entangled in the greatest legal difficulties were the least suspected because they were men of good taste and manners, handsome, clean-cut (usually with short hair), conservatively attired, athletic, and religiously committed. One was a total abstainer (rare among politicos), another had once considered entering the ministry, another was called a "straight arrow." In the Senate hearings one lashed out at those who did not grant that the president's men had a right to expose the sexual aberrations and drinking habits of a competitor for office, even if this meant suspending the Bill of Rights. How far removed was this from the Pharisee who celebrated his own righteousness and scorned the tax collector's sinfulness? This administration returned formal religion to the White House—some forty worship services had been conducted there by April 15, 1973. In chapter 9 we spoke of the danger of "court prophets" who blunt the message of God to "curry the king's favor." There can be no doubt that Billy Graham was used to make the administration appear more virtuous than it was.[23] At the administration's request, a Jewish rabbi defended everything the public record established that the president had done. Even a Jesuit priest was marched before the American public after the edited manuscripts were released to defend Nixon's ethnic slurs and profanity. "These profanities have no moral meaning, and they have very little signal value," he noted. "I see the profanity as a form of emotional drainage." In identifying his employer as "the greatest moral leader of the last third of this century," the priest continued to offer what may rank as the most unnecessary advice ever offered the American electorate: "We certainly don't want a saint in the Oval Office."[24]

If we could conclude that Watergate was a complete aberration, that it was perpetrated by culprits who were devoid of ordinary moral decency, who just happened to come to political power at a particular time, then we could rest content that justice has been reasonably served and that the whole matter can now be left to historians. But Watergate is hardly that simple. The Watergate participants reflected moral views more widespread than it is easy

---

23. Graham seemed to acknowledge this in an exclusive interview for *Christianity Today*, 4 January 1974, pp. 9-19. Graham noted that, having no ecclesiastical authority over any public leader, he could not possibly relate to a president as the prophet Nathan did to King David. He said he is a liberal on many social subjects, adding: "I am a theological evangelical. I gladly take my stand with them. However, some of the criticism hurled at evangelical theology lands on me, and I suppose when I make a mistake it hurts the evangelical cause. I sometimes put my foot in my mouth. I've made many statements I wish I could recall. I am an erring, fallible disciple of our Lord Jesus Christ and am subject to all the temptations, human frailties, and errors of other disciples of the Lord."

24. Most of the remarks of Fr. John McLaughlin, at that time a deputy special assistant to the president, are in *National Observer*, 18 May 1974.

to admit. Watergate is a mirror that reflects the general morality of American citizens.

Howard F. Stein indicted the nation for its "silent complicity" in Watergate. He quoted Sigmund Freud's observation about a murder in *The Brothers Karamazov:* "It is a matter of indifference who actually committed the crime; psychology is only concerned to know who desired it emotionally and who welcomed it when it was done."[25] Freud's insight, Stein contended, has deep implications for understanding the Watergate shenanigans as well as the celebrated assassinations of the sixties: all were triggered by a sense of latent community approval. "The question of individual guilt or innocence, with its own set of cultural meanings, will be a matter of months or years of adjudication," Stein continued. "But to focus on individual culpability is to be constrained by our set of cultural blinders that prevents us from perceiving the wider context in which crime and punishment occur, a context in which they differentiate out as symptomatic of fundamental cultural conflicts."[26] An assassin may act because he knows that his crime will be at least silently approved by society.

There is a sense, Stein argued, in which the citizenry does not have a double standard. Politicians are expected to be inherently corrupt, but also to maintain a public image of virtue and propriety. When they allow their corruptness and corruptibility to become too overt, the public cries for justice, or rather for the sham to be restored. And when the public becomes completely disillusioned and demoralized, as during the Weimar Republic, then guilt, shame, and rage combine to demand a total house cleaning and purge. Citizens tolerate and perhaps envy the less significant kinds of political corruption for they both forgive and, when necessary, cover up their own petty corruption in private affairs. For his archetypical American citizen, Stein took Archie Bunker. Archie has no qualms about covertly circumventing the law. If he is caught, he resorts to either denial or rationalization. Archie both denies his own corruption and projects it upon the world, thereby cleansing him of the gnawing guilt. Hence, there were many Watergates before the real one happened. Instead of declaring "They all do it," we might more circumspectly conclude, "we all do it—if we can get away with it."[27]

---

25. "The Silent Complicity at Watergate," *American Scholar* 43 (1973-74): 21.
26. Ibid.
27. Ibid., pp. 32, 33.

One might counter that this indictment of American society is too harsh. After all, is there not deep inside the heart of America a thoroughgoing respect for law and justice? Despite some unpopular decisions, is not the Supreme Court the most respected political institution in our land? At first thought, the answers to both questions would be affirmative. But a closer examination of public morality in the United States forces us to qualify these answers. The average American reveres Law with a capital *L*, the Constitution, the legal system, and the Supreme Court, and he believes the "Law" should apply evenly to every citizen. But he does not practice this philosophy consistently. He is more typically indifferent to rules, regulations, and laws, or he is exasperated by them. When they appear to block the path of success, he may circumvent them. The attitude is not new. Many colonists did not respect the laws regulating trade, land, or Indian affairs that were enacted in London, and they felt justified in taking the "law" into their own hands. The same attitude persisted in the nineteenth century as the West was won, railroads were flung across the continent, and the ranks of the Indians were decimated.

This generation is no more virtuous. There is simply no dodging the fact that crime has become a cancer in American society. In a survey in the late sixties, more than nine out of ten adults confessed to non-traffic offenses for which they could have been jailed.[28] The high rate of violent crime has lowered the quality of life for potential as well as actual victims. From 1961 to 1975 the rate for all serious crimes has more than doubled; robberies increased 255 percent; forcible rape, 143 percent; aggravated assault, 153 percent; and murder, 106 percent.[29] But violent crime is only part of the story. It is difficult to maintain an updated list of the major corporations that have pleaded guilty to making illegal campaign contributions; and few were ignorant of the law. Some of the most distinguished, most successful, and most honorable corporations in America have been deeply, knowingly, and willfully involved in unethical, immoral, illegal, and corrupt practices that cut to the core of our constitutional system. Bribes and kickbacks are basic

---

28. President's Commission on Law Enforcement and Administration of Justice, *The Challenge of Crime in a Free Society* (Washington, D.C.: Government Printing Office, 1968), p. 43.

29. *Time*, 30 June 1975, p. 10. As if violent crime were not serious enough, the flouting of traffic laws costs us fifty thousand deaths every year.

business expenses for trade unions, bankers, doctors, insurance agents, builders, and even publishers. Another serious problem is employee theft from the company; sometimes employees work in collusion. Shoplifting costs a nickel on every merchandise dollar. The money spent on store security tripled in five years from five to fifteen billion dollars; seminars and conventions on security are now held. Three cents on the consumer's dollar are kicked back to store purchasers, sending them on vacations or building them private swimming pools. Many doctors and lawyers have swindled Medicaid and Medicare.[30]

American youth seem to have taken to heart the example of their elders. Cheating in colleges and universities is rampant.[31] Urban schools have become cesspools of vice and violence. In the spring of 1975 a Senate subcommittee on juvenile delinquency reported that there are now more than one hundred murders in public schools each year and seventy thousand assaults on teachers. School vandalism costs $500 million a year—about the amount spent on textbooks.[32] One school superintendent conceded that one cause of this is the lax enforcement of rules, but he added, "We are a reflection of the society that we serve."[33]

The practical effect of all this is that the average American has difficulty forwarding a consistent standard for measuring integrity and justice. A commitment to Christian principles demands that if we utterly disdain the wrong-doings of the Nixon administration, we must reflect upon our own indiscreet or illegal acts. If President Nixon exceeded the law in preparing his tax returns, we cannot condemn him until we look carefully at our own returns. If we assail him for using his connections with other government agents to accomplish partisan ends, we must not ask a politician or another person of influence to get our sons or daughters admitted into a college the entrance requirements of which they cannot meet. We must not attempt to get a local official we know to "take care of a traffic violation" before court date. If Nixon broke his oath

---

30. Most of the information in this paragraph was taken from an NBC special, "The White-Collar Rip-Off," aired 1 June 1975. The saddest aspect of white-collar crime is that so little of it is ever punished.

31. *Newsweek,* 21 April 1975, pp. 97, 98.

32. *Time,* 2 June 1975, p. 39.

33. Ibid.

of office, how many millions of Americans have flagrantly violated their marriage vows? Jesus spoke tersely to the hypocrites who dragged a pathetic adultress to His feet: ". . . one of you who is faultless shall throw the first stone" (John 8:7).

Alexander Hamilton once noted that people get the kind of government they deserve. In all branches of government, our public servants are no better than what citizens demand. "If we ask ourselves on what causes and conditions good government in its senses, from the humblest to the most exalted, depends," commented John Stuart Mill in his *Considerations on Representative Government,* "we find that the principal of them, the one which transcends all others, is the qualities of the human beings composing the society over which the government is exercised."[34] Our politicians reflect the prevailing morality of our times. If we as a self-proclaimed Christian nation can see our reflection in Watergate, our moral indignation over light penalties and the presidential pardon may be replaced by real penitence and a sincere search for ways to change what needs to be changed in our society. If the voice of the church is clear and strong, Watergate will have some saving grace. If this nation seeks excellence, righteousness, and justice, our leaders will surely point the way. No one concerned about the quality of government can speak seriously of ceasing to participate. Not only is that no remedy, but it will aggravate the problem. Recall the old aphorism attributed to Edmund Burke: "All that is necessary for evil to triumph is for good men to do nothing."

Political Leadership Is Moral Leadership

A final lesson from Watergate is that our public leaders must fulfill their responsibility as moral leaders as well as political leaders. Under any form of government, and at any time and place, political leadership is by and large moral leadership. The presidency, FDR once claimed, "is not merely an administrative office. That is the least part of it. It is pre-eminently a place of moral leadership."[35] Theodore Roosevelt said, "The White House is a bully pulpit."[36] A civic leader with great power cannot choose not

---

34. (Oxford: Blackwell, 1940), p. 125.

35. Quoted in *New York Times,* 13 November 1932. See Carter, "The Pastoral Office of the Presidency," *Theology Today* 25 (1968): 52-63.

36. Quoted in Edward S. Corwin, *The Presidency—Office and Powers* (New York: New York University, 1941), p. 267.

to exercise moral leadership; he can only choose the direction of his moral leadership. We noted in chapter 8 that quantitative studies have established that the role and importance of God and of the president are mingled in the minds of preschool and early elementary school children. Except possibly for the Supreme Court, no institution plays as important a symbolic role in American political life as does the presidency.

The mystique and symbolism surrounding the American president are sui generis. Perhaps no one has emphasized this fact and its implications more than Michael Novak, especially in his volume *Choosing Our King*. To Novak, the president is an elected king whose religious leadership is just as important as his political leadership. But the president's symbolic power is greatly underestimated. The nation wants, almost desperately, to believe in its president. In this geographically inchoate, sprawling, and disparate nation, it is reassuring to know there is one man in whom all Americans can have confidence. He is the only elected official who symbolizes the entire nation. He is the nation's image of itself. "Those in high places are more than the administrators of government bureaus," stated Walter Lippmann. "They are more than the writers of laws. They are the custodians of the nation's ideals, of the beliefs it cherishes, of its permanent hopes, of the faith which makes a nation out of a mere aggregation of individuals. They are unfaithful to that trust when by word and example they promote a spirit that is complacent, evasive, and acquisitive."[37] Over the years, since Jefferson walked to his own inauguration, we have granted to our presidents the life style and trappings of royalty. The pomp and splendor that Alexander Hamilton thought so ludicrous has in fact arrived. The 1973 inaugural ceremonies cost some $4 million (the grandstand alone cost $425,000, and there were five postinaugural "galas" attended by 37,000 guests, some of whom paid $125 per folding chair to watch the president dance and hear veteran comedians crack political jokes); taxpayers provide an elegant house and one or two resort homes for retreats; the president's personal staff costs nearly $10 million annually; he rides in a car built like a tank; the Secret Service controls all of his public appearances; and the ritual of shaking the president's hand is more and more like

---

37. Quoted in a column by James Reston, *Nashville Tennessean*, 3 February 1974.

seeking the medieval "king's touch."[38] Surely the easiest virtue for our presidents to maintain is not humility.

Despite all the pomp and trappings, the presidency is not an imperial office. When a man wins that office, he soon discovers there is nothing inherently ennobling or mystic in it, nothing that will turn him from an ordinary politician into a superhuman. He is not suddenly bestowed with virtue. Instead, he finds a grand opportunity to use power wisely and responsibly. It is considered a sacred trust. Jefferson once noted that "when a man assumes a public trust, he should consider himself as public property." When the trust is extended, it must be maintained. "Where a man has been given much," Jesus declared, "much will be expected of him; and the more a man has had entrusted to him the more he will be required to pay" (Luke 12:48). Once the president loses the trust or the affection of the people, as both Lyndon Johnson and Richard Nixon did, he discovers his varied political powers dissipating. And as Lincoln once reminded us, confidence and trust are never easily regained.

What does this moral leadership entail? First, it means respecting the law and legal institutions. Without respect for law and public order, democracy is doomed to failure. Though the president is elected by a national ballot and is the only one who represents all the people, he neither embodies the nation's sovereignty nor is above the law's demands; sovereignty resides in the people and is exercised according to established laws. A Herblock cartoon once showed a father instructing his son: "And so, remember the lesson —honesty is the best policy if nothing else works." The clear lesson, of course, is that a public official or an administration should not just obey the law when there are no alternatives. Conduct must go beyond being merely legal, it must be above suspicion. It was a sad commentary on American politics when a vice president, who was later to resign because of confessed wrong-doing, had to announce, "I have full confidence in the integrity of the President," or when the president himself had to declare to the nation (Nov. 17, 1973), "I'm not a crook."

If the high and mighty do not respect the law, the effects upon

---

38. These statistics are from Robert Sherrill, *Why They Call It Politics,* 2nd ed. (New York: Harcourt Brace Jovanovich, 1974), pp. 11-18. Sherrill cited numerous other examples. See James Thomas Flexner, "The Presidency: Where More Is Less," *Time,* 4 August 1975, pp. 49-51, for an excellent survey of how the American presidency has changed vastly since its inception.

the fabric of public morality and decency will be devastating. The sixth and final report of the National Advisory Commission on Criminal Justice, "Standards and Goals," acknowledged surveys showing that the public believes government corruption to be widespread. The commission concluded that "most people in public service are honest and dedicated" but added that official corruption "results in a staggering cost to the American taxpayer, and the existence of corruption breeds further crime by providing for the citizen a model of official lawlessness that undermines any acceptable rule of law."[39] This confirms Justice Brandeis's eloquent dissent in *Olmstead* v. *United States,* a criminal justice case:

> Decency, security, and liberty alike demand that government officials shall be subjected to the same rules of conduct that are commands to the citizen. In a government of laws, existence of the government will be imperiled if it fails to observe the law scrupulously. Our government is the potent, the omnipresent teacher. For good or for ill, it teaches the whole people by its example. Crime is contagious. If the government becomes a lawbreaker, it breeds contempt for law; it invites every man to become a law unto himself; it invites anarchy. To declare that in the administration of the criminal law the end justifies the means—to declare that the government may commit crimes in order to secure the conviction of a private criminal—would bring terrible retribution.[40]

Of course the "government" in the abstract does not violate the law. The government is merely a coincidental assortment of men and women paid out of the public purse. *People* break the law. But what encouragement is it to boys to obey the rules in constructing their soap box racers when church leaders dismiss political corruption with the quip, "Everybody's doing it; Nixon's boys just happened to get caught"? How can teachers teach young people the moral, ethical, and spiritual values essential to a free society if high officials disregard the nation's traditional, high standards of morality? What incentive is there for the little man to file an

---

39. Quoted in *Time,* 31 December 1973, p. 17.

40. 277 U.S. 438 (1928). Justice Clark commented: "Nothing can destroy a government more quickly than its failure to observe its own laws, or worse, its disregard of the charter of its own existence." Mapp v. Ohio, 367 U.S. 643 (1961). In an address to the Young Men's Lyceum of Springfield, Illinois, Lincoln stressed the importance of complete obedience to civil law. Reverence for the law should become "the political religion of the nation." The address is published in *Collected Works of Abraham Lincoln,* ed. Roy P. Basler, 9 vols. (New Brunswick, N.J.: Rutgers University, 1953), 1:108-15.

honest income tax return when the administration uses the IRS to retaliate against political "enemies"?

Perhaps most important, moral leadership means facing and telling the truth. Perhaps no incident in our history has produced such an orgy of finger pointing and buck passing than Watergate. But we deny the importance of truth in larger contexts because we love to delude ourselves. Some believed that our long involvement in the jungles and rice paddies of Vietnam, our complicity in atrocities like My Lai, and the lies forwarded by the Pentagon and retracted (without apology) only when reporters uncovered too much contrary evidence—all of this brought into American living rooms by the mass media—would at last educate us as to our capacity for evil. We would then know that our "New World" is not morally superior to the "Old World," that we are not intrinsically better or worse than other nations, only wealthier and a little more self-righteous. Further, we could profit from Hannah Arendt's study of the Nazis, which revealed how evil could be rendered so commonplace and so interwoven into the social order that respectable people simply learn to live with it.[41]

Watergate was a tragedy over which no one can gloat. But it was far from unprecedented. The Old Testament details the rise and fall of men who had great potential. One example is Saul, whose lust for power drove him insane. Solomon inherited a kingdom that his father, David, had made strong and prosperous. Solomon, who was both wealthy and spiritually wise, was given this advice by his dying father: "Be strong and show yourself a man. Fulfil your duty to the Lord your God; conform to his ways, observe his

---

41. One potent example should clarify this point: The Nixon administration, acting on cues from previous ones and abetted by the popular prophets of folk religion, contrived to reinterpret the Vietnam experiences as "America's finest hour," the culmination of our dreams for a "full generation of peace." Rather than saying the war had been expensive but necessary and that the settlement was the best possible given the exigencies of time and place, the administration offered us only the rhetoric of "peace with honor" and moral righteousness. It is instructive that scores of thousands of people on both sides were killed in Vietnam in the two years after "peace with honor" officially began in early 1973.

We know now the Gulf of Tonkin incident was a kind of "dirty trick" arranged to get President Johnson a blank check from Congress to conduct the war. The war was then escalated behind a smokescreen of evasions and misstatements. Surely neither Johnson nor Nixon began his term deliberately intending to deceive flagrantly the people or to usurp the powers of Congress, but they came to perceive these actions as essential to national security. For us the real question is, How much moral leadership, how much respect for the law, and how much integrity do we really want?

statutes and his commandments, his judgments and his solemn precepts, as they are written in the law of Moses, so that you may prosper in whatever you do and whichever way you turn, and that the Lord may fulfil this promise that he made about me: 'If your descendants take care to walk faithfully in my sight with all their heart and with all their soul, you shall never lack a successor on the throne of Israel' " (I Kings 2:2-4). But Solomon's consuming passion for sensual gratification eventually led to his demise. His many wives and concubines turned his affections away from Almighty God (I Kings 11:3). After his death the kingdom was divided, and its prestige and glory were never regained. Whether for a nation or a civic leader, a grand beginning never insures a glorious conclusion. How ironic it is to read what Solomon himself wrote: "A man who is still stubborn after much reproof will suddenly be broken past mending. When the righteous are in power the people rejoice, but they groan when the wicked hold office" (Prov. 29:1, 2).

Christian Realism: Antidote to Cynicism

Are there measures that we can adopt to prevent widespread scandals like Watergate? Various measures have been proposed to deal with the following issues: First, what is a legitimate concept of national security, and how may official secrecy be curbed? How may priorities be established for declassifying mountains of unjustifiably "secret" material now sitting in Washington? Second, how can we curb both the awesome power and official burdens of the presidency? How can we curb excesses and abuses in campaign financing?

We will not discuss these questions here. We leave that to the Congress, the courts, and political philosophers and scientists. We have viewed Watergate largely in the context of Biblical morality. By now it should be clear that even the most stringent controls will not work unless there is a basic integrity, a moral consensus, at work in this nation. Laws and policies are neither self-executing nor self-justifying. Unfortunately, at times their execution rests in the hands of those who are uncommitted to them. Even when laws and policies are faithfully executed and implemented, they can only deter the illegalities and immoralities of the citizens. They cannot make men good. Only ethics or genuine religion can do this. The story of Watergate is reassuring in one respect. Though Nixon survived for twenty-six months after the break-in and for fifteen months after John Dean first implicated him in May 1973, the legal and political system worked. It worked because an aroused public forced it to. It worked because men of tenacity and courage made it work. American politics now will be cleaner, and presidents will be more open and exercise power less imperiously.

From a Christian perspective, what is ultimately needed is strong indoctrination in Christian realism. It is not realistic to dwell upon the faults of a regime and neglect the good it accomplished. There is reason to hope that détente with Communist China and Russia will do more to affect our lives and the lives of our children for good than Watergate will affect us for evil. Nor is it realistic to ignore one's own responsibility by pleading ignorance of *all* the facts, uncritically accepting all the pronouncements of cherished politicians as gospel, and impugning the loyalty and patriotism of those who are critical. Those who do are "rendering unto Caesar" more than his due.

Neither was it realistic to search for scapegoats for the malaise surrounding Watergate. The most popular scapegoat was the American press. But after several years of government hostility and harassment, the nation perceived again why a fully independent press—despite its abundant faults, biases, and excesses—is essential to the American system. The adversary relationship between the government and the press must continue. The mission of the press is to give the people an alternative to the official version of things, another perspective on reality, a measure by which to judge the rulers and their rhetoric; it is not to serve as a megaphone for any given administration. A free press can be the oil that keeps democratic machinery running smoothly.[42]

The Christian realist knows that omnipotence and sinlessness in public leaders are too much to expect. All public leaders are flawed. Our political representatives are human beings who represent different constituencies, are not particularly fond of one another, march for different causes, and yet compromise with and accommodate each other, each hoping to come out on top. In the process they will shove and jostle each other as they jockey for the public limelight. Most will use strong language in private; a few will in public. Some, like Congressman Wilbur Mills of Arkansas, will act without propriety around women. Paul taught that

---

42. See "The Good Uses of Watergate," *Time*, 14 May 1973, pp. 24, 25, and the cover story on the performance of the American press, *Time*, 8 July 1974, pp. 68-75.

all men are prone to sin (Rom. 3:23). The important matters for the Christian critic to keep foremost in mind are the substantive offenses that go to the heart of political leadership. There are enough such matters to occupy us without weighing private behavior and language, unless they are symptomatic of something far larger. After all, the Christian's full and complete confidence is in God.

Put positively, Christian realism permits us to celebrate a constitutional system that allows us to choose our leaders and shape our policy while it concomitantly reassures us that ultimately not our representatives but a system of law and justice determines how we live within that freedom. Our founding fathers did not place the government above the people, but the people above the government; they said the people have certain "inalienable" rights that emanate not from their politicians but from their Creator, and, as Thomas Jefferson said in his first inaugural, "to violate [them] would be oppression." James Madison warned that "ambition must be made to counteract ambition. . . . If men were angels, no government would be necessary."[43] Under our constitutional system it would be difficult indeed to corrupt all three major institutions at once.

Christian realism assures us that not just any one administration but all who wield civil power are susceptible to temptations to misuse that power. Because we ultimately trust only God and because Jesus' words in Luke 12 renew our courage to trust the truth no matter how unpalatable it is, we deal cautiously and mercifully with all human assertions of power and authority. With this realistic view of man, the Watergate events have proven again for Christians the wisdom of Reinhold Niebuhr's often quoted statement: "Man's capacity for justice makes democracy possible. His inclination to injustice makes democracy necessary."

---

43. *The Federalist,* no. 51.

While each of us pursues his selfish interest and comforts himself by blaming others, the nation disintegrates. I use the phrase soberly: the nation disintegrates.

John W. Gardner

The evidence is strong that human society is in a stage of comprehensive breakdown.

Norman Cousins

The situation is not dire, the situation is not threatening—the situation is catastrophic.

Alexander Solzhenitsyn

I do not see how we scientists can bring the human race much past the year 2000.

George Wald

chapter fifteen

Toward a Renewal
of the Republic

Over three decades have passed since the world officially entered the nuclear age in August 1945. The sense of relief that followed the conclusion of World War II soon dissipated into the fears of cold war. The Korean War told Americans that the settlement of World War II was not as permanent as they had hoped. In the mid-fifties Nikita Khrushchev frightened Americans with his warning "We will bury you." In the campaign of 1964 President Lyndon Johnson warned Americans not to trust Senator Barry Goldwater. Goldwater would dangerously escalate the war, and "we are not going to send American boys nine or ten thousand miles away from home to do what Asian boys ought to be doing for themselves," Johnson promised repeatedly. Johnson was elected, and he was on his way to a great record as president until the Gulf of Tonkin incident was manufactured and emergency war powers were approved almost unanimously by Congress. The only two dissenters, Gruening and Morse, were not returned to the Senate. "In war, the first casualty is truth," someone remarked, and the Vietnam experience confirmed and illustrated this statement. The war was in large or small part responsible for mass unrest among youth, Kent State, the My Lai massacre, and bawling little children running with their clothes burned off. Americans had trouble accepting the dawning realization that the most powerful nation in the world could not break the will of a backward little country whose soldiers wore black pajamas, and they suspected that many of the casualties of the 1970s could have been saved if our civic leaders could have admitted a grave mistake. On the domestic front there was rampant inflation, urban unrest, civil rights demonstrations, and growing alienation among all sectors of the citizenry. It was a period of change. All institutions helped change our society, but the Supreme Court was a major catalyst. It proscribed prayer and Bible reading in public schools, limited public financial assistance to church-related schools, legalized abortion, greatly loosened restrictions on pornography, and reformed the apportionment for state legislatures. The courts played a major role in the "equality explosion" by opening new doors for blacks, women, and even homosexuals. These are but a few of the many changes in contemporary society, some of which have affected all of society, others only certain segments, and others very few people. Watergate touched the vast majority of citizens, and we have already discussed the widespread disillusionment it engendered.

Mark Twain observed the extremes in late-nineteenth-century America and called the period "the Gilded Age." Future historians may well call ours the "flawed age" or the "tarnished age." In many ways it has been a good era. It could have been a great era. There were magnificent moments, such as July 1969 when Neil Armstrong stepped onto the moon, or six years later when American and Russian spacemen linked their two spaceships in a symbol of partnership and shook hands, or when Richard Nixon arrived in the heartland of China to further his version of world peace. There were many new inventions, many social improvements, a lift in living standards, and a quickening of the national conscience concerning our use of nature and of natural resources. But the period was flawed. "For once there was a fleeting wisp of glory—called Camelot." Camelot, or something less, ended with an assassination. The peaceful civil rights movement, already losing support among black youth, virtually ended with another assassination. The man LBJ wanted to succeed Earl Warren as chief justice left the Supreme Court altogether under a cloud of ethical insensitivity. Nixon's chief preacher of law and order "copped a plea" by resigning the vice presidency. Nixon resigned and then was pardoned. Ex-CIA agents told of the bribery, blackmail, lying, and even murder which this agency had employed to protect American "interests" at home and abroad. By then we had lost our sense of innocence, optimism, and righteousness. Little wonder our enemies seemed to outnumber our allies. All of this brought the nation to the brink of a nervous breakdown. Pessimism, gloom, despair, and fatalism still seem contagious, spreading across our land like a virus.

The United States is a bundle of paradoxes. There is the paradox of *freedom*. Having pursued freedom more successfully than any other nation, millions of Americans feel they have lost irretrievably their personal freedom—freedom to breathe clean, fresh air, to walk downtown at night, to enjoy clean beaches and see virgin forests, to express publicly religious sentiment. There is the paradox of *power*. With the greatest accumulation of economic and military power in the world, we feel impotent to export our style of peace and reform to other parts of the globe. Even the future of democracy does not look encouraging. Old democracies are losing their appeal in several nations, and no new ones are emerging to take their place. There is the paradox of *knowledge*. Two hundred years ago Jefferson proposed universal free education as an antidote for mass ignorance, alienation, and incompetence. By the mid-twentieth century colleges and universities were jammed. The federal government pumped money into all kinds of research. Never before have as many citizens possessed college degrees, yet fewer and fewer feel that they understand the world in which they live or life itself. The masses enjoy twelve years of free public education, but they appear no more capable of wise and humane government than the smaller masses of Jefferson's time. Finally, there is the paradox of *communications*. Doctorates are granted annually in the many-faceted field of communications, but never have so many people agonized so much about "the failure to communicate." Especially is this true in the American home, the smallest basic unit of our society.

What Americans long for is a renewed sense of care, of ownership and stewardship, and a reassurance that we have some control over our destiny as a nation. Can all of this be restored? Can the American civilization long survive? Can public and private life be revitalized so that American citizenship matters more than it seems to have mattered in recent times? If we wish for affirmative responses to these queries, we must concede that Christian citizens, acting individually and in groups, will have to play an important role in our national destiny. We close our study of politics and Christianity in America with a brief statement of some of the challenges that Americans must face and resolve in the immediate future. These are more than political challenges, for they summon the creative energy and talents of American citizens who would also be faithful Christians.

Creating Real Community

One great challenge is the need to restore a sense of genuine community in this nation. Rapid transit, clustered living (as in apartment complexes and condominiums), and mass communications have brought people into closer physical proximity, but they have not united them. Several times in this volume we have commented on the breakdown of a moral consensus in America. Decent communal life requires mutual trust and respect, and this requires that certain fundamental beliefs and attitudes be held in common. No large nation can be bound together for a long period of time when each citizen considers values to be strictly a personal matter. We are using *community* in the sense captured well by James Q. Wilson:

> By community I do not mean, as some do, a metaphysical entity or abstract collectivity with which people "need" to affiliate. There may be an "instinct" for "togetherness" arising out of ancient or tribal longings for identification, but different people gratify it in different ways, and for most the gratification has little to do with neighborhood or urban conditions. When I speak of the concern for "community," I refer to a desire for the observance of standards of right and seemly conduct in the public places in which one lives and moves, those standards to be consistent with—and supportive of—the values and life styles of the particular individual. Around one's home, the places where one shops, and the corridors through which one walks there is for each of us a public space wherein our sense of security, self-esteem, and propriety is either reassured or jeopardized by the people and events we encounter. Viewed this way, the concern for community is less the "need" for "belonging" (or in equally vague language, the "need" to overcome feelings of "alienation" or "anomie") than the concerns of any rationally self-interested person with a normal but not compulsive interest in the environment of himself and his family.[1]

Accepting this broader concept of community, it follows that no nation can be a community that depreciates the importance of its citizens' beliefs and opinions. And genuine community is re-

---

1. "The Urban Unease: Community vs. City," *The Public Interest* (Summer 1968); reprinted in Paul Kramer and Frederick L. Holborn, eds., *The City in American Life* (New York: Capricorn, 1970), pp. 369, 370.

lated to social routines, habits, and institutional involvement as well as to attitudes and beliefs. Charles Frankel noted that "the mutual understandings and common loyalties that sustain a social order emerge out of men's daily habits and routines, out of the concrete institutions that frame their lives."[2] The failure of many American institutions is both the symptom and the cause of the breakdown of moral consensus in America, as home life in America demonstrates. There can be little doubt that the American home is in grave trouble. The nuclear family has never encountered such heavy pressures. Statistics show infidelity more commonplace than churchmen like to concede. Faithful church attendance no longer supports morality and restrains immorality the way it did in the past. Moral discipline is slackening. And yet genuine community cannot exist in a nation half of whose citizens believe in the sanctity of monogamous marriage and pay more than lip service to sexual fidelity, while the other half hold these values in contempt, believing that libido should be given free rein, that sexual gratification shoud be virtually unlimited, that sexual variety is "the spice of life," and that orgies and group perversions are matters of personal taste. While such a nation may survive in some sense, it cannot be a real community. If businessmen cannot agree on a general code of ethics, the business world will be in ethical disarray. The same principle applies to all our public and private institutions.

We can restore genuine community in this nation if we citizens concern ourselves with the quality of life we create for our children and our aged. The mortality rate is higher in America than in any other technologically advanced nation of the West. Child abuse has become prevalent enough for organizations to be established from which parents who are willing seek help anonymously for this seemingly senseless aberration. Even more serious for the future of this nation is the abdication by parents of their responsibility to provide moral guidance; in too many homes this function has been defaulted to the mass media. While most Americans, whether moved by Christian principles or common decency, still try to follow the fifth commandment and "honor" their parents, the position of the aged in America has become critical. No longer are retirement years necessarily the "golden years." About a million, or five percent, of our elderly already live in nursing homes, most

---

2. *The Case for Modern Man* (New York: Harper, 1955), p. 84.

of them private ones, and too many of them are grim warrens of the unwanted. Nursing homes are the last option available to many older folks. And yet, as Mary Adelaide Mendelson pointed out in her thorough report, *Tender Loving Greed:* "There is widespread neglect of patients in nursing homes across the country and evidence that owners are making excessive profits at the expense of patients."[3] Many convalescents learn they must relinquish their children, their life-long friends, their resources, their rights, and, ultimately, their humanity. If present population trends continue, those over sixty-five and those under fifteen should each account for twenty percent of our population by the end of this century. A sense of genuine community cannot be restored in America if we neglect the physical, emotional, and spiritual needs of our children and our aged.[4]

The disintegration of real community in our great urban centers threatens the physical safety and psychological security of millions in this nation. The combination of conditions that we label "the urban problem"—juvenile delinquency, street crime, slums, racial tension, street gangs, and public immorality—is intricately related to the breakdown of moral consensus. Any formulation of new directions for this nation that neglects the needs of our great urban centers is doomed to failure. At work is a process by which neighborhoods, in the fullest sense, are created out of chaos in the large cities only to encounter new movements and conditions that spawn a new form of disorder. Reactionary responses such as tougher and better equipped policemen, when separated from restoration of genuine community, will bring only the most cosmetic and temporary relief.

---

3. Quoted in a cover story, "New Outlook for the Aged," *Time,* 2 June 1975, p. 46. Statistics quoted in this paragraph are from this source. I have intentionally shunned the term *senior citizens,* which to many connotes that aging is something disgraceful and embarrassing.

4. Do Americans care more for their pets than for their children and aged relatives? Probably not, but if one is in search of evidence that America is a decadent society, he need look no further than the "love affair" millions have with their pets. There are some one hundred million dogs and cats in the U.S., reproducing seven to eight times faster than humans. Many of these pets get not only more nutritious meals, but also better medical care and vastly more attention than the great majority of the world's people. Americans spend $2.5 billion annually on commercially prepared pet food alone—more than six times what they spend on baby food and more than enough to nourish the third of the world's population that goes hungry. There are pet psychiatrists and pet astrologists. See the cover story, "The Great American Animal Farm," *Time,* 23 December 1974, pp. 58-64; and *Newsweek,* 7 September 1974, pp. 74-78.

Proving what beliefs and attitudes help maintain community life is not always possible. The values of the nuclear family (a healthy sexuality and a loving concern for children, the aged, and the disadvantaged) and of strictures applied to public immoralities and indecencies are hardly subject to scientific verification in the same sense that physical laws are. Consequently we cannot reasonably demand that the government enforce all of the sanctions and applications that emerge from these attitudes and values. Herein is the great opportunity of the Christian church. No other philosophical or value system can better undergird these positive values and attitudes than New Testament Christianity. "Christianity is a quality of life rather than a fixed system of doctrine," declared Willard L. Sperry.[5] Perhaps Sperry slighted Christian doctrine, but we must not lose the thrust of his emphasis. As faithful Christian leaders and laity, we must fulfill our responsibility to help restore a sense of genuine community in America.

Overpopulation and Hunger

When God created man and woman in His image, He blessed them and commanded them: "Be fruitful and increase, fill the earth and subdue it. . . ." (Gen. 1:28). Over the long haul of human history, no command of God has been more obeyed, whether through spiritual commitment, inadvertence, or accident. It took from the time of Adam and Eve until 1830 for the world population to reach one billion. By 1930 there were two billion, and by 1960 there were three. There are now four billion, and the number is doubling about every thirty-five years. The population likely will top seven billion by the end of this century. Overpopulation is already a problem in many nations. In western Europe, which many consider densely populated, there are now about 85 people per square kilometer. South Asia, according to the most cautious estimates, will add 140 people per square kilometer over the next quarter century. The future is *now*.[6]

What does all of this have to do with Christian citizens in America? After all, is not population growth a much greater problem in the developing nations of the Third World than in the industrialized nations? Committed Christians can no longer assess

5. *Religion in America* (New York: Macmillan, 1946), p. 138.

6. Statistics for this paragraph were taken from an address entitled "On the State of Man," given by Dr. Philip Handler, president of the National Academy of Sciences, and reported in the *Nashville Tennessean,* 11 November 1974.

world problems solely in terms of how they affect life in the United States. Perhaps the most stark realization of our times is that our planet is not indestructible and its ability to sustain life is not limitless. The telecasts from outer space show the earth as an orbiting spacecraft with finite resources to sustain all of its passengers. Granted that some passengers are presently faring better than others, the situation still is precarious. Population per se would not trouble the concerned Christian, but the population explosion is intricately linked to virtually every other problem presently plaguing the human race. At stake is human decency and the quality of life. Eventually we will see that our destiny is linked with that of the other nations of the world.

The two most significant problems rooted in overpopulation are poverty and hunger. The images on our television screens and in national magazines are anything but reassuring. We see legions of the poor, feebly extending empty wooden bowls. We see aged, gaunt, hollow-eyed people wracked by beriberi and scurvy, swarming the shantytowns and refugee camps, the back alleys, river banks, and garbage dumps of the city. We see bony, weeping mothers with barely living babes sucking on dry breasts. We see little children whose stomachs are bloated because their bodies are feeding on their own substance until death comes. We turn away in repulsion when reflecting that, but for the grace of God, those children would be our own. Impinging upon our consciences, they are poor, unloved, unwanted by the world, and unlovely. And yet Jesus said, "Blessed be ye poor: for yours is the kingdom of God. Blessed are ye that hunger now: for ye shall be filled. . . ." (Luke 6:20, 21 KJV). This is no ordinary appraisal, but several philosophers of human nature concur that there is something heroic and revealing in the poor, that there is a mystery about poverty and indigence that can elevate the human race.

Famine and poverty are by no means peculiar to our age. A study of Old Testament history shows that these same conditions were dreaded in ancient times. Recall how Joseph helped to prepare ancient Egypt for seven years of famine. Disturbing to some eschatologists are Jesus' prophecies that one sign of the end of time will be famines (cf. Matt. 24:7; Mark 13:8; Luke 21:11). Just how colossal will these famines be? Estimates of the number of people who will starve to death each month before 1980 have run from one to twenty-five million. While the divine historians take into account contributing causes such as enemy invasions, lack of rain, and other natural disasters, they ultimately attribute famine and destitution to God's providential purpose for His people. The Psalmist knew that food is a gift from God. Famine was a dramatic means by which God called His people to repentance. In Biblical theology the rich do not merely save the poor; the poor save the rich. In this puzzling, paradoxical scheme of things, on an earth frightfully polarized into the enormously affluent and the desperately poor, help from the former is urgent not just to save the latter, but to save the affluent ones themselves. There are so many secular, utilitarian philosophers who find no fault with this Scriptural line of reasoning.[7]

We merely cite population and hunger as problems Christian activists must face in the immediate future. Our purpose is not to suggest what new public policies should be enacted or world conferences convened. Americans have vast resources of food, and it must be allocated and distributed by governmental bureaucrats who should be informed, inspired, and answerable to the larger and hopefully sensitive and humane community at large. Is it only ironic that those who worry about being overweight are mainly the ones who claim allegiance to the Master who was born in a stable? Compassion must not become a forgotten Christian virtue. In no greater way than by our compassion can we reflect the example and spirit of Christ—how often and how easily He was moved.

At the national level we might ask if it is compassionate and humane for the affluent nations to spend $225 billion annually on military gear and $8 billion annually on aid to poor countries. At the individual and congregational level we must remind each other that gluttony, the forgotten sin, is still a grave evil. And as we renew the Republic's compassion for a needy world, we also reiterate that life is far more than food and drink (Matt. 6:25, 32) and that our abiding meat is to do the will of the Father of all mankind (John 4:34).

Ecology and Energy

In the fall of 1973 when many Americans were coming to grips

---

7. Interestingly enough, some Christian ethicists suggest that the world's starving should be left alone. The lifeboat analogy is used. If people in the rich lifeboat give their substance to the doomed folk falling out of the others, they reduce the chances of their own survival. But they do not improve things on the other lifeboats, where food and fuel are quickly translated into more babies, who in turn push more passengers over the side to struggle in the water of starvation. See "Let 'Em Starve," *National Observer*, 29 March 1975.

with the shell-shock from the Watergate scandals, the president appeared on television to announce the Arab oil boycott and declare an energy crisis. He requested immediate and, in some cases, sacrificial action. Restricted domestic use of electricity, lower automobile speeds, less heat in winter, and fewer Christmas lights were tolerable to a majority of Americans. But the sudden realization that in postbicentennial America our entire life style would never be the same was not easily accepted. We are making the most fundamental adjustment in life style that we have ever had to make. There have been times of national sacrifice before, particularly during the two world wars, but the consensus was that times would be "good" again when the emergency ended. Now, however, our ecological and energy situation forces prudent Americans to conclude that our material and even social life may never be the same again. The cost of food, transportation, goods, and services will not significantly diminish. The value of the dollar will not increase. The cost of land, housing, and utilities will not drop dramatically. Population generally serves to compound the whole problem. Indeed the twin problems of population and hunger cannot be divorced from the problems of ecology and energy.

As we Christians face problems so complex and intractable, our first reaction may be to relegate the whole matter to political bureaucracy and then, because of our deep if not totally unselfish concern, sign public petitions in support of our president and other public officials who are grappling with it. But cannot the voice of the church be stronger and clearer on this issue? Are there no principles in the Scriptures that can be applied to the present and future problems related to ecology and energy? We cannot avoid these questions, for the management of the earth for the human good now becomes not simply a theological or philosophical abstraction but an operational necessity. Three reflections are offered.

First, Christians need to proclaim as never before that this earth is God's, and we, like our ancestors and descendants, are merely stewards of this great planet and its vast resources. "The earth is the Lord's, and all that is in it, the world and those who dwell therein," wrote the Psalmist (24:1). A central lesson of Eden is that God has entrusted the care of the earth and its resources to the creatures made in His image. David forwarded this lesson succinctly when, contemplating the place of man in creation, he declared: "Thou madest him to have dominion over the works of thy hands; thou hast put all things under his feet" (Ps. 8:6 KJV).

If the proper stewardship of our earth and its animal and mineral resources is incumbent upon us as Christians, just as it is of our time, money, and talent, it follows that we must evaluate our use of the land, the animals, fossil fuels, and other minerals from a moral perspective. Not that these moral issues are simple to resolve; indeed, quite the contrary. For centuries scientists have known that existence on our planet is possible only because millions upon millions of factors are in precise and delicate balance. Heretofore that delicate balance has not been in jeopardy, but it is now, not because the Universal Planner's cosmic design has failed but because man has intervened for his own purposes. Too seldom has he considered the consequences. We tolerated more and more until past mistakes have caught up with us.

Suddenly a new and increased wisdom is essential to keep mankind from becoming inimical to its own survival. It is clear that while we as a generation of world citizens can do nothing about the physical environment that was bequeathed to us, we can do much about the world we bequeath to our children. We can no longer tolerate our present ethic of consumption and waste. We can no longer be oblivious to the fact that we have been squandering much of the earth's precious energy in our quest for "the more abundant life."

Merchandise is deliberately manufactured for a short life. The whole range of goods and services is considered "disposable." Built into automobiles is a "planned obsolescence"; each fall's new models make all present cars seem out of date, a condition the Jones's ego cannot tolerate for more than two or three years. The modern American credo "There's plenty more where that came from" needs to be replaced by the much older but wiser adage, "Use it up, make it do, wear it out."

Second, this renewed concern for our stewardship of the earth must transcend narrow nationalistic concerns and reach out to all lands and peoples. As we noted in the last chapter, the United States, with about six percent of the world's population, now consumes between thirty and forty percent of the world's petroleum even though we have only a dwindling nine percent of the world's oil reserves. Despite efforts to cut consumption, our demand for more fuel and resources must seem insatiable to most of the world. And yet, a major theme in the political rhetoric of the energy crisis is the need for American self-sufficiency; i.e., make some minor sacrifices now, and by the 1980s we can return to our old life style without having to rely on any source of energy beyond our own.

Christians need to examine closely proposals such as "Project Independence." Are they inward-looking and selfish, designed to continue an extraordinarily wasteful life style regardless of the consequences abroad? Would they mean a brief pause before continuing our recent practice of doubling our consumption of energy every fifteen to twenty years? If so, it would mean the withdrawal of America into a kind of fortress where our life style is perpetuated at the expense of many of the nations, both developed and undeveloped, that depend economically on the United States. Indeed, our relations with some nations are already strained, as they have become unwilling to yield up their riches for our pleasure. Perhaps these underdeveloped nations are only taking America's ideals of equality, profit, and supply and demand quite seriously.

The Biblical principle of sharing our resources with those less fortunate need not be documented again with numerous narratives and proof texts. What is essential is that we apply this principle in dealing with other nations. During the oil embargo one newsmagazine noted that the Arabs sit on the world's richest oil reserves because of some "accident of geography." For Christians the phrase "accident of geography" reflects a parochial and selfish view of the situation. For Americans who have discovered a land of rich soil, plenteous forests, beautiful waters, and almost more land than we knew what to do with—and then depleted and destroyed so much of it—now to cry "accident of geography" is ludicrous. Why should not the oil belong to the Arabs, or the English, or the Chinese, or to any other nation as well as to the Americans? Are we inherently superior morally to all other nations? Are we wiser or more prudent than others in our use of the earth's air, water, land, and other natural resources? The responsible alternative to a vision of limitless energy and luxury while the rest of the world "toughs it out" is the ethic of sharing, conservation, and moderation. It rests on the premise that all the peoples of the earth are one, that ties of nationality pale when compared to ties of common blood, and that no nation is truly "Christian" that exploits and hoards essential resources at the expense of the survival and modest comfort of other peoples.

And third, the energy crisis provides us with new opportunities to practice often-neglected virtues and learn often-forgotten principles. A central lesson of the Scriptures is that adversity does more to create righteousness than does prosperity. Abstinence enriches the spirit. This is learned best if not easiest by firsthand experience, and facing the future challenges of ecology and energy may provide this experience. Nothing less is needed than a radical change in the values by which we measure life.

We have already noted that thriftiness will again become a cherished virtue. There was a time when the maxims of Benjamin Franklin ("A penny saved is a penny earned") were chiefly for elementary school children to memorize. Now the apostle of thrift seems to be just the right philosopher for the whole Western world. Patience rather than progress may become our "most important product." Families may be required to live closer together physically, which just could mean being closer emotionally and spiritually. We may search for more creative uses of our leisure time than driving many miles to some movie, ball game, or other entertainment. We may appreciate the nobility of work more once we do more things for ourselves, such as cultivating our own gardens. And with soaring food prices, those forgotten New Year's resolutions to diet again may be kept much more easily.

More important, we may learn better a principle we pay lip service to—A man's life consists not in the abundance of things he possesses. "The more abundant life" refers to a spiritual existence that is Christ-centered. This life is not rendered more abundant by a double garage filled with fully-equipped luxury automobiles, campers and trailers, color television sets, Hondas, dune buggies and snowmobiles, electric toothbrushes, and garbage compactors. It is attained, with however much difficulty, by faithfully following Christ's example and precepts no matter what our contemporary situation. And no matter what our social, political, or economic circumstances may be, this higher and unselfish life style brings results in inward peace and satisfaction and enriches human relations through Christian fellowship.

Revitalizing Bureaucracy and Insuring World Peace

Casper W. Weinberger, in his final major speech as secretary of the Department of Health, Education, and Welfare, stated that his "overriding observation after these years in Washington is of an all-pervasive Federal Government." Unless checked, he warned, "that growth may take from us our most precious personal freedoms" and "shatter the foundations of our economic system."[8] From 1970 to 1975 the federal budget increased eighty-three percent to nearly $360 billion. If social programs continue growing at the pace they have in the previous two, by the year 2000 the United States will spend half of the entire gross national product for domestic social programs. Half of the American people would support the other half. And over half the labor force might be working for the government. A renewal of our Republic is unlikely until we restructure and revitalize our massive federal bureaucracy to bring about a better life at home and to insure world peace. Of the future challenges that Christian political activists must face, this is one for which there seem to be no clear Scriptural guidelines. And yet the challenge is so great that it must be cited in any survey of future challenges facing this nation.

In just over a decade (1958-1971) the number of engineers, managers, and other employees in the top five ranks of the federal bureaucracy grew three hundred percent. There are nearly three million federal civilian employees, a vast pool of talent (thirteen percent of the permanent employees have graduate training) that seems to be less and less innovative as the problems and bureaucracy grow. Government bureaucrats are the single largest salaried group in this nation, and in many ways they are better paid and more secure in their employment than their counterparts in the private sector. The bureaucrats in Washington are exceptionally well housed, well pensioned, well vacationed, and well chauffeured. The Library of Congress has 320 miles of shelves containing the experience and wisdom of human civilization, and 4,200 men and women who help us get what we need out of sixteen million books and fifty-eight million other items. But how many of our civil servants know what to do with it all?[9] Generating its own growth, insulated from careful public scrutiny, and accountable to few, there is little wonder our bureaucracy comprises what William S. Banowsky called an "invisible government."[10]

The pervasive nature of government makes it more rather than less likely that there will be even more abuses of power than have been publicized in the past. Modern history provides disturbing

---

8. Excerpts from the speech were published in *Higher Education and National Affairs*, 25 July 1975, p. 4.

9. *Time*, 14 April 1975, p. 30, supplies the statistics in this paragraph.

10. From the "My Turn" guest column, *Newsweek*, 17 March 1975, p. 13.

examples of the evil that men will perform who are trained but who lack moral guidance or humane education. One needs only read in William Shirer's *The Rise and Fall of the Third Reich* about the atrocious experiments conducted by Nazi doctors on Jews (one example: artificially impregnated Polish women were set in ice water to induce miscarriages) to see the potential of "official" immoral conduct. The passing of history has not changed man's propensity for evil. The Bible teaches that man in all places and in all ages is sinful and needs regeneration. While human nature is basically the same, the possibility and opportunities for abusing power are much greater now than ever before. New inventions such as computer banks and electronic surveillance devices, despite their obvious usefulness, present new temptations to abuse power. Our technological bureaucracy has made great strides in this century. We have sent men to the moon. It may be within our reach to eradicate hunger, poverty, and major diseases from this continent and large sectors of others. But the same bureaucratic and technological expertise may be used to destroy land and natural resources, invade privacy, and torture and kill masses of people in new and painless ways.

How may we be assured that our present and future political leaders, bureaucrats, and technocrats will use their skills and technology for moral rather than immoral purposes? The best way is to maintain a system of humane and, if you will, Christian education and training. The simple fact is, however, that Christian people have failed to support Christian education fully. We do not suggest that Christian education is a panacea for all present and future problems, but it is one significant way in which Christians can meet these challenges. Christian education is dedicated primarily and preeminently to educating the heart or soul of man, and it should provide a rich alternative to the public university's necessarily limited version of undergraduate education. Apart from this commitment the Christian college with its higher tuition has lost its *raison d'être*. This value is more than vain rhetoric to be employed in preparing college bulletins and brochures. Its absence from our public institutions is widely recognized. One cannot read the literature of the New Left and other radical student groups without noting their unanimous conclusion that higher education engages their intellect and skills in only the most technical and specialized fields; they concur with many moderate students that college failed to afford them what they really needed: a moral and aesthetic education.

Put succinctly, higher education cannot serve higher goals by developing capacities and skills with no concern for how their students put them to use. This is not to imply that public colleges and universities cannot or do not impart needed values; such an implication would overstate our case, and perhaps they have been ahead of us in certain areas, such as race relations. They do teach values at least implicitly. What the Christian college offers is explicit instruction concerning ideals and values, and unlike any public school it can place these ideals and values in the context of Biblical authority and morality.

There are several problems that a restructured and revitalized bureaucracy could address. One is the confused welfare system in America, which allows too much "chiseling" and too often fails to provide adequately for the modest comfort and health care of the needy. An even greater and more perplexing problem is that of world peace. The continuing threat of nuclear war and the huge arms sales by the major world powers to Third World countries are undoubtedly bringing the world nearer the brink of destruction. Six nations are known to possess nuclear explosives, and a number of other nations are capable of producing them in fairly short order. Shortsighted considerations of nationalistic prestige are feeding the ambition of some nations to become nuclear powers, and nuclear proliferation is now a fact. Any country that possesses nuclear weapons can provide a grave threat to virtually any other country, a condition that threatens the virtual annihilation of life as we have enjoyed it. It may soothe our collective conscience to hear a nation assure the world that it seeks nuclear weapons or explosive devices solely for "peaceful purposes." But as Lord Palmerston of England once observed: "We have no eternal allies, we have no perpetual enemies. Our interests are eternal and perpetual, and those interests it is our duty to follow."[11] A morally enlightened political leadership and bureaucracy would not permit the combination of short-term self-interest, greed, and the business-as-usual mentality to continue expanding this grave threat to world peace.

---

11. From a report to the Senate in the spring of 1975 by Senator Stuart Symington of Missouri. See cover story, "The Arms Dealers: Guns for All," *Time,* 3 March 1975, pp. 34-44. "Common sense argues that the arms trade can scarcely advance peace. In each of the 60 military conflicts since the end of World War II, imported weapons were used almost exclusively."

The Imperative of Specific Action

We are changing the world faster than we are changing ourselves and faster than we are adapting our institutions to these changes. Christians are overawed by the magnitude of the human and political problems we have discussed in this chapter. We need not now relinquish our faith in a meaningful history under God. True, God has not guaranteed survival to any civilization or to mankind; but one theme in traditional Judaism and Christianity is that when men are in desperate straits, God performs His mighty works of salvation. The Christian believes in an eternal God whose purposes are certainly not limited to this time and planet. The least we can do is be patient with and compassionate toward those we elect and appoint to deal with these seemingly intractable problems. But the most important point of this chapter is that we can do much more.

Discussion about renewal seems decades old; success seems dubious. We have all heard sermons, lectures, and lessons on the problems of society and the church's relationship to the world. Words are a form of external behavior, and that is the problem. Too many think that talking and reading about religion and the world make them Christian activists; their commitment is not total.

One of the chief pitfalls for the church today is that we so glibly verbalize convictions but are unwilling to witness to them by our lives. Our attitudes and convictions are complete entities only when they are also given outward expression. Our identification with those in need and our concrete expressions of love precede and authenticate our verbal witness. Continue talking about fine preaching, outstanding lectures, interesting periodicals, and promising blueprints for future action—*but do not substitute these for specific actions.*

Authentic Christian love and compassion may be shown in small kindnesses as well as on grandiose achievements. Small, individual victories for humanity are more personal and private, closer to the flow and reality of direct, human interrelationships. The importance of doing what one can, but at least doing something, to meet human needs is impressively taught in the story of the feeding of the five thousand. Jesus multiplied a small amount of food, and the disciples collected what might ordinarily be wasted in order to feed hungry people again. It is estimated that Americans waste up to twenty-five percent of the food they purchase, and if we add the amount of food that contributes to obesity, we waste as much as fifty percent.[12] This one example suggests that we need not stumble blindly about for lack of immediate and complete answers to the vast complexities of this century. We do not know all the solutions to the world's present and future problems. But when they have deeply rooted moral dimensions, we can act—now, in our own manner, according to our own talents and resources, in our very own community.

---

12. From a special report, "Running Out of Food," *Newsweek*, 11 November 1974, p. 67.

Bibliographic Note

The purpose of this "note" is to give direction to readers who would like to study further any of the subjects covered in this volume. To determine the kind and amount of sources used in the writing of this book, the reader should peruse the footnotes. He will find that I have supported my arguments and analyses with extensive evidence from news periodical literature. Most of the entries which follow, however, are books.

For a study of Old Testament perspectives on God and state, I recommend Norman K. Gottwald, *All the Kingdoms of the Earth: Israelite Prophecy and International Relations in the Ancient Near East* (New York: Harper and Row, 1964). This is one of the best works in English available today that treats the international events of the prophets' day and their individual responses to them. The most valuable source I have found on the New Testament and politics is Oscar Cullman, *The State in the New Testament* (New York: Scribner's, 1956). I also recommend Alan Richardson, *The Political Christ* (Philadelphia: Westminster, 1973); and John Howard Yoder, *The Politics of Jesus* (Grand Rapids: Eerdmans, 1972). Many volumes discuss the concept of American mission, past and present. A most provocative one is Robert Jewett, *The Captain America Complex: The Dilemma of Zealous Nationalism* (Philadelphia: Westminster, 1973). Jewett's thesis is that three distinctive forms of zeal have been transmitted from the Biblical tradition to the modern world—hot zeal, cool zeal, and artful zeal. Biblical and American history are interwoven as the author discusses the sources and practice of these kinds of zeal. A general history from the perspective of this volume is Cushing Stout, *The New Heavens and New Earth: Political Religion in America* (New York: Harper and Row, 1974). Two good collections of readings from American history on the theme of mission are Conrad Cherry, ed., *God's New Israel: Religious Interpretations of American Destiny* (Englewood Cliffs, N.J.: Prentice-Hall, 1971); and Winthrop S. Hudson, ed., *Nationalism and Religion in America: Concepts of American Identity and Mission* (New York: Harper and Row, 1970).

Many books are available on political activism. Lester W. Milbrath, *Political Participation: How and Why People Get Involved in Politics* (Skokie, Ill.: Rand McNally, 1965) is a comprehensive compilation of knowledge on various forms of conventional political participation. William H. Flanigan, *Political Behavior of the American Electorate* (Boston: Allyn and Bacon, 1968) is a short analysis and summary of recent voting behavior research. Useful sources in studying the social activism of nineteenth-century evangelical churches include: Timothy L. Smith, *Revivalism and Social Reform* (Nashville: Abingdon, 1957); John Warwick Montgomery, "Evangelical Social Responsibility in Theological Perspective," in Gary R. Collins, ed., *Our Society in Turmoil* (Carol Stream, Ill.: Creation House, 1970); Bruce L. Shelley, *Evangelicalism in America* (Grand Rapids: Eerdmans, 1967); and George M. Marsden, "Evangelical Social Concern," *Christianity Today*, 12 May 1972, pp. 8-11. As this volume is being prepared, Royce Money is completing a doctoral dissertation at Baylor University on political behavior and attitudes in the Church of Christ. A great deal of statistical research and analysis indicates, if the Church of Christ is typical of other evangelical bodies, that most evangelical church members: consider themselves political moderates; rate "personal integrity" the most important characteristic of political candidates; and are independents rather than party loyalists. The overwhelming majority are not political activists beyond voting, but over sixty percent believe a Christian can hold elective office without compromising his principles.

A number of excellent volumes defend and give direction to Christian political activism. I recommend: John C. Bennett, *The*

Christian as Citizen (New York: Association, 1955) and *When Christians Make Political Decisions* (New York: Association, 1964); Robert G. Clouse, Robert D. Linder, and Richard V. Pierard, eds., *Protest and Politics* (Greenwood, S.C.: Attic, 1968), Linder and Pierard, *Politics: A Case for Christian Action* (Downers Grove, Ill.: Inter-Varsity, 1973) is easy reading that appeals to teen-agers. Clouse et al., *The Cross and the Flag* (Carol Stream, Ill.: Creation House, 1972) is a more challenging series of studies written by evangelical activists. David O. Moberg, *Inasmuch: Christian Social Responsibility in the 20th Century* (Grand Rapids: Eerdmans, 1965) is strongly rooted in Scriptural teaching and is excellent. In *The Great Reversal: Evangelism Versus Social Concern* (Philadelphia: Lippincott, 1972), Moberg continues his earlier study and emphasizes the history of American evangelicalism. William Lee Miller, *The Protestant and Politics* (Philadelphia: Westminster, 1958) is a brief study for laymen. Richard Mouw, *Political Evangelism* (Grand Rapids: Eerdmans, 1974) is an excellent brief study that greatly emphasizes New Testament doctrine. Wesley Pippert, *Memo for 1976: Some Political Options* (Downers Grove, Ill.: Inter-Varsity, 1974) consists of interesting, brief analyses from a United Press International reporter who covers the Washington scene.

Several books have been written by Christian congressmen: John B. Anderson edited *Congress and Conscience* (Philadelphia: Lippincott, 1970), and wrote *Between Two Worlds* (Grand Rapids: Zondervan, 1971) and *Vision and Betrayal in America* (Waco, Tex.: Word, 1975); and Mark Hatfield wrote *Conflict and Conscience* (Waco, Tex.: Word, 1971). *Congress and Conscience* contains six essays by congressional Christians. *Vision and Betrayal in America* gives much attention to Watergate. See also *Theology Today* 26 (January 1970) for several essays by Christian congressmen on political issues.

Some of my ideas on civil disobedience and the American Christian are dependent on the following sources: Daniel B. Stevick, *Civil Disobedience and the Christian* (New York: Seabury, 1969); Charles Frankel, "Is It Ever Right to Break a Law?" *New York Times Magazine*, 12 January 1964, pp. 17ff.; Martin Luther King, Jr., "Letter from a Birmingham Jail," a response to eight Alabama clergymen dated April 16, 1963, and reprinted in many anthologies on political science and rhetoric; Judith Stiehm, *Nonviolent Power: Active and Passive Resistance in America* (Boston: Heath, 1972); and William R. Miller, *Nonviolence: A Christian Interpretation*

(New York: Schocken, 1966). For a Christian perspective on violence and revolution in general, consult the following: Jean-Francois Revel, *Without Marx or Jesus* (Garden City, N.Y.: Doubleday, 1971); Arthur G. Gish, *The New Left and Christian Radicalism* (Grand Rapids: Eerdmans, 1970); and Vernon C. Grounds, *Revolution and the Christian Faith* (Philadelphia: Lippincott, 1971).

Concerning nationalism and American civil religion, the previously cited anthologies edited by Winthrop S. Hudson and Conrad Cherry may be consulted with profit. Sidney E. Mead, *The Lively Experiment: The Shaping of Christianity in America* (New York: Harper and Row, 1963) is an excellent historical perspective. Harry R. Davis and Robert C. Good, eds., *Reinhold Niebuhr on Politics* (New York: Scribner's, 1960) is a fine compilation of the late professor's writings revealing his political philosophy. Hans J. Morgenthau, *Politics Among Nations: The Struggle for Power and Peace,* 4th ed. (New York: Knopf, 1967) is a thorough study of nationalism. Russell E. Richey and Donald G. Jones, eds., *American Civil Religion* (New York: Harper and Row, 1974) is a collection of essays by twelve authors with different perspectives, and it contains a rather complete bibliography of related books and articles. Another important collection of essays is Elwyn A. Smith, ed., *The Religion of the Republic* (Philadelphia: Fortress, 1971). For a foreigner's slant on American morality and politics, I highly recommend Alexander Solzhenitsyn et al., *From Under the Rubble* (Boston: Little and Brown, 1974). As the introduction points out, "the central premise of the collection is that the problems of the modern world, Soviet as well as Western, can no longer be solved on the political plane. Instead, the quest for solutions must begin on the ethical level. . . . their [the contributors'] approach is spiritual in nature." Provocative reading on Christian ethics and American foreign policy is available in several booklets published by the Council on Religion and International Affairs. On this same subject see John C. Bennett, *Foreign Policy in Christian Perspective* (New York: Scribner's, 1966).

On patriotism see Leonard W. Doob, *Patriotism and Nationalism* (New Haven: Yale University, 1964). The positive and optimistic side of the American standard of living, discussed in chapter 11, is documented in Ben J. Wattenberg, *The Real America* (Garden City, N.Y.: Doubleday, 1974).

Concerning the intellectual environment of the late eighteenth century, in which the founding fathers lived and from which their ideas on church and state emerged, see: Crane Brinton, *Ideas and Men: The Story of Western Thought* (New York: Prentice-Hall, 1950); Jacob Bronowski and Bruce Mazlish, *The Western Intellectual Tradition* (New York: Harper and Row, 1960); Richard Buel, *Securing the Revolution: Ideology in American Politics, 1789-1815* (Ithaca: Cornell University, 1972); Seymour Martin Lipset, *The First New Nation* (New York: Basic, 1963); and Clinton L. Rossiter, *Seedtime of the Republic* (New York: Harcourt, Brace, and World, 1953). Buel examines the change in the political ideas of the revolutionary elite as the colonies were transformed to a nation. *The First New Nation* is a historical and sociological study of the United States as an example of nation building and a significant contribution to the study of building political institutions. *Seedtime of the Republic* is a valuable social and political history of the colonial and revolutionary periods, and it also provides an exciting picture of the men who founded the Republic. For some good insight into the nature of a responsible state in Biblical perspective, see J. Philip Wogaman, *Protestant Faith and Religious Liberty* (Nashville: Abingdon, 1967). For general discussions on the nature of law, see Lon L. Fuller, *The Morality of Law* (New Haven: Yale University, 1964); and Robert Paul Wolff, *The Rule of Law* (New York: Simon and Schuster, 1971), which is a broad view of the role of law in American society.

Most of the evidence used in the last three chapters of this volume was taken from recent periodical literature, especially newsmagazines, newspapers, and religious papers such as *Christianity Today* and *Christian Century*. For a study of the American presidency, see especially Michael Novak, *Choosing Our King: Powerful Symbols in Presidential Politics* (New York: Macmillan, 1974), which gives much attention to civil religion in America. Robert S. Alley, *So Help Me God: Religion and the Presidency, Wilson to Nixon* (Richmond: Knox, 1972) and Edward J. Richter and Berton Dulce, *Religion and the Presidency* (New York: Macmillan, 1962) are two general histories of the White House and religion. For a provocative and interesting study of Nixon's religious beliefs, see Charles P. Henderson, Jr., *The Nixon Theology* (New York: Harper and Row, 1972). For studies of political corruption in general, see: Paul H. Douglas, *Ethics in Government* (Cambridge: Harvard University, 1952); Arnold A. Rogow and Harold D. Lasswell, *Power, Corruption, and Rectitude* (Englewood Cliffs, N.J.: Prentice-Hall, 1963); Stephen K. Bailey, *Ethics and the Politician* (Santa Barbara,

Calif.: Fund for the Republic, 1960); and Arnold J. Heidenheimer, ed., *Political Corruption: Readings in Comparative Analysis* (New York: Holt, Rinehart and Winston, 1970), which includes some helpful essays. *The Annals of the American Academy of Political and Social Science* 280 (March 1952) develops the theme "Ethical Standards in American Public Life," and *Annals* 363 (January 1966) discusses the theme "Ethics in America: Norms and Deviations." A spate of books on Watergate probably will appear soon. Theodore H. White, *Breach of Faith: The Fall of Richard Nixon* (New York: Atheneum, 1975) is a thorough narrative. Ethical and political perspectives are brought to bear on Watergate and related themes in Donald W. Harward, ed., *Crisis in Confidence: The Impact of Watergate* (Boston: Little and Brown, 1974).

Index

Of Scripture

Of Persons